LITERACY DEVELOPMENT IN THE EARLY YEARS
Helping Children Read and Write

LESLEY MANDEL MORROW

Rutgers, The State University

PRENTICE HALL, *Englewood Cliffs, New Jersey 07632*

Library of Congress Cataloging-in-Publication Data

Morrow, Lesley Mandel.
    Literacy development in the early years: helping children read
and write / Lesley Mandel Morrow.
        p.   cm.
    Bibliography: p
    Includes index.
    ISBN 0-13-386541-X
    1. Language arts (Preschool)—United States.   2. Reading
(Preschool)—United States.   3. Children—United States—Books and
reading. 1. Title.
LB1140.5.L3M66   1989
372.6—dc19   88-25043
                                                    CIP

Editorial/production supervision: Susan E. Rowan
Cover design: Joel Mitnick Design Inc.
Manufacturing buyer: Peter Havens
Four line drawings, Morrow Library Corner, floor plan of a classroom, a contract, and
    bookmaking directions: Pamela Cromey
Photographs: Lenore Arone, Susan Arone, Joyce Caponigro, Lori Harrje, Milton E. Mandel,
    Franklin A. Morrow, Lesley Mandel Morrow, Andrea Shane

To Frank and Stephanie
my very special husband
and my very special daughter

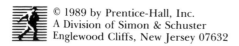
© 1989 by Prentice-Hall, Inc.
A Division of Simon & Schuster
Englewood Cliffs, New Jersey 07632

Printed in the United States of America
10 9 8 7 6 5 4 3 2

ISBN 0-13-386541-X

PRENTICE-HALL INTERNATIONAL (UK) LIMITED, London
PRENTICE-HALL OF AUSTRALIA PTY. LIMITED, Sydney
PRENTICE-HALL CANADA INC., Toronto
PRENTICE-HALL HISPANOAMERICANA, S.A., Mexico
PRENTICE-HALL OF INDIA PRIVATE LIMITED, New Delhi
PRENTICE-HALL OF JAPAN, INC., Tokyo
SIMON & SCHUSTER ASIA PTE. LTD., Singapore
EDITORA PRENTICE-HALL DO BRASIL, LTDA., Rio de Janeiro

Contents

──── 3 ────

Language as a Vehicle for Developing Literacy   38

──── 4 ────

Reading as a Vehicle for Developing Literacy   69

──── 5 ────

Developing Positive Attitudes Toward Reading Through the Use of Children's Literature   83

──── 6 ────

Developing Concepts About Books and Comprehension of Story   100

——— **7** ———

Developing Reading Through Concepts About Print   **121**

——— **8** ———

Writing as a Vehicle for Developing Literacy   **141**
Robert P. Parker with Lesley Mandel Morrow

———— 9 ————

Preparing and Organizing the Environment: A Vehicle for Literacy Development at School   171

———— Appendix A ————

———— Appendix B ————

———— Appendix C ————

———— Appendix D ————

———— Appendix E ————

———— Appendix F ————

Foreword

Dramatic changes occurred during the last decade in our understanding of early literacy development. Whereas we once thought that children learned to speak and listen during their early years and later learned to read and write at school age of 5 or 6 years, we now know that they develop language related abilities "all of a piece" (simultaneously) from the days of infancy onward.

During the last decade, we also discovered that the conditions that promote first language learning are the very same conditions that promote total literacy development. These conditions, created in the social context surrounding a child, involve immersion, approximation, opportunity to practice, feedback and modeling (Cambourne, 1984).

Lesley Morrow demonstrates the value of immersing children in the language we want them to learn—that includes the language of literature as well as the language of daily living. She provides numerous examples of children's approximations of writing and reading as she establishes the necessity of giving them unlimited opportunities to practice. Further, she illustrates the ways adults provide feedback and models for young language learners as they make attempts to read and write.

Children's literature, the area I know best, is central to Morrow's literacy environment. Literature serves as a model for language learning and provides strong motivation for learning to read and write. It is a springboard for all sorts of literacy related activities. Most importantly, literature is a way of knowing. It is shaped around story—a primary act of human minds.

Dr. Lesley Morrow knows about children's literature, too. She recognizes the impact of fathers, mothers, siblings, babysitters, grandparents, and other caregivers reading to children and enjoying the wealth of books. She shows how reading to babies influences their grasp of language and story patterns that serve them well as they learn to read and write. She illustrates how children learn concepts about print, book handling, and conventions of stories as they interact with books. Morrow establishes that adults teach by example as they enjoy shared reading and shared writing with young children. She shows the impact of having a library corner in a classroom and the effects of storybook reading aloud by a teacher. She shows that when children know authors and illustrators as real people, they want to read their works and write in a manner similar to their idols. She states that storytelling is similar to reading aloud in its impact on children. Speaking from her own experiences as a teacher, researcher, and parent, she charts a path that leads to successful literacy learning.

Lesley Morrow has taken a long view of literacy development in the early years showing the historical roots of ideas that are valid today. She also knows and draws upon the trend setting research of today's leaders because she is a member of that research community. She succinctly summarizes language theories and relates current research to shape sound practices. She has conducted much of the original research herself, testimony to the fact that she can bridge the gap between theory, research, and practice. Her examples are anchored in real classroom experiences—her own and those of other teachers with whom she works collaboratively. The examples have the ring of authenticity and add credibility to her argument.

Morrow's treatment of literacy development is on the cutting edge of current knowledge. She is well informed about her subject and makes connections among all aspects of literacy learning. She is a sensitive observer and writer as she lets children speak for themselves through their work.

Morrow states that few children learn to love books by themselves. Someone must lure them into the joys of the printed word and the wonderful world of stories. She shows us how to do that and enriches our lives and the lives of children through her work. Her contribution to the literarcy development of young children is a lasting one.

Bernice E. Cullinan
Professor of Early Childhood Education
New York University

Preface

Literacy Development in the Early Years is for teachers, reading special-
ists, administrators, students in teacher education programs, and parents.
It is appropriate for both graduate and undergraduate courses in early
literacy, and it complements texts on the teaching of reading in the elementary school, child development, the early childhood curriculum, teaching language arts in the elementary school, and children's literature.

I wrote the book because of my special interest in emergent literacy in
early childhood. I taught in preschools and kindergartens, then went on to
teach early childhood curriculum and early literacy courses on the university level. My research has focused on instructional strategies in early
literacy. A wealth of research information has been created in this area over
the past few years. That research has generated new theory and given new
strength to certain older theories of learning. It has implications for new
instructional strategies and reinforces certain older practices that had little
or no research to establish their validity. It describes a program for the
nurture of emergent literacy from birth through kindergarten and first
grade.

Although the book is about early literacy, its content has strong ram-
ifications for reading instruction in the primary and elementary grades.
The fundamental ideas presented in this volume should eventually be
incorporated in texts on reading in the elementary school. As we all recognize, there is little in education that is really new; what we know about it

simply gets refined, reorganized, or verified. In many respects, some parts of this book may sound like some of the earliest volumes on early literacy.

This book does not offer a prescription. Formula education tends to get us into trouble, and it does not reflect the traditional ideals of American education. The ideas offered in this book have been tried and they have worked, but not all of them are appropriate for all teachers or all children. The good teacher functions most effectively with teaching strategies he or she feels most comfortable with. The teacher needs to be a decisionmaker who thinks critically about the design of his or her literacy program and the selection of materials. Children, too, are individuals who come to school with different cultural backgrounds, experiences, exposures to literacy and abilities. Instructional programs can differ in different parts of the country, in different localities, and for different children in the same classroom.

Underlying this book is the merging of the art and the science of teaching. The science has developed theories based on research that has generated instructional strategies. The book carries descriptions of strategies and steps for carrying them out. But, the scientific research does not necessarily take into account individual differences among teachers and children. The art of teaching concentrates on those human variables.

Chapter 1 provides a framework of theory and research, both past and current, that has influenced strategies for developing emergent literacy. Chapter 2 discusses the strong influence of the home on the development of literacy, especially in a child's earliest years.

Chapters 3–8 deal with the areas of literacy development, oral language, reading, and writing. These chapters discuss theory, research, developmental stages, instructional strategies, and methods of assessment associated with them. The book views the development of literacy skills (reading, writing, and oral language) as concurrent and interrelated: the development of one enhances the development of the others. Furthermore, the theories, stages, acquisition, and strategies associated with each are similar, and it is difficult to separate them entirely. To make the volume more readable, however, I have treated the different areas of literacy in different chapters.

Chapter 9 discusses the preparation and organization of an environment that will help the teacher take all of the components presented earlier and implement them in a successful program. This chapter emphasizes the interrelatedness of the several areas of literacy and describes how they can be integrated into the entire school day and with content areas.

Each chapter begins with an overview and ends with suggested activities. Appendixes list materials and resources parents and teachers can use in carrying out a successful program in emergent literacy.

ACKNOWLEDGMENTS

I want to thank many individuals who helped both directly and indirectly in the preparation of this book. Thank you to my students who helped: Patricia Addonizio, Katie Farrell, Mary Ann Gavin, Laura LaBarca, Michele Preole, Mary Joyce Santoloci, and Sari Schnipper. Thank you to the teachers and their principals who helped: Joyce Caponigro, Lori Harrje, Cynthia Peters, David Harris, Dennis Monaghan, John Quintaglie. Thank you to Andrea Shane for taking many of the photographs, and to Pamela Cromey for drawing the illustrations. Thank you to those who advised and assisted: Mary Bair, Bernice Cullinan, Cynthia Lewis, Robert Parker, Shelly Wepner. Thank you to R.A. and L.K. for your continual guidance. Thank you to Susan Willig, Shirley Chlopak and Susan Rowan, the individuals at Prentice Hall who guided me through the creation of this book and to the Prentice Hall reviewers who provided helpful comments: Donna E. Alvermann, University of Georgia, Mary McDonnell Harris, University of North Dakota, and Lynn C. Smith, Southern Illinois University. Thank you to the children I've taught, my college students, and the excellent teachers I've observed from whom I've learned so much. Thank you to the researchers in early literacy who have been providing the exciting information in this field. Thank you to my parents, Mary and Milton Mandel and my sisters who provided a rich literacy environment for me; thank you to Frank Morrow, my computer consultant; and thank you to Stephanie Morrow for demonstrating the validity of many of the concepts expressed in the book.

LMM

1

Foundations
of Early Literacy Development

CHAPTER OVERVIEW

- Theory and research from the past & present indicate the need for new approaches to literacy development in early childhood education.

- Important elements in the development of literacy in early childhood are environments rich in language and social interaction with adults and peers.

- Stages of child development from birth through early childhood have implications for literacy development and include evidence of literacy development.

What a dangerous activity reading is: teaching is. All this plastering of foreign stuff. Why plaster on at all when there's so much inside already? So much locked in? If only I could draw it out and use it as working material. And not draw it out either. If I had a light enough touch, it would just come out under its own volcanic power.

S<small>YLVIA</small> A<small>SHTON</small>-W<small>ARNER</small>
Spinster

Babies begin to acquire information about literacy from the moment of birth. They continue to build on their knowledge of oral language, reading, and writing as they go through early childhood. Recently a great deal of attention has been focused on literacy development in early childhood, an area somewhat neglected in the past. Teachers, parents, and administrators tended not to perceive preschoolers as readers or writers. They emphasized oral language development and preparation for reading. Because of increased research, thinking about early literacy has changed: very young children are now viewed as individuals with literacy skills. The literacy skills of preschoolers and kindergartners are not those of adults, but children do acquire literacy traits that must be acknowledged and that have implications for instructional practice.

Over the past few years, research on literacy development in early childhood has burgeoned. That research not only has introduced new information, it has also raised concerns about certain common practices in early childhood literacy instruction and an awareness of the need for change. Like a child's first words and first steps, learning to read and write should be an exciting, fulfilling, and rewarding experience. Unfortunately, it sometimes is not. This book draws on the newer research and blends it with theory and practice that have proved successful. It presents a program for developing literacy in children from birth to seven years. It is based on the following rationale:

1. Literacy learning begins in infancy.
2. Parents need to provide a rich literacy environment to help children acquire literacy skills.
3. School personnel must be aware that children come to school with prior knowledge of oral and written language.
4. Early reading and writing experiences at school should build upon that existing knowledge.
5. Learning requires a supportive environment that builds positive feelings about self as well as about literacy activities.
6. Adults must serve as models for literacy behavior, by demonstrating an interest in books and print.
7. During their literacy experiences children must interact within a social context so that they can share information and learn from each other.

8. Early literacy experiences should be meaningful and concrete, and should *actively* involve the child.
9. A literacy development program should focus on a whole language approach, utilizing functional experiences that include the use of oral language, listening, writing, and reading.
10. Differences in cultural and language backgrounds must be acknowledged and addressed. (IRA, 1985)

The book incorporates the work of learning theorists, philosophers, educators, psychologists, and researchers who have described how young children learn. It builds on the implications their work holds for instruction and reflects the newer attitudes toward literacy development in early childhood. Throughout, it emphasizes development of literacy through the teaching of language, listening, reading, and writing in coordination with other content areas across the curriculum. Though some of the chapters concentrate on language, reading, or writing, the major concern at all times is the integration of all four dimensions of literacy.

Literacy development early in life must focus on both learning and teaching. The teacher prepares an environment rich in literacy materials and activities from which children can choose; the children are encouraged to be actively involved in learning with other children, with materials, and with the teacher. A major focus of the book is how to provide an environ-

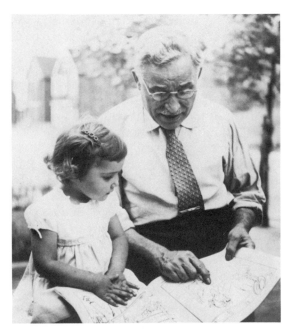

Learning requires a supportive environment that builds positive feelings about self and literacy activities.

ment that will encourage children to take an interest in reading, to associate it with pleasure, and ultimately to read by choice.

LEARNING THEORIES THAT HAVE SHAPED PRACTICES

Several important philosophers, theorists, educators, and psychologists have addressed learning in early childhood, including the issue of appropriate educational practice. Many of their ideas support the newer research in early childhood literacy or are reflected in newer practices. These ideas also represent varying responses to the question of whether learning is primarily a matter of the *nature* or the *nurture* of the child.

In the eighteenth century Rousseau (1962) strongly suggested that a child's early education be natural. That is, children should not be forced to learn things for which they are not developmentally ready. Rousseau advocated abandoning the contrived imposition of instruction on children and instead allowing children to grow and learn with the freedom to be themselves. Education follows the child's own development and readiness for learning. According to Rousseau, children learn through curiosity; forcing education upon them interferes with their learning and development. He believed that individual children had ways of learning peculiar to themselves, ways that formal instruction should not tamper with. Rousseau's philosophy suggests that the role of the educator is to use strategies that mesh with the child's readiness to learn. Rousseau strongly emphasized as little intervention by an adult as possible. He believed a child's learning "unfolds" naturally.

Pestalozzi (Rusk & Scotland, 1979) was influenced by Rousseau's emphasis on natural learning, but he added a dimension to it. He started his own school and developed principles for learning that combined natural elements with informal instruction. He found it unrealistic to expect children to learn totally on their own initiative. Although he felt that children may be able to teach themselves to read, for example, he also felt that it was necessary for teachers or parents to create the climate and conditions in which the reading process grows. The natural potential of a child develops, he believed, through sensory manipulative experiences, so he designed lessons that involved manipulating objects and learning about them through touch, smell, language, size, and shape.

Froebel's (1974) approach was similar in some ways to those of his predecessors. Like Rousseau, he believed that the adult responsible for the education of a child needs to be concerned with the child's natural unfolding. He also followed Pestalozzi's ideas and provided plans for instructing young children. But he is best known for emphasizing the importance of play in learning. He specified, however, that realizing the fullest benefits of playing-to-learn requires adult guidance and direction and a planned environment. Froebel saw the teacher as a designer of activities and experiences that facilitate learning. On this premise he designed a systematic curriculum for young children involving objects and materials that he called *gifts* and *occupations.* In handling and playing with these objects and materials, children not only use psychomotor skills but learn about shape, color, size, measurement, and comparison as well. It was Froebel who coined the word *kindergarten,* which means "children's garden." The phrase illustrates his basic philosophy that children, like plants, will grow to fruition only if they are tended and cared for. He often referred to the child as the seed being cared for by the gardener, or teacher.

Froebel was the first educator to design an organized curriculum for young children, and many of his strategies are evident in preschools and kindergartens today. Most significant among his strategies were his emphasis on guided play as a method for learning, the learning of certain concepts through manipulative materials that utilize the senses, and *circle time*—an opportunity to sing songs and learn new ideas through discussion.

John Dewey's (1966) views were not unlike Froebel's. His philosophy of early childhood education led to the concept of the child-centered curriculum. Dewey believed that the curriculum should be built around the interests of children. He agreed with Froebel that children learn best through play and in real life. He maintained that social interactions encourage learning and that interests are the vehicles for learning information and skills. He rejected the idea of teaching skills as an end unto themselves. He also believed that learning is maximized through the integration of content areas.

Froebel and Dewey have significantly influenced programs in American preschools and kindergartens throughout the twentieth century, and especially from the 1920s through the 1950s. During those decades, preschools and kindergartens typically had different areas for different activities. Shelves in a "block corner" held various sizes and shapes of blocks, small cars, trucks, and wooden figures of people. An art area contained easels with watercolors, crayons, paper, paste, scissors, construction paper, clay, and scraps of interesting materials such as fabric, plastic foam, and pipe cleaners for making collages. The dramatic-play corner was set up like a kitchen, with sink, oven, refrigerator, empty food boxes, table and chairs, telephone, mirror, dolls, and some clothing for dressing up. Still another area held manipulative toys that teach concepts about color, shape, and size. A science area revealed a water-play table, shells, interesting rocks, plants, a class animal, magnets, and magnifying glasses. The music area usually had a piano, rhythm instruments, and a record player. Sometimes there was a rug for children to sit on when they came to sing by the piano. One corner of the room had a shelf of children's literature and, depending on the teacher, soft pillows to lie on when looking at books.

The daily routine was similar in most of these settings. As children entered the classroom, they played with quiet toys. The teacher then called them to circle time to talk about the weather and the calendar. Conversation soon focused on a topic in social studies or science—animals or community helpers, for instance—with perhaps a song in keeping with the theme. Circle time was commonly followed by a long period called free play in which children could use the materials in the different areas of the room. There was minimal guidance during free play; children could explore and experiment with the materials. A snack, sometimes followed by a rest period, was an integral part of the daily routine. The day might also include a special lesson in art, social studies, or science appropriate to the unit being studied. Outdoor play allowed children to run, climb, play in sandboxes, and use riding toys. The teacher read a story daily, probably at the end of the day, often relating it to the topic being studied.

Reading and mathematics were not taught formally. Instead, the teacher might ask a child to count out enough cookies for all the children in the class, to name the date on the calendar, or to compare the sizes of different children. There were no workbooks or commercial reading materials. Teachers led some informal activities that could eventually lead to reading, but did not attempt to teach children to read. The letters of the alphabet might be found strung across the wall, the days of the week pointed out on a calendar, children's names written on their cubbies, and some other items in the room labeled with words. The general atmosphere was relaxed. The goal was to accustom children to school routines and make them comfortable in the school environment. The focus was on social, emotional, and physical development. There was no place in these programs for formal reading and writing instruction.

Maria Montessori (1965) departed from the educators and philosophers mentioned thus far. Although she believed in the use of the senses to promote learning, her emphasis on the senses was not based on the natural unfolding of the child, the child's interests, or play. Believing that children needed early, orderly, systematic training in mastering one skill after another, she supplied her teaching environment with materials for learning specific concepts in order to meet specific objectives. The materials provided the source of learning for the child. Children educated themselves by using these manipulatives, and since the materials were self-correcting, the children could determine their own errors and make corrections independently.

Montessori referred to this type of learning as *auto-education*. Like Froebel and Pestalozzi, she spoke of *sensitive periods,* when children are better able to learn certain things than at other times. It is the role of the parent or teacher to watch for these periods and take advantage of them by preparing the environment with appropriate materials and experiences for learning. In short, according to Montessori, the teacher is a guide who prepares an environment for learning. But unlike the educators already discussed, Montessori carefully designed learning materials to teach spe-

According to the concepts of Pestalozzi, Froebel, Dewey, Piaget, Vygotsky, and other philosophers and theorists, learning in early childhood will take place when youngsters have the opportunity to explore, experiment, play at real-life experiences, and manipulate materials. They need to do this sometimes by interacting with adults or other children and sometimes by working alone.

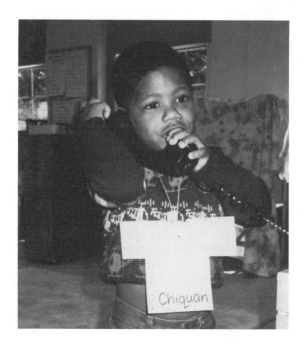

cific skills. In Montessori's curriculum, children's natural curiosity and their propensity for exploration are of less concern than their ability to work with specific materials to achieve a specific goal. Play is not as important as work since it might waste precious opportunities for goal achievement during sensitive periods for learning. Although some of her ideas are not relevant to the new thrust in early literacy, her emphasis on learning rather than teaching; her concerns about independent learning, sensitive periods for learning, and respect for the child; and her insistence on organization and a prepared environment hold implications for today's instruction.

Psychologist Jean Piaget (Piaget & Inhelder, 1969) has had a particularly strong impact on early childhood education. In describing the stages of cognitive development he recognized that children at certain stages are capable of only certain types of intellectual endeavors. Trying to involve children in abstract experiences during the preoperational stages of their early childhood, for instance, is considered inappropriate. Piaget did not advocate Montessori's systematic approach, nor did he believe in maturation as a completely natural unfolding. He believed, rather, that a child acquires knowledge by interacting with the world. Educators who have applied his theories involve children in natural problem-solving situations where they can assimilate new experiences into their existing knowledge. Children are active participants in their own learning, constantly changing and reorganizing their own knowledge.

Piaget stressed that learning takes place when the child interacts with peers and adults in a social setting as they act upon the environment. Educators who have incorporated Piaget's theories in curricula for early childhood education have designed programs that look very much like what Pestalozzi or Froebel might have created: a setting with many real-life materials, including the opportunity to play, explore, and experiment. Piaget agreed that young children should use their curiosity, inquisitiveness, and spontaneity to help themselves learn. In addition, a Piagetian preschool curriculum emphasizes decision making, problem solving, self-discipline, goal setting, planning one's own activities, and cooperating with teachers and peers in planning and evaluating learning.

Vygotsky's (1981) general theory of intellectual development also has implications for learning in early childhood. Vygotsky believes that mental functions are acquired through social relationships. Children learn by internalizing activities conducted in the world around them. Children emulate behaviors and incorporate them into their existing structure of knowledge when they are exposed to new situations in which they can actively interact with others.

The learning theories of the individuals discussed have contributed to the way we look at literacy development in early childhood education. Their ideas are the basis for early literacy instruction as it is described in this book. Particularly applicable among their concepts are these:

1. concern for a child's level of development—physical, social, emotional, and intellectual—when preparing a learning environment for that child;
2. concern for prepared environments in which learning can take place;
3. emphasis on learning rather than teaching;
4. the learner's need for social interaction with supportive adults and other children;
5. focus on learning through real experiences in meaningful and natural settings rather than by imposed, contrived objectives or techniques;
6. an awareness that children must actively participate in their own learning by engaging in manipulative experiences that are both functional and interesting.

PRACTICES IN THE PAST

Judging from professional literature of the early 1900s, little attention was paid to a child's literacy development before he or she entered school. Apparently, it was generally assumed that literacy began with formal instruction in first grade. Wielding a strong influence on reading instruction, developmental psychologists such as Gesell (1925) advocated maturation as the most important factor in learning to read. Reading instruction was frowned on until the child was ready to read. Preschool and kindergarten teachers generally ignored or avoided reading instruction. But they did follow some of the teachings of Pestalozzi and Froebel. Typically they read to children often; encouraged play, exploration, and problem solving; and led songs and discussions in circle times. Methods were child-centered, teaching units were interdisciplinary, and learning environments and instructional strategies appropriate to the child's development.

Influenced by the climate of the times, Morphett and Washburne (1931) supported the postponement of reading instruction until a child was developmentally "old enough." Their study concluded that children with a mental age of six years six months made better progress on a test of reading achievement than younger children. But whereas many educators held fast to the concept of natural maturation as the precursor of literacy, others grew uncomfortable with simply waiting for children to become ready to read. They did not advocate formal reading instruction in early childhood, but they did begin to provide experiences that would help children become ready for reading.

The growing popularity of testing during the 1930s and 1940s helped these educators in this effort and affected the next several decades of early childhood reading instruction. Generally, the standardized tests served the prevailing concept of maturation by indicating if a child had reached the maturity he or she needed to be able to learn to read. The tests usually included sections on specific skills. Unfortunately, those skills came to be seen as elements on which to base experiences that would help children to become ready to read. The term *reading readiness* came into popular use during these decades and is still with us. Instead of waiting for a child's natural maturation to unfold, educators focused on nurturing that maturation through instruction in a set of skills identified as prerequisites for reading. The concept gained strength when publishers of basal readers capitalized on the idea of readiness skills and began to prepare materials for preschool and kindergarten that would make children ready to read. Skills associated with reading readiness include *auditory discrimination,* the ability to identify and differentiate familiar sounds, similar sounds, rhyming words, and the sounds of letters; *visual discrimination,* including color recognition and shape and letter identification; *left to right eye progression* and *visual motor skills,* such as cutting on a line with scissors and coloring within the lines of a picture; and such *large motor abilities* as skipping, hopping, and walking on a line.

Early childhood literacy instruction based on the reading readiness model implies that one prepares for literacy by acquiring a set of prescribed skills. These skills are taught systematically on the assumption that all children are at a fairly similar level of development when they come to preschool or kindergarten. The system does not consider experiences or information that a child may already have about literacy, and it focuses narrowly on a set of skills perceived as those needed for learning to read. Ironically, those skills stray from the original intent of the people who were concerned with maturation. They do not reflect the developmentalist's description of children's growth during the stages of early childhood. They do not encourage activities that are meaningful or interesting to a child, nor do they capitalize on what children know about literacy from the reading and writing they experience in their social and cultural environments.

Research findings about literacy in early childhood are beginning to challenge the deep-rooted practices in reading readiness that have been evident since the 1950s. Teale (1982, p. 567) argues that the typical literacy curriculum with its progression from part to whole and its hierarchy of "skills" does not reflect the way children learn to read:

> The belief is that literacy development is a case of building competencies in certain cognitive operations with letters, words, sentences, and texts, competencies which can be applied in a variety of situations. A critical mistake here is that the motives, goals, and conditions have been abstracted away from the activity in the belief that this enables the student to "get down to" working on the essential processes of reading and writing. But . . . these features are critical aspects of the reading and writing themselves. By organizing instruction which omits them, the teacher ignores how literacy is practiced (and therefore learned) and thereby creates a situation in which the teaching is an inappropriate model for the learning.

Teale's words bring back memories of my days of teaching kindergarten during a time when reading readiness instruction flourished. Each year Froebel's and Dewey's influences diminished in the program because of the mandate for teaching skills. I questioned the relevance of some of the readiness activities for young children. The children were interested in looking at books, reading familiar words, and copying words that interested them. They approached the beginnings of literacy in ways that were meaningful, pleasurable, or functional. They carried out the reading readiness activities willingly, but it was obvious that they had no idea why they were doing them or how they were related to reading at all. This became even clearer to me in a conversation with Eric, who had chosen a worksheet on identifying initial consonant sounds.

"I see you are practicing your reading, Eric," I said.

He looked up at me and said "No, I'm not. I'm practicing my sounding."

I then said, "Right, sounding is practicing reading."

Eric looked up at me and said rather emphatically, "I'm not practicing reading, I am practicing sounding."

"But Eric," I said, "sounding is reading."

Even more annoyed, Eric responded, "Now let's get this straight: reading is reading and sounding is sounding."

That little interchange left a strong impression on me and launched my general questioning of the importance and relevance of the reading readiness program. In my observations of early childhood classrooms, I find that many teachers no longer schedule play time. Block corners and dramatic-play areas have disappeared from many rooms. Interdisciplinary units in social studies and science have been replaced with units on such skill instruction as learning the letter *t*. Classrooms are not relaxed, nor are they child-centered. Children spend most of their time working on one skill worksheet after another. Social, emotional, and physical development are no longer a major concern.

INFLUENCES FOR CHANGE IN EARLY-LITERACY PRACTICES

Researchers investigating early childhood literacy development are bringing about changes in theory and practice. Generally, they base learning and instructional strategies on what is known about cognitive development. They use varied research methodologies for data collection, including interviews and case studies in various cultural and socioeconomic settings. The research is field-based, taking place in classrooms and homes rather than in laboratories.

The first challenge to the attitudes rooted in the 1930s came in the 1960s and 1970s in studies of how children learn oral language. Although language acquisition is based somewhat on developmental maturity, much of the research concluded that children play an active role in their acquisition of language by constructing language. They imitate the language of adults and create their own when they do not have the conventional words they need to communicate their thoughts. Their first words are usually functional words, and they are motivated to continue generating language when their attempts are positively reinforced. Children who are constantly exposed to an environment rich in language and who interact with adults using language in a social context develop more facility with oral language than children lacking these opportunities (Bloom, 1972; Brown, 1973; Brown & Bellugi, 1964; Brunner, 1975; Cazden, 1972; Chomsky, 1965; Halliday, 1975; Lennenberg, 1967; McNeil, 1970; Menyuk, 1977). Findings from research on language acquisition motivated investigators to carry out similar studies of how reading was acquired. Since reading involves the use of language, many believed that the acquisition of oral language and reading might share some similarities.

Other studies investigated homes in which children learned to read without direct instruction before coming to school (Durkin, 1966; Heath, 1980; Holdaway, 1979; Morrow, 1983; Ninio & Brunner, 1978; Taylor, 1983; Teale, 1984). Such homes provide rich reading environments that include books and other reading materials from which children are free to select. These family members serve as models of involvement in literacy activities. For example, they answer children's questions about books and print. They read to children frequently and reward them for participating in literacy activities. The description of homes in which children seemed to learn to read quite naturally greatly interested those who saw in them possible implications for early literacy instruction in schools.

The phrase *learning to read naturally* is a bit misleading. It paints a picture of a child suddenly picking up a book and reading it, having had no instruction in reading at all. Actually, a great deal is happening in homes where children learn to read "naturally," without formal instruction. These homes are rich in the supportive and interactive behaviors conducive to learning to read. Specific studies of home storybook readings have provided us with information on the kinds of interaction that encourage literacy development. Analysis of the recorded questions and comments of children during shared book experiences at home have given us information on what children already know about books and print and what they are interested in finding out (Flood, 1977; Heath, 1980; Morrow, 1988a; Ninio & Bruner, 1978; Roser & Martinez, 1985; Yaden, 1985). The results of these home studies hold strong implications for change in classroom instruction.

In her research with preschool and kindergarten children, Yetta

Goodman (1984) found that many already knew certain things necessary for reading. These children knew the difference between letter characters and pictures in books, how to handle a book, and how to turn pages, and they knew that books are sources of meaning through printed words. Later work by Goodman and her colleagues concerned children's awareness of environmental print in familiar contexts and suggested that literacy-rich environments can make learning to read as natural as language acquisition.

Other researchers have looked at the acquisition of reading in early childhood from a developmental point of view. They have studied children's knowledge and acquisition of the function, form, and structure of print (Clay, 1972; Ehri, 1979; Gibson & Levin, 1975; Mason, 1980, 1982; Mason & McCormick, 1981). The work of these researchers reinforces many of the ideas found in the studies of oral language and home literacy. These authors advocate early childhood reading instruction, but not instruction that emulates first-grade practice. Rather they suggest more informal strategies similar to those discovered in homes where children learned to read without direct instruction. They also encourage activities that enhance language development and experiences in problem solving, listening to stories, and writing stories.

Another area of research in early childhood literacy is the burst of investigations on writing. Studies of children's first attempts to make marks on paper have made us aware that youngsters try to communicate in writing at a very early age. Through sample analysis of children's first attempts at writing, it is clear that they have an interest in writing, that they model adult writing behaviors, and that their scribbles, drawings, random letters, and invented spellings are early forms of writing (Clay, 1975). Many researchers now prefer to speak of reading and writing development as virtually one process. They view reading and writing as skills that build upon each other; when they are cultivated concurrently, each adds to proficiency in the other. Because it was traditionally perceived as developing after the ability to read, writing is an area that has certainly been missing from the early childhood curriculum. Research in early childhood writing has changed attitudes and promises dramatic implications for instruction. Encouraging writing in preschool and kindergarten and praising children's first attempts to write are becoming standard practices in early childhood classrooms.

The research and theories reviewed briefly here have enabled us to better understand the processes involved in becoming literate. Certain levels of maturity are required for a child to reach specific levels of ability. To acquire skill in oral language, writing, and reading, children need models to emulate and the freedom to create their own forms of reading, writing, and speaking. They must be positively reinforced and guided so that they will continue in their development.

We have come to realize that literacy development does not begin with

Tamika's early writing, attempts consisting of a mixture of letterlike forms and some real letters, need to be encouraged and positively reinforced.

formal instruction when children enter school. Children bring with them to school many concepts about literacy and certain competencies in oral language, writing, and reading. They have some command of their language and have internalized many of its rules and some of the processes for learning more about it. Many children know the difference between drawing and writing and can imitate writing in invented ways. Many children have developed reading vocabularies from such environmental print sources as road signs, food packages, and store displays. Children know that books are for reading and expect that they will be able to read books in the early stages of schooling. We cannot, therefore, rationally view literacy in early childhood as something achieved by drilling children in

Children need to be exposed to literacy early in life in the form of books and writing. Early attempts at literacy activity need to be encouraged and rewarded.

specific contrived skills. Rather, we need to build on children's existing knowledge of literacy and help their literacy evolve.

Research tells us that children learn best in situations that are meaningful and functional. Children have developed their levels of literacy in social and cultural contexts and through interaction with adults and other children. The instruction they receive should reflect to a certain extent the natural and meaningful way in which they have learned what they already know. Problems arise when the developmental, social, and natural environments in which literacy flourishes are exchanged for a systematic presentation of skills that do not reflect a child's stage of development socially, emotionally, physically, or intellectually. The chapters that follow address each of the areas involved in the process of becoming literate. They reflect both old and new ideas that have made us aware of needed changes in our approaches to early literacy instruction. Based on theory derived from recent research, they focus on oral language, writing, and reading and on how these are acquired. They also reflect the development of the child.

STAGES OF CHILD DEVELOPMENT*

Knowing what children are like developmentally, what they are capable of doing, and what they already know is important when preparing instructional environments. The following description of the developmental characteristics of children from birth through six years is provided here for reference throughout the volume.

* Adapted from Seefeldt and Barbour, 1986, pp. 63–69.

Infancy (birth through twelve months)

Physical
Develops rapidly.
Changes from waking because of hunger and distress to sleeping through the night with two naps during the day.
Changes eating patterns from every three hours to regular meals three times a day.
Develops control of muscles that hold up the head. By four months enjoys holding up head.
Focuses eyes and begins to explore the environment visually.
Begins to grasp objects at about sixteen weeks. Can grasp and let go by six months.
Rolls over intentionally (four to six months).
Holds own bottle (six to eight months).
Shows first tooth at about six months. Has about twelve teeth by age one.
Sits well alone, can turn and recover balance (six to eight months).
Raises body at nine months. May even pull self up to a standing position.
Starts to crawl at six months and to creep at nine or ten months.
May begin walking by age one.

Social
Begins to smile socially (four or five months).
Enjoys frolicking and being jostled.
Recognizes mother or other significant adult.
Notices hands and feet and plays with them.
By six months likes playing, alone or with company.
Begins to be wary of strangers.
Cooperates in games like peekaboo and pat-a-cake.
Imitates actions of others.

Emotional
Differentiates crying according to specific discomforts, such as being hungry, cold, or wet.
Shows emotions by overall body movements such as kicking, arm waving, and facial expressions.
Begins to show pleasure when needs are being met.
By six months shows affection by kissing and hugging.
Shows signs of fearfulness.
Pushes away things not liked.

Cognitive
First discriminates mother from others; later, discriminates familiar faces from those of strangers.
Explores world through looking, mouthing, grasping.
Inspects things for long periods.

As a first sign of awareness, protests disappearance of objects.

Discovers how to make things happen and delights in doing so by repeating an action several times.

Between six and twelve months becomes aware of object permanency by recognizing that an object has been taken away and by looking for a hidden object.

Begins intentional actions by pulling at an object or removing an obstacle to get at an object.

Becomes increasingly curious about surroundings.

Toddlers (one and two years)

Physical

Begins to develop many motor skills.

Continues teething till about eighteen months, develops all twenty teeth by two years.

Develops large muscles. Crawls well, stands alone (at about a year), and pushes chair around.

Starts to walk at about fifteen months; may still be wobbly at eighteen months.

Places ball in and out of box.

Releases ball with thrust.

Creeps down stairs backwards.

Develops fine motor skills. Stacks two blocks, picks up a bean, and puts objects into a container. Starts to use spoon. Puts on simple things—for instance, an apron over the head.

By end of eighteen months scribbles with a crayon in vertical or horizontal lines.

Turns pages of book.

During second year, walks without assistance.

Runs but often bumps into things.

Jumps up and down.

Walks up and down stairs with one foot forward.

Holds glass with one hand.

Stacks at least six blocks and strings beads.

Opens doors and cupboards.

Scribbles spirals, loops, and rough circles.

Starts to prefer one hand to the other.

Starts day control of elimination.

Social

At age one differentiates meagerly between self and other.

Approaches mirror image socially.

By eighteen months distinguishes between terms *you* and *me*.

Plays spontaneously; is self-absorbed but notices newcomers.

Imitates behavior more elaborately.

Identifies body parts.

Responds to music.

Develops socialization by age two. Is less interested in playing with parent and more interested in playing with a peer.

Begins parallel play, playing side by side, but without interaction.

By age two learns to distinguish strongly between self and others.

Is ambivalent about moving out and exploring.

Becomes aware of owning things and may become very possessive.

Emotional

At age one is amiable.

At eighteen months is resistant to change. Often suddenly, won't let mother out of sight.

Tends to rebel, resist, fight, run, hide.

Perceives emotions of others.

At age one, shows no sense of guilt. By age two, begins to experience guilt and shows beginnings of conscience.

Says no emphatically. Shows willfulness and negativism.

Laughs and jumps exuberantly.

Cognitive

Shows mental imagery: looks for things that are hidden, recalls and anticipates events, moves beyond here and now, begins temporal and spatial orientation.

Develops deductive reasoning: searches for things in more than one place.

Reveals memory: shows deferred imitation by seeing an event and imitating it later. Remembers names of objects.

Completes awareness of object permanence.

By age two or three distinguishes between black and white and may use names of colors.

Distinguishes one from many.

Says "one, two, three" in rote counting, but not often in rational counting.

Acts out utterances and talks about actions while carrying them out.

Takes things apart and tries to put them back together.

Shows sense of time by remembering events. Knows terms *today* and *tomorrow*, but mixes them up.

Preschoolers (three to four years)

Physical

Expands physical skills.

Rides a tricycle.

Pushes a wagon.

Runs smoothly and stops easily.

Climbs jungle gym ladder.

Walks stairs with alternating feet forward.

Jumps with two feet.

Shows high energy level.

By four can do a running broad jump.

Begins to skip, pushing one foot ahead of the other.

Can balance on one foot.

Keeps relatively good time in response to music.

Expands fine motor skills for dressing. Manipulates zippers, maybe even buttons.

Controls elimination at night.

Social

Becomes more social.

Moves from parallel play to early associative play. Joins others in activities.

Becomes aware of racial and sexual differences.

Begins independence.

By four shows growing sense of initiative and self-reliance.

Becomes aware of basic sex identity.

Not uncommonly develops imaginary playmates (a trait that may appear as early as two and a half).

Emotional

Begins enjoying humor. Laughs when adults laugh.

Develops inner control over behavior.

Shows less negativism.

Develops phobias and fears, which may continue until age five.

At four may begin intentional lying but is outraged by parents' white lies.

Cognitive

Begins problem-solving skills. Stacks blocks and may kick them down to see what happens.

Learns to use listening skills as a means of learning about world.

Still draws in scribbles at age three, but in one direction and less repetitively.

At age four, drawings represent what child knows and thinks is important.

Is perceptually bound to one attribute and characteristic. "Why" questions abound.

Believes everything in the world has a reason, but the reason must accord with the child's own knowledge.

Persists in egocentric thinking.

Begins to sort out fantasy from reality.

Early Primary (five and six years)

Physical

Well controlled and constantly in motion.

Often rides a bicycle as well as a tricycle.

Can skip with alternating feet and hop.

Can control fine motor skills. Begins to use tools such as toothbrush, saw, scissors, pencil, hammer, needle for sewing.

Has established handedness well. Identifies hand used for writing or drawing.

Can dress self but may still have trouble tying shoelaces.

At age six begins to lose teeth.

Social

Becomes very social. Visits with friends independently.

Becomes very self-sufficient.

Persists longer at a task. Can plan and carry out activities and return to projects next day.

Plays with two or three friends, often for just a short time only, then switches play groups.

Begins to conform. Is very helpful.

By age six becomes very assertive, often bossy, dominating situations and ready with advice.

Needs to be first. Has difficulty listening.

Is possessive and boastful.

Craves affection. Often has a love–hate relationship with parents.

Refines sex roles. Has tendency to type by sex.

Becomes clothes-conscious.

Emotional

Continues to develop sense of humor.

Learns right from wrong.

At age five begins to control emotions and is able to express them in socially approved ways.

Quarrels frequently, but quarrels are of short duration.

At age six shifts emotions often and seems to be in emotional ferment. New tensions appear as a result of attendance at school all day. Temper tantrums appear.

Giggles over bathroom words.

At age five develops a conscience, but sees actions as all good or all bad. At age six accepts rules and often develops rigid insistence that they be obeyed.

May become a tattletale.

Cognitive

Begins to recognize conservation of amount and length.

Becomes interested in letters and numbers. May begin printing or copying letters and numbers. Counts.

Knows most colors.

Recognizes that one can get meaning from printed words.

Has a sense of time, but mainly personal time. Knows when events take place in his or her day or week.

Recognizes own space and can move about independently in familiar territory.

ACTIVITIES

1. Observe three different preschools. Determine what theoretical influences have determined the type of practices carried out. Document your findings with specific anecdotes illustrating the theory.

2. After observing the preschools, for your own information, make constructive suggestions for improving practice; include specific materials or activities based on the theories discussed in this chapter.

3. Describe practices in the same preschools that seem to have been initiated because of the newer thinking in early childhood literacy instruction.

4. Using one of the literacy skills (reading, writing, listening, speaking), teach a lesson for preschoolers that reflects the doctrines of Piaget. Repeat for Froebel, then Montessori, and finally Dewey. In other words, teach the same lesson four different ways.

2

The Home as a Vehicle for Literacy Development

CHAPTER OVERVIEW

- "Learning to read naturally" does not just happen, nor does it require formal instruction at home.
- Homes conducive to a child's early development of literacy are rich in interaction, reading and writing materials, and emotional support.
- Schools interested in early childhood literacy development disseminate information that parents can use from the moment a child is born.

You may have tangible wealth untold:
Caskets of jewels and coffers of gold.
Richer than I you can never be—
I had a Mother who read to me.

STRICKLAND GILLILAN
The Reading Mother
from *Best Loved Poems of the American People*

Parents are the first teachers children meet. They are also children's teachers for the longest periods. Beginning at birth, children's experiences affect their success in becoming literate individuals. The success of the school literacy program frequently depends on the literacy environment at home. Studies carried out in homes have been a major catalyst for the new look in early literacy strategies. Because many children come to school already reading and writing, apparently without formal instruction, investigators began to study the characteristics of those children and of their homes. Such children were said to have "learned to read naturally," a phrase that suggests that their ability to read evolved like their aquisition of language or their learning to walk.

This line of investigation has been extremely helpful from two points of view. First, the findings reveal home practices that could be successful in school settings. Second, they provide information on the crucial role parents play in the development of their children's literacy and on how they can help. The school can disseminate this information to parents.

I can attest to the vital role of the home in the development of early literacy. From the day of my daughter Stephanie's birth I read to her. I read to her daily while she sat on my lap, always in the same chair. We looked at books. I talked about the pictures and read the stories. By five months, Stephanie would listen as I read to her. I chose mostly cardboard picture storybooks with only a few words on each page. From time to time her eyes focused intently on the brightly colored pictures. First she would be serious; next she would break into a broad smile. Sometimes she reached out to touch the book. Occasionally she made pleasant sounds that seemed attempts to imitate my reading voice. Because the experience was daily and positive, she became familiar with story readings and welcomed them.

As Stephanie grew older, her responses to the readings increased. Before she could talk, she pointed to pictures and made sounds as if naming objects or characters. As she acquired oral vocabulary, she labeled things in the book as I read. Quite naturally I responded with pleasure, reinforcing her attention and understanding of the concepts. Often I explained things beyond the words in the book. Both of us looked forward to these times we shared. They were relaxing, warm, and pleasurable. The practice has been referred to as the lap technique in storyreading (Mc-Cracken & McCracken, 1972).

By the time she was fourteen months old, Stephanie could often be found sitting on the floor reading a book—that is, reading as a four-teen-month-old can. She knew how to hold the book right side up, she knew which was the beginning of the book and which was the end, and she knew how to turn the pages. She looked at the pictures and chanted in tones similar to the sound of my reading. Except for a word here and there, most of her language was not understandable, but from a distance one might think that this baby was reading. Actually she was—not in the conventional manner, but by demonstrating early literacy behavior.

Books were all around the house. Stephanie had an accessible shelf of books in her room. We kept a crate of books with her toys on the floor of a closet, and she was free to use them at all times. There were books in the kitchen, the bathroom, and play areas. My husband and I had many books of our own, and we read a lot, both professional literature and recreational materials such as novels, magazines, and newspapers. Stephanie saw her parents reading frequently. At times she joined us with her own books just to feel like part of the group.

In addition to books, Stephanie had access to pencils, crayons, and markers, along with large supplies of different kinds of paper. Before three years it was quite natural for her to pick up a pencil and a sheet of paper, sit down and draw a picture, and even write about it. I could not identify what Stephanie had drawn, but she would talk about it. She was well aware of the difference between drawing and writing, and the squiggles of "print" looked different from the scribbles of the drawing. Although not yet capable of either drawing or writing in the formal sense, she attempted to do both and differentiated between them.

In the house and on trips to the supermarket or post office, environmental print surrounded her as it does other children. Cognizant of its importance in the development of early literacy, I pointed out STOP signs at street corners and asked her to name as many signs as she could as we drove along. At home we read cereal boxes, directions for assembling new toys, and mailing addresses. As a result, her awareness of the print around her and of its functions was heightened. She quite naturally learned to ask what labels said and looked to print for information.

When she was three and four, our story readings became more interactive. Stephanie asked questions and commented about pictures and episodes. I responded with answers and comments that expanded the discussion. She began to narrate familiar stories with me as I read. Occasionally she asked what certain words were as her attention focused more and more on print as well as on pictures.

Stephanie was sitting in the back seat of the car on the way home from our weekly trip to the library. She was looking through one of the books she had selected and began reading it out loud. It was a humorous story called *Ten Apples Up on Top* (LeSieg, 1961). The book used a limited number of words, repetitive vocabulary, and rhyme. The attractive illustrations reflected the text. As she read, I first assumed that the book was one we had read together. Suddenly I realized it wasn't. I pulled to the side of the road and with great excitement confirmed what I thought was true. Stephanie was reading, actually reading on her own! She had made the transition from half-reading, half-narrating stories.

Stephanie had reached this point in her literacy development quite gradually and naturally, unaware that her reading at four and a half was unusual. I had offered no formal reading instruction, nor was there any such instruction in her nursery school. Because of her constant exposure to books and print from birth, she had developed a large sight vocabulary as well as a number of reading skills. Her ability to read, in other words, did not just happen. Rather, it developed in a natural way within a rich literacy environment.

FACTORS IN LITERACY DEVELOPMENT IN THE HOME

According to Leichter (1984), families influence literacy development in three ways: (1) interpersonal interaction, (2) physical environment, and (3) emotional and motivational climate. *Interpersonal interaction* consists of the literacy experiences shared with a child by parents, siblings, and other individuals in the home. The *physical environment* includes the literacy materials available in the home. The *emotional and motivational climate* comprises the relationships among the individuals in a home, especially as reflected in the parents' attitudes towards literacy and their aspirations for their children's literacy achievement.

Various researchers have studied homes in which children have read early without direct instruction (Briggs & Elkind, 1973; Clark, 1976; Durkin, 1966; King & Friesen, 1972; Morrow, 1983; Plessas & Oakes, 1964; Teale, 1978). The results have consistently established that certain characteristics are common to these children and their homes. The IQ scores of early readers are not consistently high; they range from low-average to above average. Early readers can accomplish Piagetian concrete operational tasks, and are interested in pencil-and-paper activities, letters, and words. Their parents read to them, readily help them with writing and reading, and often read themselves. These parents read a great variety of material, including novels, magazines, newspapers, and work-related information. They own or borrow books, both for themselves and for their children. Reading material can be found throughout their homes, in living rooms, bedrooms, family rooms, playrooms, kitchens, and bathrooms. Parents in these homes often take their children to libraries and bookstores

(Morrow, 1983). The homes hold ample supplies of books and writing materials, and reading is generally valued as an important activity. Books are associated with pleasure, and literary activities are rewarded. The homes are well organized, with scheduled daily activities, rules, and designated responsibilities for family members. They provide a setting where interactions between adults and children are socially, emotionally, and intellectually conducive to literacy interest and growth (Holdaway, 1979).

The families of early readers tend to be small. Many of the parents have college educations, but Hansen (1969) argues that it is a literacy-rich environment, not parents' education, occupation, or socioeconomic level, that correlates most highly with children's early reading. Children with an early interest in reading tend to spend playtime at home writing and drawing with paper and crayons or looking at books. They watch television fewer hours a week than children who do not show an early interest in reading. Parents in these homes enforce rules for selecting and limiting television viewing (Whitehead, Capey, & Maddren, 1975). These children are rated by their teachers as higher than average in social and emotional maturity, work habits, and general school achievement. They also perform well on standardized readiness tests (Morrow, 1983).

Durkin (1966), Holdaway (1979), Taylor (1983), and Teale (1984) all describe home environments in which the ability and desire to read develop quite naturally. These homes provide rich reading environments that include books and other reading materials from which children are free to select. They offer social contexts in which children are actively involved with others who serve as models of involvement in literacy activity. The adults reinforce the interest of children in reading by cooperating with them in literacy activities.

Parents frequently ask teachers what they can do at home to help their children learn to read and write. In the past teachers suggested that parents drill children on the alphabet or help them with the sounds of letters. Many parents became convinced that formal teaching of skills would help their children get a head start. The newer research on early literacy suggests otherwise. When parents provide a rich literacy environment at home, teaching reading and writing becomes easier for both the teacher and the child at school. Because most children do not enter public school before age five and nursery school before age three, if at all, schools need to take responsibility for disseminating information in the community that parents can implement at home. Such information follows.

AVAILABILITY OF PRINT MATERIALS

Durkin (1966), King and Friesen (1972), and Morrow (1983) found that books were readily accessible to children who read early. Parents can provide library corners for their children, preferably in their bedrooms; even a little space is sufficient. Two cinder blocks and a piece of wood make a fine bookshelf, low enough for a child to reach. In addition, books can be made available all around the house. Kitchens and bathrooms are important, since children spend considerable time in both places. If there is a playroom or a place for toy storage, it should contain books. Virtually every room can hold books that are visible and accessible. Before babies are crawling or walking, books can be brought to them in cribs and playpens; waterproof books are available for bathtubs.

A variety of books should be selected for the home. For babies up to eighteen months, brightly colored concept books with cardboard, plastic, or cloth pages are appropriate. They must be safe, with rounded edges, and sturdy enough to withstand chewing and other rough treatment. As the child becomes a toddler, preschooler, and then kindergartener, nursery rhymes, fairy tales, folktales, picture storybooks, realistic literature, informational books, picture books, alphabet books, number books, poetry, books related to favorite television programs, and easy-to-read books (those with limited vocabularies, large print, and pictures closely associated with the text) should be made available. (See Appendix A for a list of books for children, Appendix B for children's book clubs, publishers of children's books, and awards for children's books.) Children's magazines offer attractive print material for children, and are a special treat if they come in the mail. In addition to children's literature, print material for adults, including books, magazines, newspapers, and work-related material, should be obvious in the home.

READING AS A HOME ACTIVITY

Research indicates that children who are read to regularly by parents, siblings, or other individuals in the home, and who have parents who are habitual readers themselves, are the youngsters who become early readers

Print materials such as books and magazines need to be readily available for children to use at a very young age.

and show a natural interest in books (Briggs & Elkind, 1973; Clark, 1976; Durkin, 1966; King & Friesen, 1972; Plessas & Oakes, 1964; Teale, 1978). That is not surprising. Through frequent story readings children become familiar with book language and realize the function of written language (Smith, 1971). Story readings are almost always pleasurable, which builds a desire and interest in reading (Arbuthnot & Sutherland, 1977; Cullinan, 1977; Huck, 1976; Smith & Parker, 1977; Stewig & Sebesta, 1978). Continued exposure to books develops children's vocabulary and sense of story structure, both of which help them learn to read (Chomsky, 1972; Cohen, 1968; Mandler & Johnson, 1977; Morrow, 1985).

It is quite clear that verbal interaction between adult and child during story readings has a major influence on literacy development (Cochran-Smith, 1984; Flood, 1977; Ninio, 1980). Such interaction offers a direct channel of information for the child and thus enhances literacy development (Heath, 1982; Morrow, 1987a; Ninio & Brunner, 1978). It leads children to respond to story readings with questions and comments. These responses become more complex over time and demonstrate more sophisticated thinking about printed material. Research on home storybook readings has identified a number of interactive behaviors that affect the quality of read-aloud activities. Those behaviors include questioning, scaffolding (modeling dialogue and responses), praising, offering information, directing discussion, sharing personal reactions, and relating concepts to life experiences (Applebee & Langer, 1983; Cochran-Smith, 1984; Flood, 1977; Roser & Martinez, 1985; Taylor & Strickland, 1986). Many parents engage their children in such interactive behavior rather naturally.

The following transcription from the beginning of a story reading between a mother and her four-year-old son Ian (Morrow, 1986a) illustrates how the adult invites and scaffolds responses, answers questions, offers positive reinforcement, and responds supportively to the child's questions and comments. As a result of the prompts, information, and support, Ian pursues his questions and receives additional information.

Mother: Are you ready for our story today, Ian? This is a new book. I've never read it to you before. It's about a mother and her baby bird.

Ian: (points to the title on the front cover) Hey, what's this for?

Mother: That's called a title. It says "Are You My Mother?" That's the name of the book. See, it's right here, too: "Are You My Mother?"

Ian: (long pause, then points to the words) "Are You My Mother?"

Mother: Right, you read it. See, you know how to read.

Ian: It says "Are You My Mother?" (points again with finger)

Mother: You read it again. Wow, you really know how to read!

Ian: Um, now read the book and I'll read it, too.

Ian's mother read the story. Each time they came to the words *Are you my mother?* she paused and looked at Ian, pointed to the words, and exaggerated her reading of the sentence. After two such episodes, Ian no longer needed prompting and simply read along each time they came to the phrase.

Research findings suggest that teachers should encourage parents to read to their children daily. Reading can begin the day a child is born. It must be recognized, however, that an infant's ability to listen attentively is generally limited and varies from one reading to the next. An infant may prefer to chew on the book or pound it rather than listen to it. However, babies read to from birth begin very early to be attentive in story reading situations.

From birth to three months, a child's attention to book reading is erratic. The baby who stares at the pictures and seems content and quiet can be considered receptive. If the baby wiggles, shows discomfort, or cries, the adult might just as well stop reading until the next time.

From three to six months, babies become more obviously involved in book readings. They begin to focus on pictures and to listen. Often, they will grab for the book, pound it, and try to put it in their mouth. As long as they seem content they are probably involved with the reading.

Six-to-nine-month-olds can be purposefully involved in story readings. They might try to turn pages. They might respond to changes in the reader's intonation or make sounds and movements to demonstrate in-

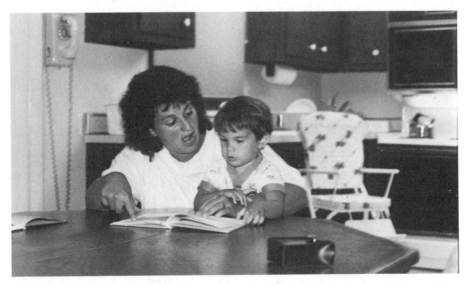

The interactive behavior between parent and child during storybook reading involves negotiating, mediating, and constructing meaning related to the print.

volvement and pleasure. They sometimes begin to show preferences for books that have been read to them before.

Babies approaching one year show strong involvement in being read to. They might take a leadership role in turning pages, or babble along in tones that sound like reading. They actively look in the book for familiar things that they remember from other readings.

By one year to fifteen months, babies who have been read to can tell which is the front and which is the back of a book and if the book is right side up or not. They begin to identify and name characters in the book. They take an active part in reading along with the adult, verbalizing a great deal (Schickedanz, 1986).

Fathers, mothers, grandparents, baby-sitters, and older siblings should all read to younger children. Let reading become a ritual, done at the same time and in the same place each day. Bedtime is a favorite time and bedtime stories are a good reading habit to establish. Both child and parent look forward to it as a time to share at the end of the day. Reading before children go to sleep has a calming effect; it establishes a routine for the children, who will eventually read by themselves before going to bed.

Spontaneous readings are encouraged as well, and if a parent finds it easier to read at different times of the day, it is certainly more desirable to do this than not to read at all. Reading to babies requires that the infant be held in the parent's arms. When the youngster is able to sit up alone, parent and child should be close to each other, preferably with the child on the adult's lap. The book with its pictures and print must be visible to the child. Children should be considered active participants in the story reading. Their comments and questions should be encouraged and acknowledged. Parents should relate comments about the story to life experiences when-

By six months the baby can be purposefully involved in story readings, pointing to pictures and demonstrating interest and pleasure.

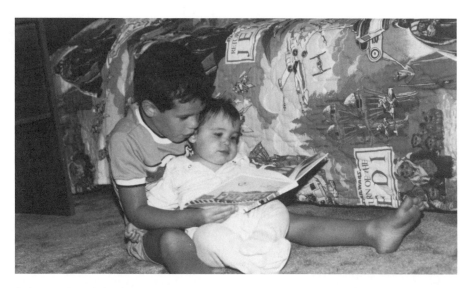

Fathers, mothers, baby-sitters, grandparents, and older siblings should read to children.

ever possible and question children about familiar things in a relaxed manner to encourage their involvement.

Parents also need to read themselves. Children learn by emulating adult behavior. Imitation is one of the major sources of language acquisition. It has been found that children whose parents read at home become avid readers themselves. The parents become models for reading behavior that the child is likely to emulate.

In addition to reading to their children and reading themselves, parents should make a point of providing time for the family to read together. Sitting all together around the kitchen table or in the den or living room, each member of the family reading his or her own book, makes for a pleasant, rich literacy activity. Talking about what each family member is reading is an important part of the experience.

AVAILABILITY OF MATERIALS FOR WRITING

Some of the researchers who reported characteristics of early readers also found that these children spend a great deal of time and show a great deal of interest in pencil-and-paper activities (Clark, 1976; Durkin, 1966; Morrow, 1983; Plessas & Oakes, 1964). The parents of many such children reported that the interest in writing began with scribbling in babyhood. Certain scholars have suggested that writing develops naturally before reading. Many children, they point out, invent writing systems of their own that seem to have meaning for them (Read, 1971). Whether reading comes before writing or writing before reading is an unsettled issue. What we have come to recognize, however, is that learning to read is enhanced by concurrent experiences with writing and that the development of writing is facilitated by experiences with reading.

One implication of these findings is that writing materials should be made available for children at home. A variety of sizes of unlined white paper is preferable, especially for babies. As children get into their preschool years and kindergarten, smaller sheets can be added to the household supply. A child approaching kindergarten might like lined paper as well. Pencils, crayons, colored pencils, a chalkboard and chalk, and markers all are appropriate home writing tools. Manipulatives such as magnetic, felt, or wooden letters are also useful. Children should be exposed to them early and have free access to them. Typewriters and home computers encourage writing and are appropriate for preschoolers. (A list of computer software for young children can be found in Appendix E.)

As with book reading, youngsters need to see their parents involved in writing activities. Parents should communicate with their children through writing as often as possible. When children begin preschool, notes can be placed in lunch boxes that say simply, "Hi! Love, Mommy and Daddy." Notes on pillows can say "Good night" or "Good morning." Children will emulate parents who take opportunities to communicate through writing.

RESPONSIVE ADULTS ENCOURAGE LITERACY

Studies of early readers reveal that the adults in their environment tended to be receptive and responsive to their interest in literacy activities (Clark, 1976; Durkin, 1966; King & Friesen, 1972; Plessas & Oakes, 1964). Parents answered children's questions about books and print, offered information, provided experiences that enhanced literacy development, and praised children for participating in literacy behaviors. Such channels of information and support systems in the home naturally encourage the development of reading. Durkin (1966) found that parents who attempted to teach children more formally were not as successful as parents who simply responded to children's requests for information about reading.

Responsiveness between parent and child needs to begin with babies and be cultivated. Responsive adults respond in many ways. Language provides a primary opportunity for developing this behavior. Responsive adults not only answer questions, they initiate activities that promote literacy. While dressing, diapering, or feeding an infant, for instance, a parent can talk, sing, recite nursery rhymes, and tell stories. The baby responds by smiling, cooing, and moving, encouraging the parent to continue, and a cycle of mutual responsiveness develops.

Environmental print surrounds children and holds meaning for them. This natural source of reading material offers a way into literacy through things whose function children are already familiar with (Downing, 1970). Children begin to read and ask about environmental print probably before they are interested in the print found in books. Parents who are aware of the importance of environmental print can point out familiar labels and other information on cereal boxes, vitamin bottles, detergent containers, and food packages. Children are naturally interested in telephone books, cookbooks, television guides, advertisements, and mail. They are particularly interested in personal letters, fliers, greeting cards, bills, catalogs, and magazines. The outside world presents a wealth of environmental print: road signs, street signs, and the names of fast-food restaurants, gas stations, and other well-known chains. Parents note the environmental print that is meaningful to children and encourage children to do the same, pointing out specific letters in these familiar words and even sounding the letters. This gamelike involvement in skills has been found to promote early literacy (Tobin, 1981).

In addition to responding to requests about books and print, parents of early readers generally respond to the need to provide varied experiences for their children. They take them to libraries and bookstores. They talk to them a great deal, which builds the children's vocabulary. Trips to zoos, fire stations, airports, and parks all foster literacy growth if they are accompanied by oral language and positive social interactions. It should be emphasized that a trip not only broadens a child's experience but allows verbal interactions between parent and child before, during, and after. Those interactions include providing the child with background about the place to be visited and the things to be seen, answering questions about the experience, offering information, reading stories related to the experience, and discussing the trip afterwards so that new ideas are absorbed. Suggesting that the child record the experience by drawing a picture about it and dictating a story for the parent to write will further expand literacy growth.

Television is part of our lives and definitely here to stay. To make the most of TV viewing, parents should watch some programs with their youngsters, posing questions, raising critical issues, and changing passive viewing into responsive interaction. Choose programs for which parallel books are available, such as "Sesame Street," "Reading Rainbow," and "Mister Rogers." When specific stories are scheduled on television, such as *How the Grinch Stole Christmas* (Seuss, 1957), borrow or purchase the book. (Books associated with TV shows are listed in Appendix D.)

In a series of interviews with parents whose children were early readers (Morrow, 1980) it became apparent that literacy was embedded in daily activities that were meaningful, functional, and part of the mainstream of their lives. Various print materials were visible in the homes. Language was used interactively and frequently, in all its forms and in a positive emotional climate. There was praise for literacy activity and pleasure and joy in reading and writing. When asked what they believed helped their children become literate so early, the parents found it difficult to answer because they had not viewed the experiences they offered their children as attempts to promote reading and writing. Most of these activities had other functions, such as keeping the house running smoothly. Many of the experiences had social objectives—to promote positive interpersonal relationships and to teach responsibility and manners, for example. Here are some anecdotes related by some of these parents:

> "I started a baby book for each of my children from the day they were born, with information about their weight and height, and I included pictures. I made sure to report major events, such as first words, first steps, likes and dislikes concerning food, and events of interest to me. I found myself looking at the book frequently and my toddler snuggling beside me showing great interest. I've continued the books and as the children are getting older they add to them and read them over and over. They are without a doubt among their favorite books."

> "Long trips can be tedious with young children in the car. To make the time pass we play games. Some games that are fun in the car are trying to rhyme words, reading road signs, and reading letters and numbers on the license plates of cars."

> "As a grandfather I don't get to see my grandchildren as frequently as I would like. In order to keep close contact, I often send them things through the mail. I'll enclose games cut from the children's section of the newspaper which I'll ask them to complete. I send them pictures of famous people and ask them to call and tell me who they think they are. Sometimes I include questions and tell them it is a contest for which they can win a prize if all their answers are correct."

> "From the time they were very young, my children were required to write thank-you notes for gifts received. At first they dictated them and I wrote down what they said. Later they were able to write simply 'thank you.' One good incentive for the task was to allow them to choose their own stationery for note writing."

> "The public library has provided many fine experiences for my children. One in particular is to help prepare them for experiences to come and allow them to relive experiences they have. Before we went to the circus, we took a circus story out of the library in preparation for our trip. After seeing the circus we enjoyed another circus story from the library. No one's home library could ever be as complete as the public library and going to the library for books is such a good habit to get into."

> "I started leaving notes for my children in surprise places before they could read. Somehow they managed to find out what the notes said, even at the pre-reading stage. Now I put messages in their lunch boxes. The notes often just say 'hello.' Sometimes I'll write a riddle or a joke, and sometimes the note may require an answer. This has become a family tradition and lately I find surprise notes addressed to me left in the most unusual places."

"The amount of TV viewing by our three- and four-year-old children was a source of aggravation to us. To make the experience a more meaningful one we read the television program guide to decide on what programs to watch and to limit the number of selections that the children are allowed to make in one day. We try to watch at least some programs with them and ask *who, what, when,* and *where* questions to elicit recall of facts. We also ask *why* questions to encourage more interpretive responses."

"I've always kept a journal recording my daily experiences. My four-year-old found me writing in it one day and asked about what I was doing. She wanted to do the same thing, so we started a joint journal. I'd write things that happened to me during the day and she'd tell me what to write for her. Soon she was able to do her own writing. Sometimes I'd ask her questions about what she'd written. I did this by writing in the journal, of course, and she would have to answer. The journal had no formal format, except that each of us wrote about an event of the day, and we would share the same journal page."

Researchers have found that home environments possessing the characteristics described here will generally instill an interest in reading, a desire to read, and the ability to read early. It should be noted that most of the data from the investigations that provided this information were correlational. Therefore, it is difficult to draw conclusions about cause and effect. There are children from homes that display all of the characteristics described who are not early readers and have difficulty learning to read. There are early readers from environments lacking the characteristics described. Obviously there are factors other than the environment that effect successful literacy development. But, it has been demonstrated that environmental factors do play a strong role in fostering literacy. A rich literacy environment at home gives children a better chance to learn to read easily and to enjoy reading as well.

School personnel should inform parents of the school's program in literacy development through orientation programs and regular newsletters. The letter can tell parents what is being studied, include samples of children's work, and offer suggestions for enriching the child's experience at home. Anecdotes concerning promoting literacy at home such as those just cited can be solicited from parents. Parents should be given lists of quality children's literature related to what is being studied and suggestions for toys that promote literacy. A list of suggested books is found in Appendix A. Finally, parents can be invited to school to help with such literacy activities as reading to children, taking story dictations, and helping with bookbinding projects.

The school also needs to take on the responsibility of getting information to homes about the need for rich literacy environments. Information can be disseminated through special meetings for expectant parents, in hospital maternity wards, in obstetricians' and pediatricians' offices, and through churches, synagogues, and community agencies. A succinct hand-out such as the one that follows will be a helpful start. (Books and pamphlets on the development of literacy at home can be found in Appendix C.)

Parent's Guidlines for Promoting Early Literacy
at Home

   Your youngster's ability to read and write depends to a great extent upon the things you do at home from the time he or she is born. As a parent you can do many things to help that will not take much of your time. The rewards from these activities will be enormous in terms of your child's reading and writing. The following list suggests materials, activities, and attitudes that are important for promoting literacy at home.

Materials
   1. Have at least twenty-five children's books available at home and add to the collection regularly.
   2. Subscribe to a children's magazine.
   3. Place some of your child's and some of your own books, magazines, and newspapers in various rooms throughout your home to encourage spontaneous reading in spare moments.
   4. Provide materials that will encourage children to tell or create their own stories, such as puppets, feltboard and felt story characters, story records, tapes of stories, and a tape recorder.
   5. Provide materials for writing, such as crayons, felt-tip pens, pencils, and plenty of white paper of different sizes.

Activities
   1. Read to your child daily and talk about the stories.
   2. If your child is able, have him or her read along with you.
   3. Visit the library at least once every two weeks.
   4. Tell stories to each other.
   5. Talk about things you've read.
   6. Provide a model for your child by reading yourself.
   7. Provide a model for children by writing.
   8. Heighten your child's awareness of the function and uses of print by pointing out words, written notes, and other items of print used in your daily life. Read environmental print such as words on cereal boxes, other food packages, and road signs. Occasionally communicate through written messages.

Fostering Positive Attitudes
   1. Reward your child's attempts at reading and writing by offering praise.
   2. Answer your child's questions about reading and writing.
   3. Let reading and writing be enjoyable experiences so that children associate them with pleasure.

ACTIVITIES

1. Observe children in a preschool. Focus on two children, one who seems to illustrate traits characteristic of an early reader and one who does not. For each child list the behaviors that determined whether you viewed him or her as an early reader or not.

2. Interview the parents of the children selected in activity 1 and determine the home activities in which each child participates. Base your interview on the guidelines for promoting early literacy at home.

3. Observe a kindergartener at home. List all the characteristics of the household that illustrate the elements that can contribute to early reading. Make a second list of things the family could do to improve the literacy environment.

4. Interview members of your family, friends, and parents of young children. Ask them to relate specific activities they have done with youngsters to promote literacy, natural events that arose from daily living. Collect the ideas, write them up in a newsletter, and share them with parents of young children.

5. The characteristics of homes of early readers are influencing practices in early childhood literacy development. Design a nursery school program including materials, activities, and teacher behaviors that is based on the characteristics of homes where children are found to read early.

6. Tape record a parent reading a story to a preschool child. Then transcribe the reading, noting the parent's comments and classifying them as informing, questioning, or supporting. Count the number of questions the child asks and classify them as well—for example, questions about meaning, about print, about parts of the book, about pictures. What types of comments do parents make the most? On the basis of the children's comments and questions, what interests them most about the book?

3

Language as a Vehicle for Developing Literacy

CHAPTER OVERVIEW

- Reading is related to language development.
- There are several theories of language acquisition.
- Stages of language development during early childhood can be identified and described.
- Strategies and techniques are available for aiding and assessing language development.

"The time has come," the Walrus said,
"To talk of many things:
Of shoes and ships and sealing-wax,
Of cabbages and kings. . . ."

LEWIS CARROLL
"The Walrus and the Carpenter"

The kind of talking to which Lewis Carroll refers in his poem is very much the language babies need to hear in their first steps toward literacy. From the moment of birth, the infant is surrounded by oral language. The language development that social context initiates is the child's first step to becoming a totally literate individual; it makes reading and writing possible. Traditional methods of initial reading instruction have been challenged by recent research on language acquisition. Using newer research methods that involve close observation of children, investigators have been able to describe the strategies by which youngsters learn and use language. Among the many things these researchers have observed is that children are *active participants* in their learning of language. In order to learn, children involve themselves in problem solving, first creating hypotheses and then interacting with those individuals around them who are generating language. They do not learn language passively; they actually construct—or reconstruct—language as they learn. This discovery laid the foundation for a new way of looking at how early reading is acquired. Researchers realized that because reading is a language process it must be closely associated with oral language.

LANGUAGE DEVELOPMENT AND READING

Now that language processes are commonly recognized as the basis for learning to read, *language learning* is considered an integral part of *learning to read*. Ruddell (1971) defines reading as the use of one's language ability to decode and comprehend. Goodman (1967) calls it the interaction between the reader and the written language. He states that reading is the attempt by a reader to reconstruct the author's message, that the graphic sequences and patterns that appear as print represent the oral sequences of language. In the process of reading, we look and listen for recognizable grammatical sequences and patterns that trigger appropriate phrasing. Using what we already know of language structure, we then test how each word fits into the context of what we are reading. Lennenberg and Kaplan (1970) tend to agree with Goodman's view. They see the reader as continually assigning tentative interpretations to the text and then checking those interpretations. As readers, we use syntactic and semantic cues that enable

39

us to predict what comes next. Our skill in processing semantics (meaning) and syntax (language structure) makes us more adept readers. As Athey (1971) points out, the reader who encounters unfamiliar language structures and unfamiliar concepts in material to be read has difficulty understanding it. Familiarity with both syntax and semantics enables even the very young reader to anticipate the format and content of sentences in print. Past theory held that it was our accumulation of letters and words that led to competent reading. Now we realize that our ability to understand what we are reading is based on our *reconstruction* of the meaning behind a printed word. Such reconstruction is based on our previous experience with the topic, our familiarity with its main concepts, and our general knowledge of how language works.

The relationship between reading and language is evident in studies of children who are early readers. It has been found, for instance, that early readers score higher on language screening tests than children who were not reading early. Early readers come from homes where rich language and a great deal of oral language are used (Snow & Perlmann, 1985). When interviewed, parents of early readers revealed that their children tended to use very descriptive language and sophisticated language structures. The youngsters invented words, used humor, and talked a lot. The mother of a four-year-old early reader reported that while watching the first snowfall of the year her youngster said, "The snow is swirling down and looks like fluffy marshmallows on the ground." One spring day a few months later the same child noted, "Look, Mommy, the butterflies are fluttering around. They look like they are dancing with the flowers."

Halliday (1975) notes that among other functions, language helps children learn how to ascertain meaning from the world around them. Early readers demonstrate an awareness of story language (Snow, 1983). They can retell stories using such literary conventions as "Once upon a time" and "They lived happily ever after." When telling stories they tend to use delivery and intonation like those of an adult reading aloud. Cazden (1972) suggests that such "book language" takes children beyond their own language patterns and is distinctively characteristic of early readers.

HOW CHILDREN ACQUIRE LANGUAGE

Although we do not have all the answers about language acquisition, there are many theories that help explain how babies learn to speak. Knowing how language is acquired has strong implications for providing environments that promote language development. It also implies how reading and writing skills develop.

The *behaviorists* have influenced our thinking about how language is acquired. Although behaviorism does not present the total picture, it still offers ideas about language acquisition that ought to be considered for instruction. Skinner (1957) defined language as the observed and produced speech that occurs in the interaction of speaker and listener. Thinking, he said, is the internal process of language; both language and thought are initiated through interactions in the environment—such interactions as those between a parent and a child, for instance. According to behaviorists, adults provide a language model that children learn through imitation. The child's acquisition of language is enhanced and encouraged by the positive reinforcement of an adult.

The behaviorist description of language acquisition is incomplete, but it is evident that children imitate adult models and are motivated to continue using language because of positive reinforcement. Children surrounded by rich language begin to use the language they hear, even though imitation sometimes occurs with erroneous comprehension or no comprehension at all. A child can imitate the sounds of the "words" of a familiar song, for instance, with no concern at all for meaning. A three-year-old girl sang "My country 'tis of thee" as "My country tis a bee." A four-year-old sang "Torn between two lovers" as "Torn between two mothers." Both children were imitating what they heard and were thus acquiring language. But when they came upon unfamiliar words in context, both substituted similar-sounding words that had meaning for them from their own experiences.

In most environments early attempts at language are rewarded. When newborns coo or make other verbal sounds, most parents are delighted and respond with gentle words of encouragement. The infant, in turn, responds to the positive reinforcement by repeating the cooing sounds. As babies get older and are able to formulate consonant and vowel sounds they try them out. It is not uncommon to hear a six-month-old playing with sounds such as *ba, ba, ba,* or *ma, ma, ma.* The responsive parent perceives such sounds as the child's first words and assumes that the child's *ma-ma* means *mommy.* The delighted adult says more warm and loving things to the baby and adds hugs and kisses. The parent might say, "Come on, now say it again, ma, ma, ma." The baby is pleased with the warm reception and tries to repeat the sounds in order to receive additional reinforcement.

As a child builds an oral vocabulary, he or she tries words more frequently. Children will point to a toy and name it. While playing with a ball, a child may say the word *ball* over and over again. The attentive parent now reinforces the child's words by extending and expanding the original language (Cazden, 1972). After the child says *ball,* the parent may say, "Yes, that is a nice, big, round, red ball." Through such extension and reinforcement of words by the adult, the child acquires new language. The adult often expands upon the baby's words by asking, for instance, "Now what can you do with that nice red ball?" Such expansion requires the child to think, understand, and act. Positive reinforcement encourages practice, which helps continue language development.

Unfortunately, the converse is also true. If a baby's babbling is considered annoying, if the parent is aggravated by the sound and responds with negative reinforcement by telling the baby in harsh tones, "Be quiet and stop making so much noise," the child is less likely to continue to explore the use of language.

Chomsky (1965), Lennenberg (1967), and McNeil (1970) have described the *nativist* theory of language acquisition. They contend that language develops innately. Children figure out how language works, say the nativists, by internalizing the rules of grammar, which enable them to produce an infinite number of sentences. They do so even without the practice, reinforcement, and modeling offered by adult language, which are considered necessary by the behaviorists. The ability to learn language must be innate to humans, the nativists believe, since almost all children develop and use language in the first few years of their lives. Language growth depends on maturation: as children mature, their language grows. Children learn new patterns of language and unconsciously generate new rules for new elements of language. The child's rule system increases in complexity as he or she generates more complex language. Lennenberg (1967), an extreme nativist, finds nothing in the child's environment to account for language development. Rather, language acquisition is motivated *inside children;* learning language is a natural ability. Although maturation does play a role in language development, newer theories offered by Piaget & Vygotsky have come to be the more accepted ideas concerning language acquisition.

Piaget's theory of *cognitive development* is built on the principle that children develop through their activity. Children's realization of the world is tied to their actions or their sensory experiences in the environment. According to this theory, children's first words are egocentric, or centered in their own actions. Children talk about themselves and what they do. Their early language as well as their general development relates to actions, objects, and events they have experienced through touching, hearing, seeing, tasting, and smelling (Piaget & Inhelder, 1969).

Vygotsky's theory of *basic learning* also has implications for language development. According to Vygotsky, children learn higher mental functions by internalizing social relationships. Adults initially provide children with names of things, for instance; they direct youngsters and make suggestions. Then, as children become more competent, the adults around them gradually withdraw the amount of help they need to give. Vygotsky describes a *zone of proximal development* (1978), a range of social interaction between an adult and child. Theoretically, the child can perform within that range, but only with adult assistance. Proximal development ends when the child can function independently. The implications for language instruction are clear: to promote language development, adults need to interact with children, encouraging, motivating, and supporting them (Sulzby, 1986a).

Brown, Cazden, and Bellugi-Klima (1968), Halliday (1975), and Smith (1973) all describe the acquisition of language as an active process. The child creates and constructs language, often making errors. But making errors is a necessary part of learning how language works (Harris & Smith, 1980), and we tend to accept language errors quite readily in a child's first years. The implications are important for early literacy development. Even though language development charts tell us when to expect certain stages of language development on average, we do not discipline babies who have not uttered their first words at eight months or their first complete sentences by two and a half years. Sometimes we even find their errors cute. We seem to respect their individuality and their right to grow at their own pace. Yet when children enter school we neglect to recognize developmental differences; we prescribe tasks based on a curriculum, not on the child.

The process of acquiring language is continuous and interactive; it takes place in the social context of the child interacting with others. Children also learn by playing with language themselves. They try out new words, involve themselves in monologues, and practice what they have learned. The acquisition of language varies from child to child, depending on their social and cultural background (Jagger, 1985). Their remarks illustrate that children do not *simply* imitate adult language. It is as if children need to express themselves but do not have sufficient conventional language to draw upon, so they create their own based on their backgrounds and their awareness of semantics and syntax.

A three-year-old saw a freckled youngster for the first time and said,

Children learn language from social interaction with a responsive adult who provides a language model and positive reinforcement for the child's early language attempts.

"Look, Mommy, that little girl has *sprinkles* on her nose." A four-year-old observed an elderly man with deep wrinkles and said, "I wonder why that man has *paths* all over his face." A father and his three-year-old daughter were toasting marshmallows; the little girl said, "Mmmm, I can smell the taste of them." After a quick summer rain, a three-year-old boy observed the sun returning to the sky and the water evaporating all around him. "The sun came out and ate up all the rain," he observed. Towards the end of the winter as the snow was melting, a four-year-old girl observed, "See how the grass is peeking out from underneath the snow."

The several theories just discussed help us to understand how language is acquired. Each has something to offer, but by itself does not present a complete picture. We *do* know, however, that children's language grows according to their need to use it, their interests, and the meaning it has for them. In other words, according to Halliday (1975), what can be said reflects what can be done. Children's language is acquired through exploration and invention and is controlled by their own maturity, the structure of the language, and its conventions.

STAGES IN LANGUAGE DEVELOPMENT

Children acquire language by moving through predictable stages. In doing so, they discover the rules that govern the structure of language—specifically, those of phonology (sound), syntax (grammar), and semantics (meaning).

There are forty-four separate sounds, or *phonemes* in English. With them we produce oral language. Children who grow up in a language-rich environment can learn these sounds quite easily. They learn appropriate articulation, pronunciation, and intonation. *Intonation* involves pitch, stress, and juncture. *Pitch* refers to how high or low a voice is when producing a sound, *stress* to how loud or soft it is, and *juncture* to the pauses or connections between words, phrases, and sentences (Hittleman, 1983).

Syntax refers to the rules that govern how words work together in phrases, clauses, and sentences. Internalizing the syntactic rules of our language helps children understand what they hear and what they read. Syntax includes rules for forming basic sentence patterns, rules for transforming those patterns in order to generate new sentences, and rules for embedding, expanding, and combining sentences in order to make them more complex. Brief examples follow:

1. Some Basic Sentence Patterns
    a. Subject–verb: *The girl ran.*
    b. Subject–verb–object: *The girl ran the team.*
    c. Subject–verb–indirect object–direct object: *Susan gave Lynn a dime.*

d. Subject–to be–noun or adjective or adverb complement: *Tom was the captain. He was happy. He was there.*

e. Subject–linking verb–adjective: *Jane is tall.*

2. Some Basic Sentence Transformations

a. Question

(1) kernel: *Jim went to the store.*

(2) transformation: *Did Jim go to the store?*

b. Negative

(1) kernel: *Jane is a cheerleader.*

(2) transformation: *Jane is not a cheerleader.*

c. Passive

(1) kernel: *Jennifer gave Lisa some bubble gum.*

(2) transformation: *Some bubble gum was given to Lisa by Jennifer.*

3. Some Embeddings (sentence expansion and combination)

a. Adding modifiers (adjectives, adverbs, adverbial and adjective phrases)

(1) kernel: *The boy played with friends.*

(2) transformation: *The boy in the red pants played with three friends.*

b. Compounding (combining words, phrases, or independent clauses to form compound subjects, verbs, etc.)

(1) kernel: *Jane ran. Jane played. Jack ran. Jack played.*

(2) transformation: *Jane and Jack ran and played.* (Morrow 1978)

Semantics deals with the meaning that language communicates, both through content words and through function words. It largely governs vocabulary development. *Content words* carry meaning in themselves. *Function words* have no easily definable meanings in isolation, but they indicate relationships between other words in a sentence. Function words include prepositions, conjunctions, and determiners (Pflaum, 1986).

Although we have identified stages of language growth, the pace of development may differ from child to child. An individual child's language development also tends to progress and then regress, so that the stages of growth are not always easily recognized. However, language development has been studied to the extent that it can be described generally (Grieve & Hoogenraad, 1979).

From Birth to One Year

In the first few months of infancy, oral language consists of a child's experimenting or playing with sounds. Infants cry when they are uncomfortable and babble, gurgle, or coo when they are happy. Parents are able to distinguish cries. One cry is for hunger and another is for pain, for instance. Infants learn to communicate specific needs by producing different cries. They communicate nonverbally as well by moving their arms and legs to express pleasure or pain.

When a baby is about six months old, its babbling becomes more sophisticated. Children at that age are usually capable of combining a variety of consonant sounds with vowel sounds. They tend to repeat these combinations over and over. As mentioned earlier, it is at this stage that parents sometimes think they are hearing their child's first words. The repeated consonant and vowel sounds, such as *da, da, da,* or *ma, ma, ma,* do sound like real words, ones that the parents are delighted to hear. Most parents tend to reinforce the child's behavior positively at this stage. Repetition of specific sounds and continued reinforcement lead the child to associate the physical mechanics of making a particular sound with the meaning of the word the sound represents.

From eight to twelve months, children increase their comprehension of language dramatically; their understanding of language far exceeds their ability to produce it. They do, however, tend to speak their first words, usually those most familiar and meaningful to them in their daily lives: *Mommy, Daddy, bye-bye, baby, cookie, milk, juice,* and *no,* for instance. As they become experienced with their first words, children use holophrastic speech—one-word utterances, that express an entire sentence (Smith, 1972). For example, a baby might say "cookie," but mean "I want a cookie," "My cookie is on the floor," or "I'm done with this cookie."

From One to Two

A child's oral language grows a great deal between one and two. Along with one-word utterances, the child utters many sounds with adult intonation as if speaking in sentences. These utterances are not understandable to adults, however. Children begin to use telegraphic speech from twelve months on—the first evidence of their knowledge of syntax. Telegraphic speech uses content words, such as nouns and verbs, but omits function words, such as conjunctions and articles. In spite of the omissions, words are delivered in correct order, or syntax: "Daddy home" for "Daddy is coming home soon," or "Toy fall" for "My toy fell off the table."

Language grows by leaps and bounds once the child begins to combine words. By eighteen months most children can pronounce four-fifths of the English phonemes and use twenty to fifty words (Biehler, 1976).

From Two to Three

This year is probably the most dramatic in terms of language development. Typically, a child's oral vocabulary grows from 300 words to 1000. The child can comprehend, but cannot yet use, 2000 to 3000 additional words. Telegraphic sentences of two or three words continue to be most frequent, but syntactic complexity continues to develop, and the child occasionally uses such functional words as pronouns, conjunctions, prepositions, articles, and possessives. As their language ability grows, children gain confidence. They actively play with language by repeating new words and phrases and making up nonsense words. They enjoy rhyme, patterns of language, and repetition (Brown, 1973). Consider the following transcription of Jennifer's dialogue with her dog. Jennifer was two years ten months at the time. "Nice doggie, my doggie, white doggie, whitey, nicey doggie. Good doggie, my doggie, boggie, poggie. Kiss doggie, kiss me, doggie, good doggie." Jennifer's language is repetitive, playful, silly, and creative, demonstrating some of the characteristics of language production typical for a child her age.

From Three to Four

A child's vocabulary and knowledge of sentence structure continue to develop rapidly during the fourth year. Syntactic structures added to the child's repertoire include plurals and regular verbs. Indeed, children of this age are prone to overgeneralization in using these two structures, mainly because both plural formation and verb inflection are highly irregular in our language (Jewell & Zintz, 1986). Four-year-old Jonathan illustrated both problems when he had an accident in class and came running over very upset. He said, "Mrs. Morrow, hurry over, I knocked over the fishbowl and it broked and all the fishes are swimming on the floor." Jonathan knew how to form the past tense of a verb by adding *ed* but he didn't know about irregular verbs such as *broke*. He also knew about adding an *s* to form a plural but again was unaware of irregular plural forms such as *fish*.

As they approach age four, children *seem* to have acquired all the elements of adult language. They can generate language and apply the basic rules that govern it. However, although their ability with language has grown enormously and they sound almost as if they are using adult speech, they have really acquired only the basic foundations. Language continues to grow throughout our lives as we gain new experiences, acquire new vocabulary, and find new ways of putting words together to form sentences. At the age of three to four, children talk about what they do as they are doing it. They often talk to themselves or by themselves as they play. It seems as if they are trying to articulate their actions (Seefeldt & Barbour, 1986). While painting at an easel, four-year-old Christopher said to himself, "I'm making a nice picture. I'm making colors all over. I'm painting, pit, pat, pit, pat. I'm going back and forth and up and down. Now I'm jumping as I paint." He carried out this monologue while painting this picture. As he talked and painted, he did exactly what he said, words and actions coinciding.

From Five to Six

Five- and six-year-olds sound very much like adults when they speak. However, their vocabularies are always increasing, and so is the syntactic complexity of their language. They have vocabularies of approximately 2500 words each, and they are extremely articulate. Many, however, still have difficulty pronouncing some sounds, especially *l, r,* and *sh* at the ends of words. They become aware that a word can have more than one meaning. When they are embarrassed or frustrated at misunderstanding things, they say something silly or try to be humorous. They also tend to be creative in using language. When they do not have a word for a particular situation, they supply their own. Adults often find the language used by children of this age to be very amusing as well as delightful and interesting (Seefeldt & Barbour, 1986).

For example, Benjamin ran into school very excited one morning. "Mrs. Morrow," he said, "you'll never believe it. My dog grew puppies last night!"

My husband and I were going to a formal dance one evening. My five-year-old daughter had never seen us dressed up like this before. When I walked into the room wearing a long gown and asked Stephanie how I looked, she said,"Mommy, you look soooo pretty. What is Daddy's costume going to be like?"

Escorted by her mother, Allison was on her way to her first day of kindergarten. She seemed a little nervous. When her mother asked her if she was okay, Allison replied, "Oh, I'm fine, Mommy. It's just that my stomach is very worried."

There are other characteristics of kindergarteners' language. Kindergarteners have discovered bathroom talk and curse words and they enjoy shocking others by using them. They talk a lot, and begin to use language to control situations. Their language reflects their movement from a world of fantasy to that of reality.

HALLIDAY'S THEORY OF LANGUAGE DEVELOPMENT

Halliday (1975, p. 7) describes language development as a process by which children gradually "learn how to mean." According to his theory of developmental language, what a child can do during interactions with others has meaning, and meaning can be turned into speech. In other words, children's initial language development is based on function: what can be said reflects what can be done. Halliday (1975, pp. 19–21) identifies seven functions evident in the language of young children:

1. *Instrumental:* children use language to satisfy personal needs and to get things done.
2. *Regulatory:* children use language to control the behavior of others.
3. *Personal:* children use language to tell about themselves.
4. *Interactional:* children use language to get along with others.
5. *Heuristic:* children use language to find out about things, to learn things.
6. *Imaginative:* children use language to pretend, to make believe.
7. *Informative:* children use language to communicate something for the information of others.

LANGUAGE DIFFERENCES

A major instructional concern in early childhood literacy programs is the varied language backgrounds of the many children who come to day-care centers, preschools, and kindergartens. Any given group may contain children using words, syntax, and language patterns quite different from those of standard English. Particularly in the United States, there are many forms of English usage that differ from the standard English expected in schools. There are, for example, distinct grammars in rural New England, Appalachia, and in some black communities. There are children whose families have immigrated from Latin America, the Middle East, or Asia. Foster (1982, p. 14) compiled six categories that represent the diverse language abilities of preschool children:

1. Recent immigrants with little or no English.

2. Children whose home language is something other than English, but who are themselves likely to know at least some English because of their experiences with television and their contacts outside the home.

3. Children who speak both English and another language fluently. Such children are usually easily assimilated into the majority group. Often English becomes the major language with which they communicate. They then risk losing the advantages that fluent bilingualism gives them.

4. Children who speak mainly English but who have poor skills in their parents' or family's language. Often these children speak English at home, but their parents speak to them in another language. Children in this group sometimes deny their heritage and are ashamed of the cultural differences between themselves and their majority classmates at school.

5. Children who speak nonstandard English because the English spoken at home is nonfluent or a dialect. Although they need to learn standard English at school, they must not be made to feel that their home language is inferior.

6. The vast majority of children, those who are monolingual in a pluralistic society. Their "understanding and appreciation of the various cultures in America," said Foster, "would be greatly enhanced through study in another language besides English."

All six categories represent major concerns because a firm base in oral language bears a strong relationship to literacy development. A child fluent in any form of nonstandard English will have difficulty reading and writing without proficiency in standard English. Along with this concern for skill development are affective concerns. Unfortunately, teachers have been known to look down on children with language differences and to classify them as students with potential learning problems. We have come to realize, however, that differences do *not* mean deficits. Linguists have found, for example, that black English is a systematic, rule-governed dialect that can express all levels of thought (Robinson, Strickland, & Cullinan, 1977). Teachers must be sensitive to the differences in language among youngsters in their classrooms. Children must not be embarrassed or made to feel inferior because they do not speak standard English. Teachers need to respect language differences and help children take pride in their backgrounds. Diversity in language and heritage should be shared in classrooms to enrich the classroom experience.

Pragmatically, children must become fluent in the language used at school. If they are expected to read standard English, they need a firm foundation in speaking standard English. According to Pflaum (1986), young children do not have a great deal of difficulty acquiring new language. She suggests that the typical preschool seems to provide a linguistic environment that enables young children to learn standard English if they are required to speak it. An environment that provides varied experiences and opportunities to converse helps the child acquire the ability to speak the language. Children who speak nonstandard dialects, such as black English, need the opportunity to use their own dialects in school during creative dramatics or in storytelling and discussions. Any child given the opportunity to use language frequently and effectively, even if it is not standard English, will be receptive to language learning in general (Robinson, Strickland, & Cullinan, 1977). Frequent opportunity to use language in varied situations will help children become more fluent. As Gonzales-Mena has pointed out (1976, p. 14):

> 1. Children are eager to learn English or any other new language when there is an openness and an acceptance of them, their culture, and their native language.
>
> 2. Language should not be taught in isolation from any of the other basic school activities, but as a part of the total, integrated program, which includes focus on language development. Listening, speaking, reading, and writing are all a part of math, social studies, art, and science.
>
> 3. Children learn through their senses, including their muscles. Concepts as

well as new words and phrases are learned better when children can participate in some action. They need to examine and explore real objects and act out new expressions. Pictures can help, but action imprints the message in a stronger fashion.

STRATEGIES FOR LANGUAGE DEVELOPMENT

The review of theory and research suggests how we can help children acquire and develop language pleasantly, productively, and appropriately. Children acquire language by emulating adult models and experiencing positive reinforcement for their efforts. If language is innate, it can develop naturally as individuals pass through common stages of development at certain times in their lives. As children mature, they become capable of generating ever more complex language structures. They learn language by doing, by acting upon and within familiar environments. Their first spoken words are those that are meaningful for them within their own experiences. Their earliest language is an expression of needs. They learn language through social interaction with individuals more literate than they, whether adults or older children. Children also create their own language, play with it, and engage in monologues.

Using what we know of language acquisition and developmental stages as guidelines, we can begin to create and prepare appropriate materials, activities, and experiences in a suitable atmosphere to nurture a youngster's language development. The following objectives are formulated for a program fostering language development in children from birth to seven.

OBJECTIVES FOR THE DEVELOPMENT OF RECEPTIVE LANGUAGE

1. Children will be provided with an atmosphere in which they will hear language frequently.
2. Children will hear language associated with pleasure and enjoyment.
3. Children will be given opportunities to discriminate among sounds heard.
4. Children will be exposed to rich sources of new words.
5. Children will be given opportunities to listen and comprehend what others say.
6. Children will be given opportunities to learn to follow directions.

OBJECTIVES FOR THE DEVELOPMENT OF EXPRESSIVE LANGUAGE

1. Children will be given opportunities to use their own language freely at any stage of development. Their desire to communicate will be encouraged, accepted, and respected.
2. Children will be encouraged to pronounce words correctly.

3. Children will be given opportunities to increase their speaking vocabularies.
4. Children will be encouraged to speak in complete sentences at appropriate stages in their development.
5. Children will be given opportunities to expand their use of various syntactic structures, such as adjectives, adverbs, prepositional phrases, dependent clauses, plurals, past tense, and possessives.
6. Children will be encouraged to communicate in such a way that they are understood by others.
7. Children will be given opportunities to use language socially and psychologically by interpreting feelings, points of view, and motivation and by solving problems by generating hypotheses, summarizing events, and predicting outcomes.
8. Children will be given opportunities to develop language that involves mathematical and logical relations, such as describing size and amount, making comparisons, defining sets and classes, and reasoning deductively.

Language is best learned when integrated with other communication skills and other content-area subjects in a meaningful environment. Isolating that objective and trying to teach that skill to a child does not promote the development of lifelong literacy. For growth, natural settings are optimal.

Strategies for Language Development from Birth to Two

"Hi, Michael. How's my great big boy today? Let's change your diaper now, upsy-daisy. My goodness, you're getting heavy. Now I'll put you down right here on your dressing table and get a nice new diaper for you. Here, want this rubber ducky to hold while I change you? That's a good boy. You really like him. Let's clean you up now. This is the way we clean up Michael, clean up Michael, clean up Michael. This is the way we clean up Michael, so he'll feel so much better. You like that singing, don't you. I can tell. You're just smiling away, and cooing. Want to do that again? This is the way we clean up Michael, clean up Michael, clean up Michael. This is the way we clean up Michael, so he'll feel so much better. Wow, you were singing with me that time. That's right, ba-ba-ba-ba, now do it again. Mmmmm, doesn't that smell good? The baby powder is so nice and smooth."

Michael was four months old when his mother's conversation with him was taped. Here in print, it reads like a monologue; in reality it was not. Michael was a very active participant in the conversation. He stared intently at his mother's face. He cooed, he waved his arms, he smiled, he became serious. His mother was providing a rich language environment for her baby. She encouraged his participation in the dialogue, and acknowledged his responsiveness in a positive way. She provided him with the environmental stimuli necessary for his innate language ability to flourish. She engaged him in this type of conversation during feedings and while changing, bathing, and dressing him. She talked to him even when he was in his crib and she in another room or while in the same room but involved in other things. The baby knew that communication was occurring since he responded to the talk with body movements, coos, babbles, and smiles. When he responded his mother responded in turn; response brought response, back and forth.

Infants need to be surrounded by the sounds of happy language. Whether from mother, father, care-giver at home, or teacher or aide in a day-care center, sounds and interaction should accompany all activities. Adults responsible for babies from birth through the first year need to know nursery rhymes, chants, finger plays, and songs. It is important for children simply to hear the *sounds* of language as well as the meanings. Thus, adults can make up their own chants to suit an occasion, as Michael's mother did when she spontaneously adapted "Here We Go Round the Mulberry Bush" to the situation at hand. Such experiences make the baby conscious of the sounds of language. Children learn that they can have control over language and that oral language can be a powerful tool as well as fun.

In addition to the conversation of nearby adults, infants should experience other sounds and other voices: soft music from a radio, record player, or music box. They need to hear the sounds of "book language," which differs in intonation, pitch, stress, juncture, and even syntax from normal conversation. They need familiarity with language in all its variety so they can learn to differentiate among its various conventions and patterns. Speaking to infants, singing to them, reading to them, and letting them hear the radio and television provide sources of language that help their own language grow. In addition, there are sounds in the immediate environment that need no preparation and are not the sounds of language but that provide practice in auditory discrimination—the ringing of the doorbell, the hissing of the teapot, the chimes on the clock, the hum of the vacuum cleaner, a dog barking, a bird singing, a car screeching, and so on. Bring them to the baby's attention, give them names, and heighten the child's sensitivity to them.

In addition to hearing a variety of sounds, the baby needs objects to see, touch, smell, hear, and taste. They should be placed in the baby's immediate environment—the crib or playpen. They will stimulate the baby's activity and curiosity and become the meaningful things within the environment from which language evolves. Some of the objects should make sounds or music when pushed or touched. They can have different textures and smells. They should be easy to grab, push, kick, or pull. They can be placed so they are visible and within the child's reach, and at least one item should be suspended overhead: stuffed animals, rubber toys, music boxes made of soft material, plastic or wooden mobiles that can be kicked or grasped, mechanical mobiles that hang from the ceiling and

Reading to young children provides book language—a source of new vocabulary and new sounds with different stress, pitch, and intonation.

rotate by themselves, and books with smooth edges. Books can be propped open against the side of the crib or playpen when the baby is lying on its back, or against the headboard when the baby is on its stomach. Certain familiar objects should always remain, and new objects frequently made available. In addition to allowing the child to play independently with these objects, the adults in charge need to talk about them, name them, occasionally join the child in playing with them, and discuss their characteristics and what they are capable of doing. Objects should have different textures and scents, make different sounds, and provide different visual effects. Some should be chewable.

From three to six months the baby gurgles, coos, begins to laugh, and babbles. Recognize an infant's sounds as the beginning of language. Reinforce the infant positively with responses aimed at encouraging the sounds. When the baby begins to put consonants and vowels together, again reinforce the behavior, imitating what the baby has uttered and urging repetition. When the baby becomes aware of the ability to repeat sounds and control language output, he or she will do these things. Babies will also begin to understand adult language, so it is important to name objects, carry on conversations, and give the baby directions. At the end of its first year, assuming he or she has experienced appropriate sounds of language as well as encouragement and pleasant interaction, the baby will be on the verge of extensive language growth during its second year.

Through the second year of a child's life the adults in charge need to continue the same kinds of stimulation suggested for developing oral language during the first year. However, since during the second year the baby is likely to develop a vocabulary of up to 150 words and to produce two- and possibly three-word sentences, additional techniques can be used to enhance language growth. As described earlier, one- and two-word utterances by children at this age usually represent sentences. When a twelve-month-old points to a teddy bear and says "bear," the child probably means "I want my bear." Parents and care givers at home or in day-care centers can begin to expand and extend the child's language at such times by helping to increase the number of words the child is able to use in a sentence or by increasing the syntactic complexity of their own utterances.

One method for helping a child develop ability with language is a kind of modeling called *scaffolding* (Applebee & Langer, 1983). In scaffolding, an adult provides a verbal response for a baby who is not yet capable of making the response itself. In other words, the adult provides a language model. When the baby says "bear," for instance, the adult responds, "Do you want your teddy bear?" or "Here is your nice, soft, brown teddy bear." In addition to expanding on the child's language, the adult can extend it by asking the youngster to do something that demonstrates understanding and extends his or her thinking. For example, "Here is your nice, soft, brown teddy bear. Can you hug the teddy? Let me see you hug him." In addition to questions that require action, the adult can ask questions that require answers. Questions that require answers of more than one word are preferable—for example, "How does it feel to hug your teddy?" *How, why,* and *tell me* questions encourage the child to give more than a yes/no answer and more than a one-word response. *What, who, when,* and *where* questions, on the other hand, tend to elicit only one-word replies. As the child's language ability develops, the adult provides fewer and fewer such "scaffolds"; the child learns to build utterances along similar models.

Select songs, rhymes, and books for one-to-two-year-olds that use language they can understand. They are capable of understanding a great deal of language by now, and the selections should help extend and expand their language. Both vocabulary and conceptual understanding are enhanced by experiences. For the one-to-two-year-old, frequent outings are desirable. Visits to the post office, supermarket, dry cleaners, and park provide experiences to talk about and new concepts to explore. Household tasks taken for granted by adults are new experiences that enrich children's language. Involve them in activities. For example, an eighteen-month-old can put a piece of laundry into the washing machine or give one stir to the bowl of gelatin or some other food that is being prepared. During such daily routines, surround the activity with language, identifying new objects for the baby and asking for responses related to each activity.

As the child becomes more verbal, the adult sometimes wants to correct the child's mispronunciations or overgeneralization of grammatical rules. The child who says, "Me feeded fishes," for instance, has simply overgeneralized the rules for

* forming most past tenses (*feeded* for *fed*);
* using pronouns (objective *me* for subjective *I*); and
* forming most plurals (*fishes* for *fish*).

Children can also overgeneralize concepts. A child who has learned to associate a bird with the word *bird* might see a butterfly for the first time and call it a bird, thinking that anything that flies is a bird. Correcting such an overgeneralization is best done positively rather than negatively. Instead of saying, "No, that's not a bird," simply refer to the butterfly as a *butterfly*, commenting on its beauty, perhaps, and thus extending the child's verbal repertoire. Eventually, with positive reinforcement and proper role models in language, the child will differentiate between birds and butterflies as well as between regular and irregular grammatical conventions and forms.

Correcting overgeneralizations negatively as absolute error, on the other hand, is not likely to help young children understand the error or use proper tense and plural forms the next time. Rather, it is likely to inhibit the child from trying to use language. In learning, children need to take risks and make mistakes. Hearing good adult models will eventually enable them to internalize the rules of language and to correct their errors themselves. At least until age five the child should be allowed to experiment and play with language without direct concern for 100 percent correctness in syntax and pronunciation. The English language is extremely complex and irregular in many of its rules; in time, the child will master these rules in all their complexity and nuance, given good adult models and plenty of verbal interaction. At the same time, encouraging "baby talk" simply because it is cute, for instance, is likely to inhibit growth since children will use whatever language they believe will please the adults around them.

Materials for the one-to-two-year-old should be varied and more sophisticated than those in the first year. Now that the baby is mobile in the home or day-care center, books need to be easily accessible to the child. Toys should still include items of various textures, such as furry stuffed animals and rubber balls. Other toys should require simple eye–hand coordination. Three-to-five-piece puzzles, trucks that can be pushed and pulled, dolls, a child-size set of table and chairs, crayons and large paper, and puppets are examples. Choose objects that require activity, for activity encourages exploration, use of the imagination, creation, and the need to communicate.

Strategies for Language Development in Early Childhood Classrooms

From three to seven a great deal of language development occurs. Children who demonstrate most of the developmental traits previously discussed are ready for language acquisition in instructional settings. They should continue to hear good models of language. They need continued opportunities to use language in social situations with adults and other children. Their oral language production must be reinforced positively. They must be actively involved in meaningful experiences that will expand their knowledge and interest in the world around them. Language should be purposeful and its development integrated with other subjects rather than taught separately as a content area unto itself.

To accomplish these continuing goals, early childhood teachers provide an environment in which language will flourish. They organize centers of learning, one for each content area, that include materials for encouraging language use. A science center, for instance, can include a pair of gerbils. Gerbils are active, loving animals, fun to watch and handle. Children surround the cage often and generate talk just from watching the animals. Gerbils reproduce in twenty-eight-day cycles. When litters arrive, the birth process can be observed, the new babies causing a great deal of excitement and generating questions, comments, and unlimited conversation.

In my own classroom, our parent gerbils reproduced a second litter twenty-eight days after the first and before the first babies had been weaned. The mother looked tired and thin from feeding and caring for ten baby gerbils. One morning one of the children noticed that the mother was not in the cage. We couldn't imagine what had happened to her. A few days later, having almost given up hope, we found her hiding behind the refrigerator in the teachers' room. We never figured out how she got out of the cage, but we hypothesized all kinds of possibilities, and there was a great deal of discussion about why she left. No teacher alone could provide a lesson in which language flourished and grew the way it did during that incident, simply because gerbils were part of the classroom.

Here are some examples of centers of learning and appropriate materials in early childhood classrooms that will help to generate language.

Science: aquarium, plants, magnifying glass, class pet, magnets, thermometer, compass, prism, shells, rock collections, stethoscope, kaleidoscope, microscope, books reflecting topics being studied.

Social studies: maps, a globe, flags, community figures, traffic signs, current events, artifacts from other countries, books reflecting topics being studied.

Art: easels, watercolors, brushes, colored pencils, crayons, felt-tip markers, various kinds of paper, scissors, paste, pipe cleaners, scrap materials (bits of various fabrics, wool, string, and so forth), clay, play dough, food and detergent boxes for sculptures, books about famous artists, books with directions for crafts.

Music: piano, record player and records, tape recorder with musical tapes, rhythm instruments, songbooks.

Mathematics: scales, rulers, measuring cups, movable clocks, stopwatch, calendar, play money, cash register, calculator, dominoes, abacus, number line, height chart, hourglass, numbers (felt, wood, and magnetic) fraction puzzles, geometric shapes, number books.

Literacy: children's literature, tape recorder, headsets and taped stories, pencils, writing paper, stapler, construction paper, three-by-five cards for recording words, hole punch, letter stencils, typewriter, computer, puppets, storytelling devices such as felt-board and roll movies, stationery with envelopes, letters (felt, wood, and magnetic), sets of pictures for different units (Halloween, seasons, animals, and so on), rhyme games, color games, cards for associating sounds and symbols, alphabet cards, pictures and words representing out-of-school environmental print (*Burger King, Dairy Queen, Exxon*). (The literacy center also includes a library corner, a writing center, oral language materials, and language arts manipulatives, all of which are described in later chapters.)

Dramatic play: dolls, dress-ups, telephone, stuffed animals, mirror, food cartons, plates, silverware, newspapers, magazines, books, telephone book, class telephone book, cookbook, note pads, cameras and photo album, table and chairs, broom, dustpan, child-size kitchen furniture such as refrigerator, sink, ironing board, and storage shelves. (The dramatic-play area can be changed from a kitchen to a grocery store, beauty shop, gas station, business office, or restaurant with the addition of appropriate materials.)

Block area: blocks of many different sizes and shapes and figures of people, animals, toy cars, and trucks.

Workbench: wood, hammer, screwdriver, saw, pliers, nails, worktable.

Outdoor play: sand, water, pails, shovels, rakes, gardening area and gardening tools, climbing equipment, riding toys, crates, playhouse, balls, tires, ropes.

Children need opportunities to use such areas for interacting with each other and the teacher, and they should be given enough time to touch, smell, taste, listen, and talk about what they are doing. Exploring and experimenting with the materials in the centers are creative, imaginative, problem-solving, decision-making experiences in which children use language and thereby give it the opportunity to grow. The opportunity to *use* language is one of the key elements in language development.

Some materials remain permanently in the centers; others are replaced or supplemented from time to time so that new items of interest become available. Materials added to the centers are often coordinated with units of instruction. For example, if a unit on Indians is introduced, Indian dolls and artifacts are added to the social studies center, and books about Indians to the literacy center. The different content-area centers provide

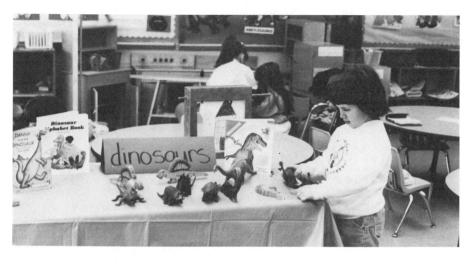

Experiences in science lead to new discoveries, new vocabulary, and reasons to talk and discuss.

Varied art experiences with different media encourage descriptive language and develop the manual dexterity needed for writing.

sources for language use and development; the literacy center is devoted *primarily* to language development. Units of instruction that integrate all areas make learning more meaningful and expand concepts. (Interdisciplinary instruction is described more fully in Chapter 9.)

　　Each new unit of instruction offers specific language experiences that extend vocabulary, syntax, pronunciation, and the ability to understand others and be understood. Again, these experiences should incorporate all content areas and make use of the senses. The suggestions that follow can be used each time a new unit of instruction is initiated. They reflect or describe activities designed to aid language growth in early childhood classrooms. For purposes of illustration, assume that the topic throughout these suggestions is *winter*. (Virtually any other topic can be substituted.)

Playing with puppets will encourage children to tell stories and create their own. Participating in dramatic play will stimulate language from real life.

1. Hold discussions about the unit topic. What is the weather like in winter? What kind of clothing do the children need to wear in winter? What fun things can they do in winter that they can't do at other times of the year? What problems does winter bring?

2. Ask the children to name every word they can that makes them think of winter. Your list might eventually include: *snow, ice, cold, white, wet, freezing, sleds, snowman, mittens, scarf, hat, slush, skiing, ice skating, snowballs, fireplace,* and *snowflakes.* Classify the words on the list into how winter feels, looks, smells, sounds, and tastes, or what you can and cannot do in winter. List the words on a chart, and hang the chart in the room. Leave the chart hanging when you go to the next unit. When the wall gets too crowded, compile the charts in a class book.

3. Provide pictures of winter scenes for discussion, each depicting different information about the season.

4. Hold a sharing period during which children bring things from home related to the topic. Give all the children an opportunity to share if they wish, but assign different children for different days, since sharing by more than five or six children in one period can become tedious. Sharing objects from home is an important activity. It gives children confidence since they talk about something from their own environment. Even the shyest children will speak in front of a group if they have the security of sharing something familiar from home. Encourage children to relate the items to the unit topic, if they can. Model language for children to encourage them to speak in sentences. Coordinate the activity with parents, informing them of their children's scheduled sharing and the general topic under discussion.

5. Carry out a science experiment related to the topic being studied. Involve the children actively. Discuss the purpose and hypothesize what is likely to happen. Encourage children to discuss what they are doing while

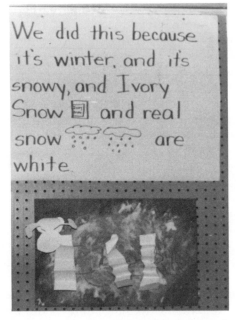

Experiences related to topics of study generate oral language that can be written down and then read.

they are doing it. When the experiment is complete, discuss the results with the class. (Example: Allow water to freeze, then melt.)

6. Carry out an art activity related to the topic; the activity should be process-oriented rather than teacher-directed. Allow children to create their own words rather than making them follow specific directions that yield identical results from child to child. Discuss the project and the available materials before the activity. Provide interesting materials and encourage children to touch, describe, and compare them. While children are creating, it is natural for them to converse about what they are doing. Encourage such conversation. For example, provide blue construction paper, tin foil, white doilies, cotton, wool, tissue paper, and chalk for a winter collage. Discuss why these colors and objects were selected. What is there about them that makes people think of winter? Suggest creating a picture that makes someone think of winter. Discuss the textures of the materials and what can be done with them.

7. Sing songs about winter, such as "It's a Marshmallow World in the Winter." Music is enjoyable and lyrics help build vocabulary and sensitivity to the sounds and meanings of words. Listen to music without words, music that creates images concerning the topic. Ask the children for words, sentences, or stories that the music brings to mind.

8. Prepare food related to the unit. Make hot soup, flavored snowballs, or popcorn. Discuss food textures, smells, taste, and appearance. Do they change during preparation? Follow directions and recipes, developing sequence as well as quantitative sense. Allow children to help prepare the food, then enjoy consuming it together, encouraging discussion and conversation throughout about the activity. Food preparation can be a source of new vocabulary, especially since many of its terms take on special meanings—*stir, blend, boil, measure.*

9. Add items related to the topic to the dramatic-play area—mittens, hats, scarves, boots for dress-up, for instance. Introduce them by placing each in a separate bag and asking a child to reach in, describe what it feels like, and identify it without peeking. The sense of touch elicits descriptive language.

10. Encourage spontaneous language and frequent problem-solving situations during outdoor play. For example, provide snow shovels, sleds, pails, and cups during playtime in the snow. Discuss outdoor play before going out, and again after coming in.

11. Discuss weather and dates during daily opening exercises. Encourage children to talk about news concerning themselves: a new pair of boots for the snow, a grandparent's visit, a birthday party. Make plans for the school day.

12. Take the class on a trip, bring in a guest speaker, or show a film. All three activities can generate language and encourage its use.

13. Read stories to the children on the topic under study. Books such

as *Katy and the Big Snow* (Burton, 1943) enhance information and expand vocabulary.

14. Provide the children with a title, such as "The Big Winter Snowstorm," and let them think of a story about it.

15. Encourage children to retell stories. This activity, of course, encourages them to use book language and incorporate it into their own. Retelling is not always an easy task for young children, so props can be very helpful—puppets, felt-boards and felt characters, roll movies, and pictures in a book. With these same props, children can be encouraged to make up their own stories as well.

16. In any of these activities, children should be encouraged as often as possible to select their favorite Very Own Words about winter. Favorite Very Own Words can be selected from discussions, art lessons, science experiments, songs, books, poems, cooking experiences, or any other activity. Early in the school year, encourage children to collect their favorite Very Own Words. After a particular experience, ask them to name a favorite word. Record children's favorite Very Own Words for them on three-by-five cards and store them in each child's own file box or on a binder ring. When children are capable of recording their own words, assist them with spelling when they ask for help. Favorite Very Own Words enhance vocabulary and are a source for reading and writing development.

17. Summarize the day's events at the end of the school day, encouraging children to tell what they liked, did not like, and want to do the next day in school.

Among more general suggestions, select and offer children's literature that represents varieties of language and experience. Some children's books feature the sounds of language; they aid auditory discrimination or incorporate additional phonemes into a child's language repertoire—for example, *Too Much Noise* (McGovern, 1967). Others help develop the syntactic complexity of a child's language through embeddings and transformations and the use of numerous adjectives and adverbs—for example, *Swimmy* (Lionni, 1963). Craft books require children to follow directions. Wordless books encourage them to create their own stories from the pictures. Concept books feature words such as *up, down, in, out, near,* and *far,* or involve children in mathematical reasoning. Realistic literature deals with death, divorce, loneliness, fear, and daily problems. Discussion of such themes leads to sociopsychological language, interpretation of feelings, sensitivity to others, and problem solving. Books of riddles, puns, jokes, and tongue twisters show children how language plays on meaning in certain situations. Poetry introduces children to rhyme, metaphor, simile, and onomatopoeia and encourages them to recite and create poems. (Children's books are listed by these and other categories in Appendix A.) When children hear and discuss the language of books, they internalize what they have heard; the language soon becomes part of their own language. Research studies have found that children who have had stories read to them frequently develop more sophisticated language structures and increased vocabulary (Chomsky, 1972; Cohen, 1968).

Two anecdotes illustrate how children incorporate into their own language the language of books that have been read to them. My kindergarten class was playing on the playground one early spring day. A few birds circled around several times. Melissa ran up to me and said, "Look, Mrs. Morrow, the birds are fluttering and flapping around the playground." Surprised at first by Melissa's descriptive and unusual choice of words, I thought for a moment, then remembered. The words that Melissa was using came directly from a picture storybook we had read shortly before, *Jenny's Hat* (Keats, 1966). In the book, birds *flutter* and *flap* around Jenny's hat. Melissa had internalized the language of the book and was able to use it in her own vocabulary.

One day after a big snowstorm, my daughter asked, "Mommy, can I go out and play? I want to build a smiling snowman." I was surprised and pleased with this sophisticated language being uttered by my four-year-old. *Smiling snowman,* after all, represents a participle in the adjective position, a syntactic structure usually not found in the language of children before the age of seven or eight. Then I noticed that Stephanie had a book in her hand, *The Snowy Day* (Keats, 1962). In it Peter goes outside and builds a *smiling snowman*. Stephanie had used the book's language and made it her own.

The activities just suggested can be repeated throughout the school year with each new unit of study. Such adaptation and repetition makes it possible to introduce children to hundreds of new vocabulary words, concepts, and ideas. They will assure children of opportunities to participate in new kinds of spontaneous language as topics and structured experiences change. Word lists and other materials produced during each unit can be maintained and made available for review and reuse.

Most of the suggestions can be followed at home as well as at school. Parents should not be expected to create elaborate centers or carry out units of instruction. But, daily living offers holidays, seasons, family events, and other topics and events of special interest. Parents can tap such meaningful occasions for their potential enhancement of language development. They can discuss events, list words, help children collect favorite Very Own Words, involve children in cooking and household chores, take trips, read stories, sing songs, and generally encourage the use of language as a pleasurable activity and a useful skill.

In the learning environment described throughout this chapter, language development is spontaneous and also encouraged. Modeling, scaffolding, and reinforcement make this environment interactive between child and adult, and it guides and nurtures language development to an extent that children are not likely to achieve on their own.

ASSESSING CHILDREN'S LANGUAGE DEVELOPMENT

It is important to assess children's language to determine if it follows expected stages of development. Assessment also determines how much a child has progressed. The word *assessment* implies several rather frequent measures by which to judge progress. Assessment should reflect instructional objectives and strategies. It should include evaluation of a wide range of skills used in many contexts. A certain child, for example, may perform better in an interview than on a pencil-and-paper test. Both kinds of evaluation, therefore, should be used. Literacy includes a wide range of skills; it is important to evaluate a child for as many as possible to determine strengths and weaknesses. Unfortunately, many assessment instruments are quite narrow in scope and frequently do not tap a child's total abilities (Glazer & Searfoss, 1988; Teale, Heibert, & Chittenden, 1987).

There are several ways to measure children's language development in early childhood. *Checklists* are practical since they provide concise outlines for teachers and appropriate slots for individual children. They

Checklist for Assessing Language Development			
	Always	Sometimes	Never
Makes phoneme sounds			
Speaks in one-word sentences			
Speaks in two-word sentences			
Identifies familiar sounds			
Differentiates similar sounds			
Understands the language of others when spoken to			
Follows verbal directions			
Speaks to others freely			
Pronounces words correctly			
Has appropriate vocabulary for level of maturity			
Speaks in complete sentences			
Uses varied syntactic structures			
Can be understood by others			

Teacher Comments:

are most effective if used periodically over the school year. Three to four evaluations during the year can provide sufficient data to determine progress. Program objectives offer criteria to include on checklists.

Anecdotal records are another form of language assessment. They tend to be time-consuming, but can reveal rich information. Loose-leaf note-books and file cards offer two means for keeping anecdotal records. These records require no particular format. Rather, the teacher or parent simply writes down incidents or episodes on the days they occur. Samples of a child's language or situations involving language can both be recorded. Like checklists, anecdotal samples are necessary periodically to determine growth over a school year.

Tape recordings are another means of evaluating language. The process can take the form of an open interview or a hidden recording. (Videotaping equipment can serve the same purpose, but is not readily available in most early childhood classrooms.) Children who are unaware that their conversation is being recorded are likely to be more spontaneous and uninhibited (Genishi & Dyson, 1984). It is often difficult, however, to place a tape recorder where it will record language clear enough to transcribe and analyze. Interviews with children become more natural when an adult familiar to the child does the interviewing. Allow the tape recorder to become such a familiar tool in the classroom that the child uses it often in the language arts center. Under such circumstances the machine is not threatening when used in an assessment interview. Children become accustomed very quickly to using tape recorders.

To record samples of natural language, discuss the child's experiences. Ask about home, favorite games or toys, TV programs they like to watch, brothers and sisters, trips they have taken, or birthday parties they have recently attended. What you are hoping to collect is a corpus of spontaneous language that provides a typical sample of the child's ability with language.

Tape assessment samples three or four times a year. Let children hear their own recorded voices, enjoying the experience and learning a bit about themselves. Then, for assessment purposes, transcribe the tapes and analyze them on such items as numbers of words uttered and numbers of words spoken in a single connected utterance (for example, "Tommy's cookie" or "Me want water"). The lengths of such utterances can be averaged to determine mean length. Length of utterance is considered a measure of complexity (Brown, 1973). When children begin to speak in conventional sentences, such as "That is my cookie," measure the length of the t-units. A *t-unit* is an independent clause with all its dependent clauses attached, assuming it has dependent clauses. It can be a simple or a complex sentence. Compound sentences are made up of two t-units. Length of t-units, like length of utterances, is a measure of language complexity. It typically increases with the user's age, and usually the more words per unit, the more complex the unit (Hunt, 1970).

Further analysis of taped utterances and t-units can determine which elements of language a child uses—number of adjectives, adverbs, dependent clauses, negatives, possessives, passives, plurals, and so on. The more complex the transformations, embeddings, and syntactic elements used, the more complex the language overall (Morrow, 1978). Data from several samples over the course of a year can be most revealing.

I have discussed oral language separately from the other communication skills in this chapter in order to describe its developmental stages and the theories of how it is acquired. This separation is somewhat artificial, however, since oral language is as important to literacy development as are reading and writing. The *whole-language* approach to early literacy has demonstrated that communication skills develop concurrently, each helping the growth of the others. Coordination and integration of the several communication skills in a single program are described in Chapter 9.

ACTIVITIES

1. Collect one language sample each from two-, three-, four-, five-, six-, and seven-year-old children. Elicit language by encouraging the children to talk about favorite television shows, pets, friends, family members, or trips. Or, show them pictures to discuss. Tape-record each sample and transcribe it.
    a. Check the characteristics of the children's language development according to the descriptions in this chapter and decide if each child is above, below, or at a level appropriate for his or her age.
    b. Check each sample for length of utterances, length of t-units, and number and type of syntactic elements used.

2. Collect three additional language samples at different times of the year from one of the children recorded in activity 1. Evaluate the new samples as you did the first, and check for growth.

3. Tape-record children involved in free play. Try to identify which characteristics of their language can be described by the various theories of language acquisition. For example, imitation could be explained by the behaviorist theory.

4. Select an objective for language development. Prepare a lesson integrated with another content area that will help a child to achieve the goal. Identify the theories of language acquisition used in your lesson plan.

5. Observe a preschool, kindergarten or first grade class. Note the amount of time children are given to talk, the amount of time the teacher talks, and the amount during which there is no verbal interaction. Compare the three figures. Then classify talk in the classroom into the following categories:

    a. questions and answers;
    b. whole-class discussion;
    c. small-group discussion;
    d. interactive discussion among children;
    e. interactive discussion between teacher and children.
        Based on the results of this mini-study, ask yourself how much opportunity the children were given to use language, and in how many different contexts or situations.

4

Reading as a Vehicle
for Developing Literacy

CHAPTER OVERVIEW

- Implications of the concept of emergent literacy have challenged some of the practices and attitudes traditionally known as *reading readiness*.
- As a concept, emergent literacy draws on cognitive, social, and psycholinguistic theories and research.
- Descriptions of early literacy development are founded in current research and tend to follow earlier descriptions of child development as well.

Thomas Jefferson articulated three fundamental beliefs about literacy and education that have become part of our national ethos: (1) the ability of every citizen to read is necessary to the practice of democracy, (2) it is therefore the duty of the general public to support the teaching of reading for all youngsters, and (3) reading should be taught during the earliest years of schooling. Among the reasons he cited, "none is more important, none more legitimate, than that of rendering the people safe, as they are the ultimate guardians of their own liberty."

THOMAS JEFFERSON
IN KOCH & PEDEN, 1974, P. 265
The Life and Selected Writings of Thomas Jefferson

As noted in Chapter 1, early developmentalists believed in the natural unfolding of the child. At a certain level of maturity, they felt, a child is ready to read, instruction is appropriate, and the child will learn to read. Some educators became impatient with the notion of simply waiting for maturation, even though they held to the idea that certain levels of maturation were necessary before reading could be taught formally without detriment to the child. This attitude led to instructional programs in reading readiness.

In general, reading readiness programs view getting ready to read as a set of social, emotional, physical, and cognitive competencies. If a child possesses these competencies, adherents say, formal reading instruction can take place. Conversely, a child who has not mastered particular tasks is not considered ready for reading instruction. Strategies for readiness instruction depend on lists of skills in the four areas of development. Typically, these lists include characteristics such as the following, on which children are tested.

1. *Social and Emotional Development:* The child
   a. shares;
   b. cooperates with peers and adults;
   c. demonstrates confidence, self-control, and emotional stability;
   d. completes tasks;
   e. fulfills responsibilities.
2. *Physical Development:* The child
   a. demonstrates large motor control by being able to run, hop, skip, trot, gallop, jump, throw, and walk a straight line;
   b. demonstrates fine motor control by being able to hold a pencil properly, color within lines, and cut with scissors;
   c. demonstrates eye–hand coordination;
   d. can write name, copy letters, draw a human figure;

   e. is generally healthy and vigorous;
   f. shows no visual or auditory defects;
   g. has established dominance (hand, eye, foot).
3. *Cognitive Development:* The child
   a. demonstrates auditory discrimination by identifying familiar sounds, differentiating sounds, recognizing rhyming words, identifying initial and ending consonant sounds, and possessing an auditory memory;
   b. demonstrates visual discrimination by understanding left to right eye progression, recognizing likenesses and differences, identifying colors, shapes, letters, and words, possessing visual memory, and showing a sense of figure–ground perception.

Many such lists go on and on, and often it is assumed that a child must master all behaviors on the list before entering formal reading instruction. There are sad stories of kindergarten teachers who have not promoted children who were unable to master skipping or trotting or galloping. Parents have become frantic and children brought to tears by teachers' insistence on mastery of motor skills. It still is not uncommon to see classes of kindergarten children undergoing skipping lessons to the teacher's cadence of "step-hop, step-hop, step-hop, step-hop."

At least two misguided assumptions lie behind such an approach: (1) children know nothing about literacy before coming to school; (2) they therefore need an instructional program in readiness. In actuality, some of the listed competencies are irrelevant and inappropriate for early literacy development. Many lists do not include awareness of book and print characteristics that are necessary and important for reading. Instructional practices motivated by the readiness-skills approach abstract activities away from the act of reading. There have been reports of children who had accomplished few of the tasks on a list of reading readiness skills but were nonetheless already reading. Their ability to read went unrecognized by their teachers because reading readiness tests and activities never do ask children to read. There are also children who can carry out the tasks on a list and still experience difficulty learning to read.

Recent research in cognitive development, language acquisition, early readers, and what children learn before school about books, print, and writing has changed attitudes and ideas about early childhood instructional strategies and literacy development. Until recently, reading, writing, listening, and speaking were thought of as separate skills taught independently of one another. Our teacher education programs have tended to separate courses in the teaching of reading from those in language arts. We now realize, however, that literacy involves all of the communication skills and that each skill enhances the other as they are learned concurrently.

New concepts are replacing older ideas of reading readiness. The phrase *emergent literacy*, first used by Marie Clay (1966), has caught the attention of educators interested in early literacy. Emergent literacy assumes that the child acquires some knowledge about language, reading, and writing before coming to school. Literacy development begins early in life and is ongoing. There is a dynamic relationship between the communication skills; each influences the other in the course of development. Development occurs in everyday contexts of the home and community. Children at whatever age possess certain literacy skills, though these skills are not fully developed or conventional, as we recognize mature reading and writing to be (Teale, 1986). Emergent literacy acknowledges as rudimentary writing a child's scribble marks on a page, even if not a letter is discernible. The child who knows the difference between such scribbles and drawings certainly has some sense of the difference between writing and illustration. Similarly, when a child narrates a familiar storybook while looking at the pictures and print, and gives the impression of reading, we acknowledge the activity as legitimate literacy behavior, even though it cannot be called reading in the conventional sense.

THEORIES ON THE ACQUISITION OF READING

To speak of the acquisition of reading apart from that of writing and speaking is somewhat artificial if literacy is viewed as the concurrent development of communication skills. In this text, however, the several communication skills are addressed in separate chapters, primarily because much of the relevant research discusses them rather discretely. Their concurrent development and their integration in pedagogy are addressed in Chapter 9.

Reading Is Acquired Through Socially Interactive and Emulative Behavior

Teale (1982) views literacy as the result of children's involvement in reading activities mediated by literate others. It is the social interaction accompanying these activities that makes them so significant to the child's development. Not only do interactive literacy events teach children the societal function and conventions of reading; they also link reading with enjoyment and satisfaction and thus increase children's desire to engage in literacy activities. Teale's emphasis on the social aspects of reading development reflects Vygotsky's (1981) more general theory of intellectual development. Vygotsky asserted that "all higher mental functions are internalized social relationships." This movement from interpsychological learning to intrapsychological learning is apparent as children become

increasingly able to engage independently in reading activities that previously required interaction with more literate others.

Holdaway's (1979) theory of literacy development is consistent with
Teale's. Holdaway writes:

> The way in which supportive adults are induced by affection and common
> sense to intervene in the development of their children proves upon close
> examination to embody the most sound principles of teaching. Rather than
> provide verbal instructions about how a skill should be carried out, the parent
> sets up an emulative model of the skill in operation and induces activity in the
> child which approximates towards use of the skill. The first attempts of the
> child are to do something that is like the skill he wishes to emulate. This
> activity is then "shaped" or refined by immediate rewards. . . . From this point
> of view, so called "natural" learning is in fact supported by higher quality
> teaching intervention than is normally the case in the school setting. (p. 22)

Holdaway contends that this form of "developmental" teaching is appropriate for school-based literacy instruction. Characterized by self-regulated, individualized activities, frequent peer interaction, and an
environment rich with materials, Holdaway's model is derived from observations of home environments where children have learned to read without
direct instruction, homes such as those described in Chapter 2.

Holdaway (1986) explains four processes that enable children to acquire reading ability. The first is *observation* of reading behaviors—being
read to, for example, or seeing adults reading themselves. The second is
collaboration with an individual who interacts with the child, providing
encouragement, motivation, and help when necessary. The third process is
practice. The learner tries out alone what has been learned—role playing,
for instance, or other reading activities—and experiments without direc-

Interactions during literacy events play a significant role in learning to read. The interaction can occur
between adult and child or between children.

tion or adult observation. Practice gives children opportunities to evaluate their performances, make corrections, and increase skills. In the fourth process, *performance,* the child shares what has been learned and seeks approval from adults who are supportive, interested, and encouraging. The ideas expressed by Holdaway (1986) are also articulated in work on literacy development by Calkins, 1983; Clark, 1976; Read, 1975; and Smith, 1983.

Children Acquire the Ability to Read as a Result of Life Experiences

Some children already have considerable information about reading and writing before they enter school for formal instruction. Some are reading before they come to school; others have had little exposure to literacy at all. Even though children's strengths in literacy vary with the individual, most children have a general command of their language and a sizable vocabulary and have internalized rules of language. They know the difference between drawing and writing and they associate books with reading. They can read environmental print and they realize the functional purposes of reading. Because their knowledge about literacy to this point is based on meaning and function, they expect that reading will be an activity that makes sense.

Research over the past thirty years has made us aware of early childhood competencies and literacy skills. Studies such as those by Clark (1976), Durkin (1966), Krippner (1963), and Torrey (1969) have revealed that many children read early—that is, before starting school and without formal instruction. Investigations have also revealed how the environment supports literacy development. Children as young as three are able to read such common words in their environment as *Burger King, McDonald's, Exxon,* and *Sugar Pops* (Goodman & Altwerger, 1981; Harste, Woodward, & Burke, 1984; Hiebert, 1986; Mason, 1980; Ylisto, 1967). The results of these investigations indicate that very young children are aware of print, letters, and words, and that their ability to identify familiar printed symbols constitutes the beginning of reading. According to Goodman (1984), the "roots of literacy" are established in early childhood by most children in literate societies. Environmental print helps children discover how print is organized and used as well as what it is used for. Young children also demonstrate such knowledge of books and book handling as (1) where to begin reading, (2) the difference between pictures and print, (3) awareness of the left-to-right progression of print, (4) the difference between the beginning and the end of the book, and (5) how to turn pages (Wiseman & Robeck, 1983). Efforts to expand their reading abilities into reading fluency need to build on their strengths and on what they already know and expect of reading (Jewell & Zintz, 1986).

The psycholinguistic definition of reading is based on this last premise. It strongly recommends capitalizing on children's prior strengths, knowledge, and past experiences. Goodman (1967) described reading as a psycholinguistic "guessing game" in which the child attempts to reconstruct, in light of his or her own knowledge, what the author has to say. Young children bring with them to school concepts and understanding from past experiences. Their awareness and use of oral language are particularly helpful. When they read they anticipate what the written message is likely to say. Reading is an active process. Children search the printed page for cues based on what they already know. They search for *graphic* cues, or cues about print—whether a squiggle is a letter or a word, for instance. There are *syntactic* cues. For example, in the case of *The boy ran down the* _____, the child's internalized knowledge of syntax indicates that the word in the blank must be a noun such as *hill, stairs,* or *street*. A verb would make no sense: *The boy ran down the jumped.* From *semantic* clues, children know which words make sense in the slot and which do not. Few if any would guess that the sentence reads *The boy ran down the sky,* for example. Using these graphic, syntactic, and semantic cues, children predict, guess, expect, make associations, and correct themselves to derive meaning from the printed page. The meaning comes from what they know about language and from their own experiences. The most meaningful cues are those in whole pieces of print, rather than in isolated words. All the processes of reading are brought to bear at once within the reader.

It is difficult for us as adults to understand and appreciate the various processes involved in learning to read since we have been reading for so many years. To better understand the nature of learning to read, put yourself in the place of the learner. With a contrived alphabet called the Confusabet, I have taken college students back to when they were five and six and first taught to read. Whole words are introduced in the unfamiliar alphabet, accompanied by picture clues and context clues. They are reinforced with worksheets. After being introduced to about twenty-five words, the students are given a book containing pictures and stories that use these words. They are called upon to read just as they were in a reading group in an early childhood classroom.

After the lesson we discuss how they have just learned to read with the Confusabet. Students consistently report similar strategies: They try to relate information they already know about reading to the situation. They realize quickly that Confusabet words have the same number of letters as words written in the regular alphabet, and their knowledge of words in general helps them make sense of Confusabet words. Certain similarities in letter forms help them figure out words. They use context and picture clues as much as possible. Their knowledge of syntax (language structures) and the meanings of words surrounding an unknown word helps them determine words they cannot otherwise identify. They skip around within a sentence looking for words they might know. Some rely on the first letter of a word to identify it. Many try to memorize words by the "look–say" method. Most agree that words with unusual shapes or lengths are easiest to identify. They acknowledge that to learn they have to involve themselves actively in the reading process. In short, they guess, make mistakes, and correct themselves.

My observations of their behavior also reveal that they look to others for help and share successes and failures with those around them; they agree that such social interaction is an important part of their learning. They demonstrate a natural curiosity as they flip eagerly through new materials. In their descriptions of how they have learned to read material written in the Confusabet, the students define the psycholinguistic nature of the reading process. In all cases they sought meanings. They approached a printed message as a whole and not by segmenting it into little parts. Granted, these college students draw on many more experiences and associations with print and reading than can the typical kindergarten child or first grader, but this only indicates more emphatically how important it is for initial reading experiences to be based on meaning and function.

Illustration of the Confusabet

Children Acquire Reading Skills
When They See a Purpose and a Need for the Process

Children are more likely to become involved in formal reading if they have seen reading, writing and speaking as functional, purposeful, and useful. Studies of early reading behaviors clearly illustrate that young children acquire their first information about reading and writing through their functional uses (Goodman, 1980; Heath, 1980; Mason, 1977; Mason & McCormick, 1981; Taylor, 1983). Grocery lists, directions on toys, packages, household equipment, and medicine containers, recipes, telephone messages, school-related notices, religious materials, menus, environmental print inside and outside the home, mail, magazines, newspapers, storybook readings, TV channels, telephone numbers, conversation among family members, and letters represent but a sample of the functional literacy information with which a child comes in contact daily. Children are familiar with such forms of literacy, they participate in them, they pretend to use them at play, and they understand their purpose. Parents and day-care, preschool, and kindergarten teachers need to provide experiences with reading similar to experiences children have already had. Children expect learning to read to be meaningful and functional.

Being Read to Plays a Role
in the Aquisition of Reading Skill

Research indicates that reading to a child benefits the child's acquisition of reading ability. It aids development of literacy skills, increases interest in books and in learning to read, enhances background information and sense of story structure, and familiarizes children with the language of books as opposed to oral language (Chomsky, 1972; Cohen, 1968; Cullinan, 1977; Huck, 1976; Morrow, 1985). A well-structured story has a *setting* (a beginning, time, place, and introduction of characters), a *theme* (the main character's problem or goal), *plot episodes* (a series of events in which the main character tries to solve the problem or achieve the goal), and a *resolution* (the accomplishment of the goal or solving of the problem and an ending). From hearing many well-formed stories, children can predict what will happen next in an unfamiliar story on the basis of their awareness of its structural elements (Morrow, 1985). That the language of books is different from oral language is quite evident in such passages as these:

> One bad day a tuna fish, fierce, swift and very hungry, came darting through the waves. (Lionni, *Swimmy*, 1963)

> The wild things roared their terrible roars, gnashed their terrible teeth, and rolled their terrible eyes. (Sendak, *Where the Wild Things Are*, 1963)

Often, children benefit in terms of comprehension skills from their assimilation of and familiarity with vocabulary and syntactic structures in books that have been read to them. Children who have been read to frequently and early tend to read earlier than others and to learn to read more easily (Clark 1984; Durkin, 1966; Hiebert, 1981; Schickedanz, 1978). Furthermore, as pointed out earlier, reading to children at school or at home generally leads them to associate reading with pleasure and provides them with models for reading. In fact, when children begin to read on their own, they often choose books read to them earlier. After I had read *The Little Engine That Could* (Piper, 1954) to a four-year-old, she said to me, "Show me where it says 'I think I can, I think I can.' I want to see it in the book. "When I showed her the words, she repeated them while pointing to them and then asked to see them again in another part of the book. She proceeded to search through the rest of the book, reading with great enthusiasm each time she found the line "I think I can, I think I can."

Researchers have found that reading to children enhances the development of reading in many ways. Repeated reading of the same story is an important strategy as well. (Morrow, 1986; Sulzby, 1985; Yaden, 1985). Smith (1978) suggests that reading to children gives them an understanding of the functions of print, a sense of how print is used and of what people are doing when they are reading. Children with storybook experience learn how to handle a book and are sensitive to its front-to-back progression; a story's beginning, middle, and end; and the concept of authorship (Clay, 1979; Torvey & Kerber, 1986). Mason (1980) found not only that reading to children contributes to their awareness of the functions, form, and conventions of print, but that children develop metacognitive knowledge about how to approach reading tasks and how to interact with teachers and parents. *Metacognition* is one's own awareness of how learning is taking place; it thus nurtures one's own learning.

Children who are read to develop positive attitudes towards reading. The warmth that accompanies storybook readings by a caring adult lasts beyond the experience. It involves ritual, sharing, and mutual good feelings. Certain books take on special meanings between an adult and child through repetition or because they are favorites of the one or the other. My daughter and I have had a special relationship with the book *Alexander and the Terrible, Horrible, No Good, Very Bad Day* (Viorst, 1972). I first read it to Stephanie when she was four, and whenever things seemed to go wrong for her I found myself saying, "I guess you're having a terrible, horrible, no good, very bad day." Soon, when things were not going well for me, Stephanie would say, "I guess you're having a terrible, horrible, no good, very bad day."

One day, when she was in the seventh grade, Stephanie came home from school looking terrible. She was wearing only one sneaker, her hair was not combed, and she looked generally distraught.

"What's the problem?" I asked.

"Someone stole one of my sneakers, I got yelled at for talking when my friend asked me a question in class and I answered her, I have tons of homework, and I lost my assignment notebook."

Being read to plays an important role in the acquisition of reading skills.

"I guess you're having a terrible, horrible, no good, very bad day," I said.

She smiled and said, "You're right. I think I'll go to Australia."

"Some days are like that, even in Australia," I replied.

We both laughed. The familiar words of a familiar book have created a special ritual between us by which one tries to cheer the other. Good feelings gained in story readings transfer to the act of reading itself (Hiebert, 1981; Taylor, 1983).

Children who have been read to often begin to concern themselves with strategies for independent reading. It is not just the reading itself but the interaction between adult and child that motivates the interest. Studies carried out in school settings illustrate that active participation in literacy experiences enhances comprehension of story and sense of story structure. Role-playing stories they have heard, retelling them, and reconstructing them through pictures enable children to relate parts of a story, integrate information, and interact with teachers and other children (Brown, 1975; Morrow, 1985b; Pellegrini & Galda, 1982).

Studies of home read-aloud sessions clearly illustrate that active social interaction between parents and children during these sessions is a major factor in literacy development. This interaction offers a direct channel of information for the child. Initially, children are interested in the illustrations and label items pictured or repeat words said by the adult who is reading the story (Yaden, 1985). Such interactive behavior leads children to respond with questions and comments, which become more complex over time and demonstrate more sophisticated thinking about printed material. Eventually, children's remarks about story content reflect interests in narration, evaluation, interpretation, association, prediction, information, and elaboration. These remarks focus sometimes on title, setting, characters, and story events (Morrow, 1988; Roser & Martinez, 1985), and at other times on print characteristics, including names of letters, words, and sounds.

One of the primary goals of reading aloud is the reconstruction of meaning through the interaction between adult and child. The adult helps the child understand and make sense of the text through their cooperative personal interpretation of the written language based on their experiences and beliefs (Atwerger, Diehl-Faxon, & Dockstader-Anderson, 1985). Particularly helpful behavior includes prompting children to respond, scaffolding responses for children to model when they are unable to respond themselves, relating responses to real-life experiences, answering questions, and offering positive reinforcement for children's responses. (See Chapter 2.)

The emphasis thus far is the child's understanding of whole concepts, not such isolated reading skills as letter–sound relationships and decoding. The development of such specific skills has been overemphasized and pursued almost exclusively in recent decades. Their overemphasis has often led to inappropriate home and classroom practices. Yet, we cannot ignore them since research has been done that supports their role in literacy development. For instance, children who are taught letter–sound relationships have been found to get off to a better start in learning to read than other children (Baumann, 1984; Chall, Conrad, & Harris-Sharples, 1983; Williams, 1985). On the other hand, there is evidence that teaching many phonic rules does not greatly help most youngsters learn to read, since most of these rules are irregular. Rather, only the most regular letter–sound relationships should be taught. Once those are clear to a child, the best way to refine and extend them is to give the child repeated opportunities to read. What needs to be stressed is that the teaching and learning of the alphabet, letter–sound relationships, and decoding skills are only a very small part of reading instruction. The time spent on them should be minimal, and the strategies selected for instruction appropriate for young children.

STAGES OF READING DEVELOPMENT

The concept of emergent literacy suggests that one does not suddenly learn to read; rather, becoming literate is a process that begins at birth and continues throughout one's lifetime. Children differ in their rates of literacy achievement; they must not be pressured into the accomplishment of tasks or placed on a predetermined time schedule. Stages in reading development are not as precise as we might like them to be. Certain traits of literacy do seem to be acquired by many youngsters before others, but the dividing lines among traits and among youngsters are not always distinct. Different children pass through stages at different levels of maturity. Although it is helpful to recognize the various stages and to monitor a child's progression through them, we must not be trapped into believing that all children must pass through all stages or all at the same time and in the same order. In planning for instruction, we must never presume that the stages are fixed, or that a child cannot operate at a "later" stage before an "earlier" one.

Mason (1980, 1984) suggests that there are three strands of reading behavior, which develop separately but concurrently—attention to the *functions, forms,* and *conventions* of print, with the first of these predominating in initial reading development. Other researchers, too, have found that children learn how print *functions* as a first step toward reading (Goodman, 1984; Smith, 1971). Often, the first words a child reads are those with meaning and purpose in the child's life—family names, food labels, road signs, and names of fast-food restaurants. It is this stage of development that Goodman (1984) referred to as the "roots of literacy." In the second stage, the learner is concerned more with the *forms* of print. Details about names, sounds, and configurations of letters and words serve the child's learning more than does observation of how print functions. The third stage, identifying and using *conventions* of print, involves the recognition that print is read from left to right, that punctuation serves certain purposes in printed material, that spaces serve to demarcate letters and words, and so forth. In other words, although recognition of the functions of print dominates the first stage of reading development in early childhood, the child is at the same time, but to a lesser degree, acquiring notions about the form and conventions of print (Mason, 1984). As the child matures as a reader, the form of print becomes more important in reading development, and finally the conventions of print become a focus.

Sulzby (1985) found developmental trends in two-to-five-year-olds in her work on attempted reading of familiar storybooks. Children's first attempts at "reading" familiar stories were governed by pictures, their stories were not well formed, the children sounded like they were telling a story rather than reading, and they paid no attention to print. In later attempts, the children approached conventional reading behaviors. They attempted to read the print, their stories were well formed, and their language sounded as if they were reading.

In a study of what children know about reading and of their skill in letter and word recognition, McCormick & Mason (1981) established three developmental levels in word recognition. Children first identified words through context, then used letter–sound cues, and finally relied on sounding out words.

Studies of young children's responses to story readings also reveal developmental trends that follow Mason's basic three-strand paradigm. Children's initial questions and comments during story readings are related to the pictures and the meanings of the stories. As they gain experience with story readings, their questions and comments begin to concern the names of letters, the reading of individual words, or attempts to sound out words (Morrow, 1987a; Roser & Martinez, 1985; Yaden, 1985). Again, the function of print dominates early responses, the form of print becomes more important in later responses.

Judging from the research, then, there seem to be categtories of reading development in early childhood. Yet reading is obviously a complex process, and individual case studies vary between children. One must never forget that each child is an individual developing at his or her own pace.

STRATEGIES FOR READING DEVELOPMENT

According to Teale (1987), studies on emergent literacy suggest that to become literate young children must learn about the functions and uses of literacy, conventions of written language, decoding and encoding strategies, and comprehending and composing strategies. They must also develop positive attitudes toward reading. From the theories on reading acquisition and the categories of reading development we can formulate four objectives for emergent readers from birth to seven.

1. to develop positive attitudes toward reading;
2. to develop concepts about books;
3. to develop comprenhension of story;
4. to develop concepts about print.

These objectives are intended simply as basic guidelines for helping teachers design strategies for instruction.

The instructional strategies described in the next three chapters are designed to serve these objectives. Chapter 5 emphasizes the use of children's literature and concentrates on the first objective. Chapter 6 deals with the second and third objectives, and Chapter 7 with objective four.

ACTIVITIES

1. Observe a preschool, kindergarten, or first grade. List those activities that seem characteristic of an emergent literacy approach to instruction and those that seem characteristic of a reading readiness approach.

2. Reading is acquired through a child's (1) interaction with and emulation of adult reading behaviors, (2) association of print materials with real-life experiences, (3) recognition of purpose in reading, and (4) recognition of a need for reading as a result of having been read to. Review each of these areas. Then observe a nursery school, kindergarten, or first grade, and classify the activities by the area they represent.

3. Observe a child between the ages of three and seven. Identify his or her emergent reading behaviors or reading developmental characteristics.

5

Developing Positive Attitudes Toward Reading Through the Use of Children's Literature

CHAPTER OVERVIEW

- The goal of literacy instruction is not just to promote the ability to read, but to nurture and accommodate a desire to read.
- Children's literature is an ideal resource in literacy development.
- Well-planned and efficiently managed classroom library corners encourage voluntary reading.
- Creative teachers are key facilitators in developing positive attitudes toward reading.
- Recreational reading periods allow children to practice skills learned during reading instruction and enjoy reading for pleasure.

Children who read only when in a reading group are not being taught a love of reading. The best index of the success of reading instruction is the eagerness with which children approach reading.
  Love of reading is not taught, it is created.
  Love of reading is not required, it is inspired.
  Love of reading is not demanded, it is exemplified.
  Love of reading is not exacted, it is quickened.
  Love of reading is not solicited, it is activated.

RUSSELL STAUFFER, 1970, P. 288
Wilson Library Bulletin

Becoming a Nation of Readers (Anderson, Hiebert, Scott, & Wilkinson, 1985) states, among other things, that learning to read requires (1) the motivation and desire to read, (2) practice to the point of proficiency, and (3) continuous and lifelong involvement so that fluency is maintained. One of the first goals in early literacy development is the nurture of positive attitudes toward reading. Those attitudes usually result in voluntary readers. If children learn to read but have little desire to use their ability, we have not accomplished much (Spiegel, 1981). In a 1984 report to Congress entitled *Books in Our Future,* Daniel Boorstin, then Librarian of Congress, warned that *aliterates*—individuals who can read but choose not to—constitute as much of a threat to our democratic tradition as illiterates. Voluntary reading, or the lack of it, he wrote, "will determine the extent of self-improvement and enlightenment, the ability to share the wisdom and delights of our civilization, and our capacity for intelligent self-government" (p. iv).

Unfortunately, substantial numbers of children and adults read neither for pleasure nor for information. Greaney (1980) found that 22 percent of the fifth-grade students he surveyed chose not to read at all, and that those who did read spent only 5 percent of their leisure time at it. Morrow (1982) and Morrow and Weinstein (1982) observed that few primary children chose books during free-choice time in school. A 1972 Gallup survey revealed that 80 percent of the books read in the United States were read by only 10 percent of the population; half the adults sampled had never read a book all the way through (cited by Spiegel, 1981). An extensive investigation by the Book Industry Study Group (1984) indicated that the number of young people under twenty-one identified as readers dropped from 75 percent in 1976 to 63 percent in 1984.

One reason for such distressing reports may be that most instructional programs in reading have been skills-oriented, providing little opportunity for students to read for enjoyment (Lamme, 1981; Spiegel, 1981). Children's reading habits develop early in life (Bloom, 1964). If schools do not deliberately and thoughtfully entice children to read during their early years, the desire and motivation to learn to read and to acquire the reading habit may never develop.

Apart from the common belief that voluntary reading is desirable, there is considerable empirical evidence that it correlates with success in school. Children identified as voluntary readers in elementary and middle grades demonstrated high levels of reading achievement in comprehension and in vocabulary development (Anderson, Wilson, & Fielding, 1985; Greaney, 1980; Whitehead, Capey, & Maddren, 1975). Morrow (1983) found that in comparison with children whose interest in books was low, kindergarteners who demonstrated a strong interest in books scored significantly higher on standardized reading readiness tests and were rated higher by teachers on work habits, general school performance, and social and emotional development. Chomsky (1972) found that children who are introduced to literature at an early age tend to develop sophisticated language structures. Cohen (1968) concluded that the language structures and vocabulary children gain from early exposure to literature correlate with their subsequent success in learning to read. Both vocabulary and language structures can be improved significantly in youngsters by regular listening to stories read aloud. Children who experience literature early accumulate background knowledge, appreciate books, and show increased interest in learning to read. As we saw in previous chapters, they often begin to read early or learn to read more easily (Durkin, 1966). Bissett (1970) contends that discussing books provides a foundation for comprehension skills because of the language development, background knowledge, and sense of story structure acquired thereby.

Researchers have repeatedly stressed the importance of providing children with daily opportunities to experience literature pleasurably; to discuss stories through literal, interpretive, and critical questioning; to relate literature activities to content-area learning; and to share the books they read or look at (Arbuthnot & Sutherland, 1977; Cullinan, 1977, 1987, 1989; Huck, 1976; Smith & Parker, 1977; Stewig & Sebesta, 1978.) More recent research (Morrow & Weinstein, 1982, 1986; Morrow, 1987b) has shown that children's use of literature increases dramatically when teachers incorporate enjoyable literature activities into the daily program and design attractive classroom library corners.

The information in Chapter 2 for parents of infants and toddlers focuses on techniques and practices to develop positive attitudes toward books that are appropriate as well for aides and professionals in day-care centers. For that reason, the discussion in this chapter focuses on techniques for use with two-to-seven-year-olds (much of this information is applicable to younger children, too).

PREPARING A LITERACY-RICH ENVIRONMENT

Before planning instruction that will entice children to books, the teacher must prepare appropriate materials and a physical setting that sets the stage for pleasurable literacy experiences. As Plato said, "What is honored in a country will be cultivated there." Teachers who honor the development of literacy demonstrate that attitude by providing within their classrooms a rich environment where the use of books can be cultivated. Their students honor literacy development by assimilating the attitudes and atmosphere presented by the teacher.

A classroom library corner is essential for children's immediate access to literature (Beckman, 1972). Bissett (1969) found that children in classrooms with literature collections read and looked at books 50 percent more often than children in classrooms without such collections. Coody (1973) and Huck (1976) both report that the efforts spent in creating an inviting atmosphere for a classroom library corner are rewarded by increased interest in books. Studies by Morrow and Weinstein (1982, 1986) and Morrow (1987b) showed that well-designed classroom library corners significantly increased the number of children who chose to participate in literature activities during free-choice periods. Morrow (1982) observed library corners in nursery schools, kindergartens and first and second grades and identified specific design characteristics that correlated with children's use of the corners during free-choice periods. Conversely, Morrow (1982), Rosenthal (1973), and Shure (1963) found that poorly designed library corners were among the least popular areas during free-choice periods in early childhood rooms. Suffice it to say that the physical features of a classroom library corner can play an important role in enticing children to use the corner voluntarily.

FEATURES OF WELL-DESIGNED LIBRARY CORNERS

A classroom library corner should be a focal area, immediately visible and inviting to anyone entering the classroom. For an atmosphere of privacy and physical definition, it should be partitioned on two or three sides with bookshelves, a piano, file cabinets, or freestanding bulletin boards. The dimensions of the library corner will vary with the size of the classroom. Generally, it should be large enough to accommodate five or six children comfortably. (See page 87.)

Well-designed library corners have two kinds of bookshelves. The first houses the bulk of the books, which are shelved with the spines facing out. The other type is open-faced, allowing the covers of the books to be seen, which is important for calling attention to special books. Featured books, changed regularly, are placed on the open-faced shelves for easy

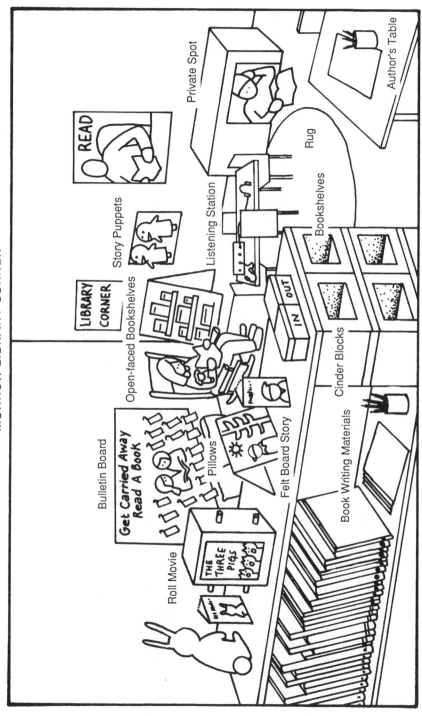

MORROW LIBRARY CORNER

access. An alternative to open-faced shelving is the circular wire rack, commonly found in bookstores.

Books in the collection should be shelved by category and color-coded according to the type of book. Identify all animal books, for example, byplacing blue dots on their spines and clustering them on a shelf marked *Animals,* with a blue dot next to the label. Another color might distinguish books about holidays, a third color poetry, and so on. Color coding introduces children to the idea that books in libraries are organized so as to be readily accessible.

The library corner should be furnished with a throw rug and pillows or beanbag chairs, since much of the activity there takes place on the floor. If possible, it should also be furnished with a small table and chairs where children can use headsets to listen to taped stories and make their own books. A rocking chair allows comfortable reading.

Children are given little privacy in the typical school. It has been found that many children relish privacy. Because it is partially partitioned from the rest of the room, the library corner provides some privacy. Listening to recorded stories on headsets offers even more privacy, and an oversize carton, painted or covered with contact paper, makes a cozy private reading room.

Attractive posters that encourage reading are available from the Children's Book Council (67 Irving Place, New York, NY 10003) and the American Library Association (50 East Huron Street, Chicago, IL 60611). Stuffed animals also belong in a library corner, especially if they are related to books available in the corner—a stuffed rabbit next to *Peter Rabbit* (Potter, 1902), for instance. Children enjoy reading to stuffed animals or simply holding them as they look at books. A felt-board, with figures of story characters from favorite books, is one of the more heavily used

The library corner is a cozy place where children can relax and read, sitting on a rug, leaning on soft pillows, and hugging stuffed animals.

materials in a library corner, as are roll movies. Viewmasters with story wheels are a source of literature for young children, and puppets aid the acting out of stories. The corner should also include materials from which children can make their own books, felt stories, and roll movies.

Huck (1976) recommends five to eight books per child in a classroom library. Books are not difficult to accumulate. They can be purchased very inexpensively at flea markets. Teachers can borrow as many as twenty books a month from most public libraries, ask for book donations from parents, and hold fund-raisers for book purchases. Children's paperback book clubs offer inexpensive books and free bonus books for bulk purchases.

Children's magazines and newspapers belong in the classroom library, even if they are not current. For the cost of mailing and shipping, some publishers and local magazine agencies will donate outdated periodicals to schools.

Children should be involved in the planning and design of a library corner. They can develop rules for its use, be in charge of keeping it neat and orderly, and select a name for it, such as Book Nook.

To ensure continued interest in the library corner, the teacher must introduce new books and materials and recirculate others. Approximately twenty-five new books should be introduced every two weeks, replacing twenty-five that have been there for a while. In this way, "old" books will be greeted as new friends a few months later. Recirculation compensates for limited budgets.

Books from the library corner should be available for students to check out and take home for a week at a time. The check-out system should be simple. At specified times during the school day, children might bring the books they want to borrow to the teacher, who notes the date, name of borrower, and book title. Some kindergarten children have been taught to check out books themselves by copying titles and recording dates on five-by-eight cards filed under their own names. Other youngsters enjoy keeping track of books borrowed by recording titles and dates on three-by-five cards hung on curtain-rod hooks or key rings mounted on a bulletin board, one hook or ring per child.

Books and other materials selected for the corner should appeal to a variety of interests and span a range of grade levels. It is advisable to stock multiple copies of popular books. Children sometimes enjoy reading a book because a friend is reading it (Morrow, 1985a). Several types of children's literature should be represented:

Picture concept books are appropriate for the very young child who cannot yet read. Most picture concept books do not have story lines, though they often have themes, such as animals or toys. Each page usually carries a picture identified by a printed word. Many picture books are made of cardboard, cloth, or vinyl to withstand rigorous handling. Alphabet and number books are also considered picture concept books.

Traditional literature includes nursery rhymes and fairy tales, familiar stories that are part of our heritage and originated in the oral tradition of storytelling. We assume that children are familiar with *Goldilocks and the Three Bears* (Izawa, 1968a) and *The Three Little Pigs* (Brenner, 1972), yet many youngsters have not been exposed to these traditional stories. Children who *do* know the stories welcome them as familiar territory.

Picture storybooks are most familiar to us as children's literature. Their texts are closely associated with their illustrations. Picture storybooks are available on a wide range of topics, and many are known for their excellence. The Caldecott Medal is awarded annually to the author or illustrator of an outstanding picture storybook. Many of these books have become classics and their authors renowned—Robert McClosky, Dr. Seuss, Ezra Jack Keats, Tomie DePaola, Maurice Sendak, and Charlotte Zolotow, to name just a few. Every child should be given the benefit of hearing some of these books read. In particular, the earliest emergent readers will often find the vocabulary and syntax too sophisticated to read them on their own.

Realistic literature—really a category of picture storybooks—deals with real-life issues. *Bedtime for Frances* (Hoban, 1960), for example, is about the fears and concerns a child faces when told to go to sleep, and *Peter's Chair* (Keats, 1967) handles the problems that arise with a new baby in the house. Some touch on very sensitive issues, such as divorce and death. Many can be read to the entire class if they address issues that all share. Teachers can also recommend specific titles to parents of children who face particular problems.

Easy-to-read books are designed to be read by emergent readers themselves. They have limited and repeated vocabularies, and many of them rhyme, which makes them predictable and aids independent reading. Because of their limited language, few easy-to-read books rate as quality literature, but many preschool and kindergarten children begin to read independently with them.

Fables and folktales retell many of the myths and traditional stories that are available in picture-book style for the younger child. Many of these stories originate in other countries and cultures and therefore broaden a child's experience and knowledge base.

Informational books offer nonfiction for emergent readers. There are books about holidays, plants, animals, foreign countries, communities, dinosaurs, and famous people. They broaden a child's background information, explore new ideas, and often stimulate deep interest in particular topics.

Wordless books carry very definite storylines, but use no words. They are often thought appropriate for very young children and are confused with picture books. They are designed not for babies but for children three and older. The child creates the story by reading the pictures, some of which are intricate.

Poetry is too often forgotten in collections of children's literature at home and in school. Many themed anthologies have been compiled for young children, and they are an important part of the library corner.

In addition to these categories of books, young children enjoy joke and riddle books; participation books, which involve them in touching, smelling, and manipulating; books in a series built around a single character; and books related to television programs appropriate for their age. Children particularly enjoy literature that is predictable, since it helps them to understand the story line more easily and enables them to read along with the individual reading to them. Predictable literature contains rhyme; repetition; catch phrases; conversation; familiar sequences, such as days of the week or numbers; cumulative patterns, in which events are repeated or added on as the story continues; stories about familiar topics; familiar or popular stories; books with uncluttered illustrations that match the text; and stories that have well-developed story structures (setting, theme, plot, episodes, and resolution). (Selected children's books are listed in Appendix A, children's book clubs and publishers of children's literature in Appendix B, and television programs that feature children's literature in Appendix D.)

THE TEACHER AS FACILITATOR

The teacher plays a critical role in influencing children's attitudes toward voluntary reading.

> If children live associating reading only with repetition of skill, drill, teach, and test, they will never reach for a book on their own. If, on the other hand, children live in an environment that associates reading with pleasure and enjoyment as well as with skill development, they are likely to become voluntary readers. How children live and learn at home and in the classroom ultimately determines whether they will live their lives as literate or aliterate individuals. (Morrow, 1985a, p. 20)

Chapter 2 dealt with literacy activities appropriate for home use and intended primarily to provide parental models for literacy behavior and to help children associate reading with pleasure. The school must follow a similar agenda. "One of the clear points to emerge from research into reading failure is that there was no association between reading and pleasure. . . . The role of teachers in stimulating voluntary reading among children and young people is . . . potentially the most powerful of all adult influences upon the young" (Irving, 1980, p. 7).

Programs that incorporate pleasurable experiences with literature create interest in and enthusiasm for books that in turn increase children's voluntary use of books (Morrow, 1982, 1983, 1987b; Morrow & Weinstein, 1982, 1986). Among other specific activities in early childhood classrooms, teachers should read or tell stories to children daily. Interest heightens when stories are discussed both before and after being read, especially if they are related to issues that reflect children's real-life experiences or current school topics. Literal, inferential and critical questions can be introduced even at the preschool level.

I recently led a discussion with four-year-olds after reading *Goldilocks and the Three Bears.* I asked who were the good and the bad characters. Hands waved in the air and Jennifer answered, "Goldilocks was good and the bears were bad." When I asked Jennifer why she thought that, she said, "Well, the bears scared Goldilocks."

Another hand went up and Tim said, "No, that's not right. The bears are good and Goldilocks is bad. Goldilocks went into the bears' house when they weren't home. She ate their food and didn't even ask."

"That's right," said Megan, "and she broke their chair and went to sleep in their bed and didn't even ask if it was okay."

Chris chimed in, "Yeah, Goldilocks was really bad. She did a lot of bad things because she didn't ask if she could."

"Would you go into a stranger's house and do the things Goldilocks did?" I asked. The whole group called out in unison "Nooooo." I asked why not. Sara answered, "Because that is bad. It's like stealing. She was naughty. If the cops found out, I bet they will arrest her."

Discussion about authors and illustrators also arouses interest. Reading different stories by the same author or a series of books about the same character, such as Madeline (Bemelmans, 1939) or Curious George (Rey, 1941), increases interest as well. Read different kinds of literature to the class and as often as possible coordinate stories with topics being discussed. If the topic is spring, bring a cocoon to class, discuss the life cycle of a butterfly, and follow the discussion with *The Very Hungry Caterpillar* (Carle, 1970), the story of the caterpillar's transformation to a butterfly. Read and recite poetry together regularly. Recruit older children, the principal, the custodian, the nurse, the librarian, parents, and grandparents to read to classes, to small groups, and to individuals. Encourage children to share books with one another. Books from home should be shared with the group and children encouraged to take books home from school.

Many popular folk songs have been made into picture storybooks, such as *Go Tell Aunt Rhody* (Quackenbush, 1973) and *Old MacDonald Had a Farm* (Quackenbush, 1972). These books are particularly good to read to children since the children are familiar with the words and very much want to pretend to read the books themselves and to another person. Cooking is another pleasurable activity that can be related to literature. Many picture storybooks feature food—*Blueberries for Sal* (McCloskey, 1948) and *Bread and Jam for Frances* (Hoban, 1964) for instance. After such stories have been read, the class can make blueberry muffins or bread and jam or whatever food is appropriate. Art activities can also be motivated by story readings. After reading *The Snowy Day* (Keats, 1962), have the children create a winter collage from blue construction paper, white cotton, wool, doilies, chalk, and silver foil. After reading *Where the Wild Things Are* (Sendak, 1963), ask kindergarteners and first graders to think of a wild thing and draw a picture of it. Gather their pictures into a class book. Class books become favorites and are read frequently by children. Children also enjoy filmstrip and movie stories, which motivates their interest in reading the associated book.

MAKING STORY READING PLEASURABLE

To make story readings as enjoyable and pleasurable as possible, select good pieces of literature—well-structured stories with well-delineated characters, clear and uncluttered illustrations, catch phrases, rhyme, and repetition. Read to youngsters in a relaxed atmosphere in a location designated for such readings. Each day let a different child sit close to you while you are reading, with the other children in a semicircle. If the children are on the floor, sit on a low chair. If they are sitting on chairs, you can sit on your own-size chair. Because children enjoy seeing illustrations in books during story readings, hold the book so it faces the group or turn the book at appropriate pauses so its pictures can be seen. Before reading a story to a group, practice reading it aloud to yourself.

Be expressive in your reading, change your voice when a different character speaks, and highlight special events. Use facial expressions. A story reading is like a dramatic presentation. Read slowly and with a great deal of animation. Record or videotape your readings to improve your technique. Begin a story with an introduction such as, "Today I'm going to read a story about a little girl who wanted to get a present for her mother's birthday. She can't think of anything and asks a rabbit to help her. The title of the story is *Mr. Rabbit and the Lovely Present* [Zolotow, 1962]. The author's name is Charlotte Zolotow and the illustrator is Maurice Sendak. While I read the story think of which part of the present you like the best." When you have finished reading the story, begin a discussion with a question such as "Who would like to tell me which part of the present you liked best?"

STORYTELLING: SOME CREATIVE TECHNIQUES

Storytelling strongly attracts children to books (Morrow, 1982; Morrow & Weinstein, 1982, 1986). It has a power that reading stories does not, for it frees the storyteller to use creative techniques. It also has the advantage of keeping him or her close to the audience. The storyteller establishes direct eye contact with the group. Telling a story produces an immediate response from the audience and is one of the surest ways to establish rapport between the listeners and the storyteller. Long pieces of literature can be trimmed so that even very young children can hear whole stories in one sitting. Considered an art, storytelling can be mastered by most people.

It is not necessary to memorize a story, but be sure you know it well. Use all the catch phrases and quotes that are important to the story. Use expression in your presentation, but don't let your dramatic techniques overshadow the story itself. Look directly at your audience and take their attention into consideration. Storytelling allows you to abridge stories as you go if attention spans seem to grow short. It is important to have the original book at hand when you have finished telling a story so that the children can see it and enjoy it again through its pictures and printed text.

Creative techniques help storytelling come alive. They excite the imagination, involve the listeners, and motivate children to try storytelling themselves and create their own techniques. Take clues for creative technique from the story. Some stories lend themselves to the use of puppets, others are perfect for the felt-board, and still others can be worked up as chalk talks.

Felt-boards are a popular and important tool in a classroom. You can make characters or purchase them commercially. Prepare your own with construction paper covered with clear contact or laminate. Attach strips of felt or sandpaper to the backs of the cutouts so they cling to the felt-board. Stories that lend themselves to felt-board retelling are those with a limited number of characters who appear throughout the story—*Ask Mr. Bear* (Flack, 1932), for example, or *Caps for Sale* (Slobodkina, 1947).

Prop stories are quite easy to develop. Simply collect stuffed animals, toys, and other articles that represent characters and objects in a story. Display the props at appropriate times during the storytelling. Three stuffed bears and a yellow-haired doll aid in telling *Goldilocks and the Three Bears* (Izawa, 1968a), several toy trains in *The Little Engine That Could* (Piper, 1954).

Stories strong in dialogue are best suited to the use of puppets. There are many kinds of puppets, including finger, hand, stick, and face puppets. Shy children often feel secure telling stories with puppets. Such stories as *The Gingerbread Boy* (Holdsworth, 1968) and *The Little Red Hen* (Izawa, 1968b) are appropriately told with puppets because they are short, have few characters, and repeat dialogue.

Another technique that attracts the listener is the chalk talk. The storyteller draws the story while telling it. Chalk talks are most effective when done with a large chalkboard so that the story can keep going in sequence from beginning to end. The same technique can be carried out on mural paper hung across a wall. The storyteller simply uses crayons or felt-tip markers instead of chalk. The chalk talk technique can also be adapted to easel and chart paper or an overhead projector. Choose a story with simple illustrations. Draw only a select few pictures as you tell the story. There are stories that have been written as chalk talks, including an entire series, *Harold and the Purple Crayon* (Johnson, 1955).

Sound-story techniques allow both audience and storyteller to provide sound effects when they are called for in a plot. The sounds can be made with voices, rhythm instruments, or music. When preparing to tell such a story, first select those parts of the story for which sound effects will be used. Then decide on each sound to be made and who will make it. As the story is told, students and storyteller chime in with their assigned sounds. Record the presentation, then leave the recording in the library corner with the original book. Among books that adapt easily to sound-story techniques are *The Noisy Book* (Brown, 1939), *Too Much Noise* (McGovern, 1967), and *Mr. Brown Can Moo: Can You?* (Seuss, 1970).

Other creative techniques, plus the opportunity to create your own, offer endless possibilities for storytelling (Morrow, 1981). By serving as a model of creative storytelling, you can excite children about literature and motivate them to try their own creative storytelling as well.

RECREATIONAL READING PERIODS

Once the environment, materials, and activities are designed and implemented to draw children to literature, the children need time to look at books and become immersed in literature independently during the school day. In the past, such periods have been called *sustained silent reading (SSR)*.

Sustained silent reading has generally been defined as very quiet time, with little socialization and little student choice beyond selection of the particular book the child chooses to read. If we expect them to become interested in reading, young children (and perhaps older children as well) require more options and greater flexibility than have been characteristic of SSR periods. Setting aside fifteen to thirty minutes three to five times a week for looking at books as well as for engaging in other activities related to literature allows the variety, free choice, social interaction, and flexibility children need if they are to be enticed into voluntary reading. Recent research indicates that children of different ability levels worked together during recreational reading periods. In one study, it was found that although many options were available, including felt-boards, roll movies, and taped stories, 70 percent of the free-choice activities selected by children involved the reading of books. Other materials and options attract children into a free-choice literacy area, but they lead children to choose books (Morrow & Weinstein, 1982, 1986).

Here are some ways you can help children function effectively during a recreational reading period:

1. Introduce the materials in a library corner to the children. You

During recreational reading periods, children read alone and to each other.

Headsets with taped stories and the accompanying storybooks provide a good reading model for the child and a popular, enjoyable activity.

might do so by drawing on different materials for each day's lesson, then placing those materials in the library corner for the children's further use.

2. Discuss the care of the books and other materials and indicate where everything belongs so that children can find and return whatever they want. Instill the Montessori concept of building respect for the materials (Morrison, 1984).

3. Ask children to decide beforehand what they will do during each recreational reading period. Let children change activities, but only after they have replaced materials they have already been using.

4. Allow children to work alone or with other children, and let them

During recreational reading, children may choose to tell a roll movie story or a felt-board story. All activities are literature-related and are accompanied by the original book.

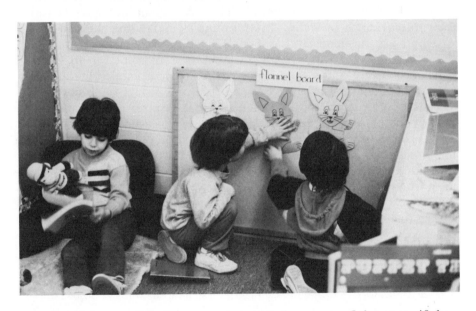

take materials out of the library corner to other parts of the room if they want.

5. Point out that the recreational reading period is generally a quiet time because some classmates are looking at books or listening to stories, but that quiet talk and some movement are okay.

These rules are based on Montessori's instructional procedures. Children as young as two are able to assimilate them and work well within the structure they establish. The rules allow freedom of choice in activities while defining limits for working with materials.

When children first begin to participate in recreational reading periods, it is the teacher's responsibility to circulate among them to see what they are doing and to help them become involved, if help is needed. Once the children have become familiar with the procedures and can work independently, the teacher can also participate directly in recreational reading period activities. It is most desirable for teachers to model behavior by reading themselves. The recreational reading period exposes children to reading in many forms and gives them the opportunity to make choices. It is a positive approach toward activating interest in voluntary reading.

The recommendations in this chapter for developing positive attitudes towards reading incorporate Holdaway's (1979) developmental approach to literacy. This approach highlights less teaching and more learning, learning that is self-regulated rather than regulated by adults. It has been suggested here that the teacher provide an environment rich with materials and activities from which children are invited to select, plus a social context in which children are actively involved with other children, with the teacher, and with materials. The environment is emulative rather than instructional, providing lively examples of reading skills in action. Teachers present themselves as models involved in literary activities. They serve as sources of support and positive reinforcement for appropriate behavior patterns in the child. Through regularly scheduled literary activities and ready access to attractive and comfortable classroom library corners stocked with books and materials that inspire interest and active participation, children associate reading with pleasure and develop an appreciation for books. Given time to use the library corner and participate in recreational reading activities, children reinforce their learning of skills through enjoyable, self-selected practice. The outcome can only be children who not only learn to read, but who choose to read voluntarily.

Much of the information in this chapter represents the results of studies that involved classroom observation and intervention. Teachers and children who were interviewed during some of those studies offered instructive comments. Among the comments of the children were these:

> "I like the library corner because you get to do things with your friends. We look at books together, listen to them at the listening station, and do felt stories."

> "I like the library corner. I can cuddle up on a pillow with a book or crawl into the private spot, and you can take the books home. It's nice."

> "I like the things at recreational reading period. It's fun. It makes you like the books."

Here are some comments from the teachers:

> "I was surprised that space could be made in my room for a library corner and that so many materials could fit into such a small area."

> "You could tell that the children were enjoying themselves during the

recreational reading period. We seldom had discipline problems during this time and everyone participated."

"I never realized that children's involvement in this type of program was beneficial in promoting interest in books and a desire to learn to read, yet also developed skills. I sort of thought of these things as what you do after worksheets were finished. I suddenly realized that because they were immersed in literature activities children were learning concepts about books and print and also having the opportunity to practice and reinforce the things I teach them."

"Participating in the study demonstrated to me how important the teacher's involvement, enthusiasm, and encouragement are in making children more interested in books." (Morrow, pp. 18–19, 25, 1985a)

ASSESSING CHILDREN'S ATTITUDES TOWARD BOOKS

Direct observation of children's behavior while they are listening to stories or looking at books is probably the most effective method of assessing their attitude toward books. How much attention do they give to the books they are looking at? Do they simply browse? Do they flip through the pages quickly, paying little attention to print or pictures? Do they silently study the text, sustaining attention to pictures and print throughout? (Martinez & Teale, 1988). The teacher should also note how frequently children select looking at books when faced with other options. In occasional interviews with individual children, asking what they like to do best in school and at home might reveal interest in reading. During conferences, ask parents if their children voluntarily look at books or pay close attention when they are read to. At the same time, ask parents how often they read to their children. Gather facts about the home literacy environment that will help you understand the child's attitude towards books.

ACTIVITIES

1. Observe in an early childhood classroom. If there is a library corner, list all the characteristics that reflect criteria described in this chapter. List items that need to be included.

2. Observe in an early childhood classroom for five different sessions. List all the literacy activities carried out there that you believe contribute to developing in the children a positive attitude toward reading.

3. Select a piece of children's literature and choose a creative storytelling technique that is appropriate to it. Create materials for the story and tell it to a group of children. Evaluate your performance according to the criteria discussed in this chapter about storytelling.

6

Developing Concepts About Books and Comprehension of Story

CHAPTER OVERVIEW

■ Varied active participation in literature experiences such as story retelling, directed listening-thinking activities, small group and one-to-one readings help young children develop book concepts and comprehension of story.

■ Interactive behavior between adult and child during story book reading is an important factor in helping children construct meaning from print.

■ Sense of story structure enhances a child's comprehension of story.

Few children learn to love books themselves. Someone must lure them into the wonderful world of the written word, someone must show them the way.

ORVILLE PRESCOTT
A Father Reads to His Child

Investigators have found a number of instructional strategies that nurture children's concepts about books and help them to comprehend stories. Those practices include children's role-playing, retelling, and reconstructing with pictures stories that have been read to them. The active involvement of children in experiences with literature enhances their comprehension of stories, their sense of story structure, and their language development. Through experiences with literature, young children integrate information and learn the relationships among a story's various parts (Brown, 1975; Morrow, 1985b; Pellegrini & Galda, 1982). The fact that interactive behavior plays a leading role in such learning seems to reinforce a model of generative learning: the reader or listener understands prose by actively engaging in construction of and relationships with the textual information he or she hears or reads (Linden & Wittrock, 1981; Wittrock, 1974, 1981).

Teale (1984) has utilized Vygotsky's (1978) definition of higher mental functions as internalized social relationships and applied it to literacy. Literacy develops, according to Teale, from children's interactions with others in specific environments of which reading and writing are a part. Holdaway's (1979) model of developmental teaching, derived from observations of middle-class homes, indicates that a child benefits when early experiences with storybooks are mediated by an interactive adult who provides problem-solving situations. The child is asked to respond and the adult offers information when necessary. In such situations, children and adults interact to integrate, construct, and make relationships with printed text. The strategies to be described in this chapter follow the theory, research, and models just outlined.

PRACTICES THAT DEVELOP CONCEPTS ABOUT BOOKS AND COMPREHENSION OF STORY

The many benefits of reading to children have been discussed throughout this volume. Strategies for reading to infants and toddlers that are applicable in the home and in day-care centers have been described, as have techniques for reading stories to children that will arouse their interest and entice them to books. The following sections suggest strategies for using children's literature to develop children's concepts about books and the meanings to be found in books.

Activities that Emphasize Concepts about Books

A child who has a good concept of books:

1. knows that a book is for reading;
2. can identify the front and the back of a book as well as the top and the bottom;
3. can turn the pages of a book properly;
4. knows the difference between print and pictures;
5. knows that pictures on a page are related to what the print says;
6. knows where one begins reading on a page;
7. knows what a title is;
8. knows what an author is;
9. knows what an illustrator is.

Adults take such concepts for granted. To many two-to-six-year-olds, however, those concepts are totally unfamiliar. To help children master them, point them out at every opportunity when you read to children. You can introduce a story reading, for instance, by pointing appropriately as you say, "The title of the story that I'm going to read is *Mr. Rabbit and the Lovely Present* [Zolotow, 1962]. This is the title on the front of the book. The author of the book, the person who wrote it, is Charlotte Zolotow. Here is her name. And the illustrator, the person who drew the pictures, is Maurice Sendak. Here is his name. All books have titles and authors, and if they have pictures they also have illustrators. The next time you look at a book, see if you can find the title. It is always on the front cover."

The repetition of such dialogue familiarizes a child with the concepts, which they assimilate easily. Similar dialogues explain other concepts. Point to a picture, then to print. Identify each, then ask, "Which do we read, the picture or the print?" As you get ready to read to them, ask children to point out the top and bottom of the book, the title, and where you should begin reading on a page. Not only will you give the children the opportunity to learn the concepts, you can at the same time determine which children have the concept and who needs help. These activities and dialogues can be carried out during story readings to small groups or to individual students. A child's independent exploration of books will reinforce what the teacher has pointed out or explained.

Activities That Develop Comprehension of Story

A child is developing story comprehension when he or she:

1. attempts to read well known story books which results in well formed stories;
2. retells a story without the help of the book;
3. includes elements of story structure in story retellings: setting (beginning, time, place, characters), theme (main character's problem or goal to be

achieved), plot episodes (events leading toward a solution of the main character's problem or attainment of his or her goal), resolution (problem solution, goal achievement, ending);

4. responds to story readings with literal questions and comments;
5. responds to story readings with interpretive and critical questions and comments;
6. participates in story reading by saying words and narrating stories as the teacher is reading them;

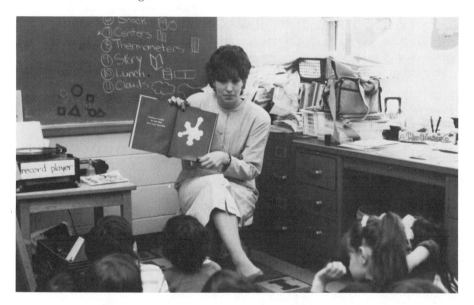

Children learn concepts about books when they are read to by adults who point out features such as the print and the pictures.

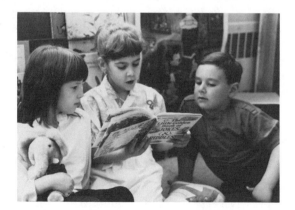

Children learn concepts about books by interacting with other children as they browse through the pictures and by looking at books themselves.

Children's literature is especially appropriate for developing a child's sense that print conveys meaning. The stories are generally attractive, they relate well to a child's real-life experiences, and they are typically well structured, containing clearly delineated settings, themes, plot episodes, and resolutions. Furthermore, the use of children's literature offers ample opportunity for developing such traditional comprehension skills as literal, inferential, and critical thinking. Children exhibit literal understanding when they can recall details of a story, recognize its sequence, or follow directions. Inferential and critical skills enable a child to recognize cause and effect, understand relationships, identify main ideas, predict, anticipate outcomes, make associations, relate story episodes to life experiences, make judgments, evaluate, and draw conclusions.

Directed Listening–Thinking Activities

Reading to children should always be purposeful, whether it be simply for pleasure, to complement content area learning, or to develop specific concepts about books. The format of the directed listening–thinking activity (DLTA) can with frequent use be internalized by the child and transferred when new material is presented (Anderson, Mason, & Shirley, 1984; Morrow, 1984; Stauffer, 1980). Whatever a DLTA's specific objective, its framework offers the listener a direction and strategy for organizing and retrieving information from the text being read. In the following DLTA outline for *The Little Red Hen* (Izawa, 1968), there are two main objectives: to emphasize the sequence of events and to involve children in making inferences and judgments from the text.

A. Prepare for listening with prequestions and discussion.
1. Build a background by introducing the story: "Today I'm going to read a story entitled *The Little Red Hen*. Let's look at the pictures to see if you can tell me what it is going to be about." Encourage children to respond as you turn the pages. After they have offered their ideas say, "The story is about a hen who wants to bake some bread and asks her friends for some help."
2. Ask prequestions that build additional background for listening and that set a purpose for listening. Relate the questions to real-life experiences whenever possible: "Have you ever asked people for help? What kind of help? Did they help you? Has anyone ever asked you for help? What kind of help? Were you able to help the person? How? While I'm reading, try to decide if you think the little red hen did the right thing with her bread at the end of the story, and why. Try also to remember what happened first, second, third, and at the end of the story."
3. When the children have gained enough experience with your prequestions, you can ask them to think of their own: "Now that I've told you a little about the story, what do you want to find out when I read it to you?"

When prequestioning, show the pictures in the book to the children as further preparation for their listening.

B. Read the story.   Be sure also to show the children the pictures as you read the story. Stop a few times for reactions, comments, or questions from the children. Model or scaffold responses to guide them in their thinking, keeping in mind the objectives for this particular DLTA: "Can you remember what help the little red hen has asked for so far? How have the other animals acted about giving help?" If the children do not respond, scaffold or model responses by changing questions to statements: "These animals aren't very helpful to the little red hen. Each time the hen asks for their help the animals all answer, 'Not I.' " Ask also for children's predictions of what will happen next.

C. Have a discussion after reading.   The post-discussion should be guided by the objectives set for listening: "What did the little red hen want help with first? Second?" And so on. Ask children to retell the story; retelling will demonstrate their knowledge of sequence. Allow children to use the pictures of the book to help them follow sequence. Finally, focus on the second goal, making inferences and judgments: "What would you have done if you were the little red hen? What lesson can we learn from this story?"

A DLTA can have any of many different objectives. The framework, however, is always basically the same: (1) preparation for listening—prequestions and discussion; (2) reading the story; and (3) discussion after the reading. All three steps are focused on the DLTA's specific objectives. A DLTA can focus on *literal responses* (such as recall of facts and sequencing) *inferential responses* (such as interpreting characters' feelings, predicting outcomes, and relating the story to real-life experiences), and *critical responses* (such as evaluating, problem solving, and making judgments). It can focus on elements of story structure, such as *setting* (introduction, time, place, characters); *theme* (the goal or problem faced by the main character); *plot episodes* (events leading to solution of the problem or achievement of the goal); *resolution* (problem solution or goal achievement, story ending). It helps youngsters draw meaning from the print. Research has demonstrated that a DLTA can increase the story comprehension of young listeners (Morrow, 1984), just as a DRTA (directed reading–thinking activity) can increase the story comprehension of young readers (Danford, 1973; McGraw & Groteleuschen, 1972; Pearson, Hansen, & Gordon, 1979; Richards, 1979).

SMALL-GROUP AND ONE-TO-ONE STORY READINGS

Although teachers share literature with children most commonly by reading to whole classes, the importance and benefits of reading to small groups and to individuals must not be overlooked. Too often considered impractical in school settings, one-to-one and small-group readings yield such tremendous benefits that they must be incorporated into school programs. The most striking benefit of one-to-one story readings at home is the interactive behavior it involves, along with the direct channels of information it gives the child. It also provides the adult with insight into what children already know and want to know. In a recent study (Morrow, 1988a) it was determined that similar readings in a school setting had similar positive results with preshoolers from lower socioeconomic backgrounds, even though the youngsters had little previous experience interacting with adults. Teachers in the study practiced the same interactive behaviors identified by researchers who had studied home storybook readings (Applebee & Langer, 1983; Cochran-Smith, 1984; Flood, 1977; Heath, 1980; Ninio & Brunner, 1978; Roser & Martinez, 1985; Teale, 1981). These teacher behaviors are as follows;

Guidelines for Teacher Behavior During Storybook Reading

1. *Manage*
   a. Introduce story.
   b. Provide background information about the book.
   c. Redirect irrelevant discussion back to the story.

2. *Prompt Responses*
   a. Invite children to ask questions or comment throughout the story.
   b. Scaffold responses for children to model if no responses are forthcoming. ("Those animals aren't very nice. They won't help the little red hen.")
   c. Relate responses to real-life experiences. ("I needed help when I was preparing a party, and my family shared the work. Did you ever ask for help and couldn't find anyone to give it to you? What happened?")
   d. When children do not respond, ask questions that require answers other than yes or no. ("What would you have done if you were the little red hen and no one helped you bake the bread?")

3. *Support and Inform*
   a. Answer questions as they are asked.
   b. React to comments.
   c. Relate your responses to real-life experiences.
   d. Provide positive reinforcement for children's responses.

   (Morrow, 1988a)

Frequent readings by teachers who followed these guidelines increased the number and complexity of the children's responses. The youngsters offered many questions and comments that focused on meaning. Initially, they labeled illustrations. Later, they gave increased attention to details, their comments and questions became interpretive and predictive, and they drew from their own experiences. They also began narrating—that is, "reading" or mouthing the story along with the teacher. As the program continued, some children focused on structural elements, remarking on titles, settings, characters, and story events. Eventually, after many readings, the children began to focus on print, questioning names of words, letters, or sounds. They also began to recognize letters and words and read them as they were able (Morrow, 1987a). Compared with one-to-one readings, reading to small groups of children seems to encourage more and earlier responses. Children tend to repeat one another's remarks, and they are motivated to respond to and elaborate on what their peers have said.

The following segments from transcriptions of small-group story readings illustrate the various questions and comments children make when they are involved in the activity, and the wealth of knowledge and information they receive from the responding adult. The transcriptions also illustrate what the children already know and what their interests are, which helps us design instruction.

Story: *The Very Hungry Caterpillar* (Carle, 1970) (questions about a part of the book)

Jerry: (pointing to the picture on the front of the book) Why does it have a picture on it?

Teacher: The cover of the book has a picture on it so you will know what the story is about. Look at the picture. Can you tell me what the book is about?

Jerry: Ummm, I think that's a caterpillar. Is it about a caterpillar?

Teacher: You're right, very good. The book is about a caterpillar, and the name of the story is *The Very Hungry Caterpillar*. When you look at the pictures in a book, they help you find out what the words say.

Story: *Caps for Sale* (Slobodkina, 1947) (asks for a definition)

Teacher: I'm going to read a story today called *Caps for Sale*.

Jamie: What are caps?

Teacher: A cap is a little hat that you put on your head. See, there is cap in the picture.

Jamie: I never knew that before. I knew about hats, but I never heard about caps.

Story: *Chicken Soup with Rice* (Sendak, 1962) (attends to print)

Chris:	Wait, stop reading. Let me see this again. (He turns back to the page that talks about the month of June.) How come they're the same? (He refers to the words *June* and *July.*)
Teacher:	What do you mean?
Chris:	Look at the letters, J–U, J–U . . . They look alike.
Teacher:	Look more closely at the ends of the words. Are they the same?
Chris:	Ohh, nooo, just at the front part.

Story: *Caps for Sale* (Slobodkina, 1947) (predicts)

Colleen:	I wonder why those monkeys took the caps?
Teacher:	I don't know. Can you think why?
Colleen:	Well, the peddler was sleeping and those monkeys looked at the caps, and and maybe they think they're for them. Or, I know! Maybe they're cold so they want a cap.
Teacher:	Those are good ideas, Colleen.

Story: *Madeline's Rescue* (Bemelmans, 1953) (relates to real life experience)

Jamie:	What's the policemen going to do?
Teacher:	He's going to help Madeline. Policemen are nice; they always help us.
Jamie:	Policemans aren't nice. See, my daddy beat up Dominic and the policeman came and took him away and put him in jail for no reason. And my Daddy cried. I don't like policemans. I don't think they are nice.

Segments such as these reveal children's understandings. Do their comments and questions relate to literal meanings? Do they raise interpretive and critical issues by associating the story with their own lives, make predictions of what will come next in a story, or express judgments about characters' actions? Do comments or questions relate to matters of print, such as names of letters, words, and sounds? Recording and then analyzing one-to-one and small-group story readings reveals what children know and want to know (Morrow, 1987a). The coding sheet that follows aids such analysis.

Coding Children's Responses
During Story Readings

Child's name_____ Date_____ Story_____

(Read one story to one child or a small group of children. Encourage the children to respond with questions and comments. Tape record the session. Transcribe or listen to the tape, noting each child's responses by placing checks in the appropriate categories. A category may receive more than one check, and a single response may be credited to more than one category. Total the number of checks in each category.)

1. Focus on Story Structure
   a. setting (time, place)   _____
   b. characters   _____
   c. theme (problem or goal)   _____
   d. plot episodes (events leading toward problem
      solution or goal attainment)   _____
   e. resolution   _____

2. Focus on Meaning
   a. labeling   _____
   b. detail   _____
   c. interpreting (associations, elaborations)   _____
   d. predicting   _____
   e. drawing from one's experience   _____
   f. seeking definitions of words   _____
   g. using narrational behavior (reciting parts of the
      book along with the teacher)   _____

3. Focus on Print
   a. questions or comments about letters   _____
   b. questions or comments about sounds   _____
   c. questions or comments about words   _____
   d. reads words   _____
   e. reads sentences

4. Focus on Illustrations
   a. responses and questions that
      are related to illustrations   _____

Although whole-class readings are more practical and have tremendous value in simply exposing children to literature, the interactive behavior between adult and child in one-to-one readings and small-group readings do not occur in the large group setting. If we review transcripts of story readings in all three settings, several things become apparent. In whole-group settings no one child can ask questions or comment repeatedly throughout the story without interfering with the story line for the other children. The teacher might never get through a coherent reading. Dialogue that does occur is managed by the teacher to such an extent that the teacher often says more than the children. A truly interactive situation does not exist due to the size of the group. In small-group and one-to-one readings, by contrast, a teacher may initially do a lot of managing and prompting, but only to encourage and model responses for children. In a short time the roles reverse: most dialogue is initiated by children through questions and comments, and the teacher offers positive reinforcement and answers questions posed by the children (Morrow, 1987a).

Children who come from homes that do not offer them one-to-one readings are at a disadvantage in their literacy development. It is necessary to carry out such strategies in school to compensate for what is not provided at home as well as to provide the other benefits. Gains both in literacy skills and in positive attitudes toward books can occur. To learn to associate books with warmth and pleasure, children who have not had the benefit of the lap technique at home can experience it at school. It is difficult to provide one-to-one readings in school because of time limitations and the number of children, but asking aides, volunteers, and older children to do so helps solve the problem. So does reading to small groups of youngsters from time to time, perhaps replacing some of the traditional instruction in reading groups. Many school districts enjoy federal funding for work with young children identified as having potential learning problems. Ratios in such programs may be as low as five children per teacher. Certainly those settings allow one-to-one readings as part of a literacy development program.

SHARED BOOK EXPERIENCES

Shared book experiences (Holdaway, 1979) are a whole-group approach. In one way or another, they enable children to participate in the reading of a book. They also help develop listening skills, for children must listen attentively in order to participate.

Predictable stories are ideal for shared book experiences because they allow children to guess what will come next, thereby encouraging participation. Predictability takes many forms. The use of catch phrases, such as " 'Not I,' said the dog," " 'Not I,' said the cat," and so on, in *The Little Red Hen* (Izawa, 1968b), encourages children to chant along. Predictable rhyme enables children to fill in words, as in *Green Eggs with Ham* (Seuss, 1960). Cumulative patterns contribute to predictability. New events are added with each episode, for example, then repeated at the next, as in *Drummer Hoff* (Emberley, 1967). *Are You My Mother?* (Eastman, 1960) repeats phrases and episode patterns as its central character, a baby bird, searches for his mother by approaching different animals and asking the same question.

Conversation can contribute to predictability, as in *The Three Billy Goats Gruff* (Brown, 1957) or *The Three Little Pigs* (Brenner, 1972). All stories become predictable as children become familiar with them, so repeating stories builds up a repertoire for shared book experiences. Fairy tales such as *The Three Little Pigs* are already familiar to most children and therefore often predictable to a group. Books that carry familiar sequences, such as days of the week, months of the year, letters, and numbers, are predictable—*The Very Hungry Caterpillar* (Carle, 1970), for instance. Books gain predictability through good plot structures and topics familiar to children. Books in which pictures match text page by page tend to be predictable to children, especially if everyone in the group can see the pictures as the story is being read.

Predictable books are excellent for emergent readers in shared book experiences as well as independently. They allow the child's first experience with reading to be enjoyable, and successful with minimal effort. Such immediate success encourages the child to continue efforts at reading. (A list of predictable books is provided in Appendix A.)

One shared book technique involves reading from a Big Book (Scholastic, 1986) or a similar book made by the class or the teacher. Such a book is designed so that everyone in the group can see the pictures and the words of the story clearly while it is being read. If the book is a new one for the class, the children are asked to listen during the first reading. If it is being read for the second time or is otherwise already familiar, immediate participation is encouraged. Often the teacher uses a pointer during the reading to emphasize left-to-right progression and the correspondence of spoken and written words. Big Books stand best on an easel or against a wall. Since they are twenty-four by thirty-six inches or larger, they are hard to handle manually. The teacher encourages participation by stopping at predictable parts and asking children to fill in words and phrases. As the children become more and more familiar with the books, they begin to know them by memory, which enables the children to begin to associate words as they say them with the printed words the teacher points to on the page. Big Books and regular-size copies of the same book should be available for children to use independently after a first Big Book reading.

Shared book experiences can involve children in dramatizations of a story, art activities, or other extended experiences after the story has been read. Shared book experiences can be recorded and made available in the listening station. So can tapes of teachers' readings and commercially recorded tapes. These will provide fluent models with good phrasing and intonation for children to emulate. Shared book experiences can easily be adapted to the DLTA format, as long as it is emphasized that shared book experiences are to be pleasurable, relaxed, participatory, and enjoyable read-aloud events.

Shared book experiences involve the children in some way during the story reading. Often Big Books are used so that they can be seen easily by all and so children can see the print as the teacher reads and points to it.

REPEATED STORY READINGS

Children enjoy repetition, as we all do. Being familiar with an experience is comfortable, like singing a well-known song. Besides offering the pleasure of familiarity, a repeated story helps develop concepts about words, print, and books. One study (Morrow, 1987a) compared responses of two groups of four-year-olds. One group listened to three readings of each of three stories, the other group a different story at each of nine sessions. The repeated-reading group increased the number and kind of their responses, and their responses differed significantly from those of the different-story group. Their responses became more interpretive, and they began to predict outcomes and make associations, judgments, and elaborative comments.

They also began to narrate stories as the teacher read (their first attempts at reading) and to focus on elements of print, asking names of letters and words. Even children of low ability seem to make more responses with repeated readings than with a single reading (Roser & Martinez, 1985).

The following dialogue is taken from a transcription of a child's responses to a third reading of *The Little Red Hen*. For the sake of brevity, this excerpt includes primarily the child's comments and questions and the teacher's responses; most of the story text has been omitted.

Teacher: Today I'm going to read the story *The Little Red Hen*. It is about a hen who wanted some help when she baked some bread. (The teacher begins to read the story.) . . . Who will cut this wheat?

Melony: "Not I," said the cat. "Not I," said the dog. "Not I," said the mouse.

Teacher: That was good, Melony. You are reading. (The teacher continues reading.) . . . Who will take this wheat to the mill to be ground into flour?

Melony: "Not I," said the cat. "Not I," said the dog. "Not I," said the mouse with the whiskers.

Teacher: Very nice, Melony. (The teacher continues to read.)

Melony: I want to read that part, but I don't know how.

Teacher: Go ahead and try. I bet you can. I'll help you: The cat smelled it.

Melony: The cat smelled it and she said *umm* that smells good, and the mouse smelled it, and it smelled good.

Teacher: (continuing reading) . . . Who will eat this cake?

Melony: The mouse, the doggy, the kitty!

Teacher: You're right again, Melony. (The teacher reads to the end of the story.) Did you want to say anything else about the story?

Melony: He was bad so he couldn't have no cake. (Melony searches through the pages.) That's the wrong part.

Teacher: Show me the part you are talking about.

Melony: There it is, almost at the end. She's going to make a cake and she'll say who's going to bake this cake for me. And the cat says, "Not I," the dog says, "Not I," the mouse says, "Not I." And then when she's cooking it they smell a good thing and then they wanted some, too, but they didn't have any, 'cause they didn't plant the wheat.

Teacher: You're so right. They didn't help do the work, so they didn't get to eat the cake.

Melony: Where does it say "Not I"? Show me the words in the book.

Teacher: Here it is. Can you find it again?

Melony;   (flipping through the pages) I'm looking for where she bakes the cake. Here it is. Yea. And he smelled it. And he smelled it. And the mouse smelled it. (She turns pages.) They're going in the kitchen. And she said, "All by myself, I cut the wheat. All by myself, I took it to the mill to get it into flour. All by myself I baked the cake. All by myself I'm going to eat it.

Teacher: That's terrific, Melony. That's what the hen said.

Melony: (pointing to the dog) The dog was not happy. Where does it say *dog*?

Teacher: You're right. He doesn't look happy. Here is where it says *dog* (pointing).
Melony: There's the word, *dog, dog, dog.* How does that dog look?
Teacher: He looks hungry and mad that he can't have any bread.
Melony: You're right. But it's his fault. He didn't help. And that's the end.
             (Morrow, 1987a)

Besides illustrating the value of repeated readings in the responses generated by the child, this exchange demonstrates the encouragment, reinforcement, and rapport that can evolve from one-to-one storybook sessions.

STORY RETELLING

Letting a listener or reader retell a story offers active participation in a literacy experience that helps a child develop language structures, comprehension, and sense of story structure (Morrow, 1985b). Retelling engages the child in holistic comprehension and organization of thought. It also allows for personalization of thinking as children mesh their own life experiences into their retelling. Retelling contrasts with the more traditional piecemeal approach of teacher-posed questions that require a child to recall bits of information (Gambrell, Pfeiffer, & Wilson, 1985). With practice in retelling, children come to assimilate the concept of story structure. They learn to introduce a story with its beginning and its setting. They recount its theme, plot episodes, and resolution. In retelling stories, children demonstrate their comprehension of story details and sequence, organizing them coherently. They also infer and interpret the sounds and expressions of characters' voices.

Retelling is not an easy task for children, but with practice they improve quickly. To help children develop the practice of retelling, tell them before they read or listen to a text or story that they will be asked to retell it (Morrow, 1985b). Further guidance depends on the teacher's specific purpose in the retelling. If the immediate intent is to teach or test sequence, for instance, the children should be instructed to concentrate on what happened first, second, and so on. If the goal is to teach or assess the ability to integrate information and make inferences from text, children should be instructed to think of things that have happened to them like those that happen to characters in the story. Props such as felt-board characters or the pictures in the text itself can be used to help the students retell the story. Pre- and post-discussion of the story help to improve retelling ability as well as the teacher modeling a retelling for children (Mitchell, 1984; Morrow, 1985b). The following procedure is helpful in guiding a child's retelling:

1. Ask the child to retell the story. "A little while ago, I read the story [name the story]. Would you retell the story as if you were telling it to a friend who has never heard it before?"
2. Use the following prompts only if needed:
   a. If the child has difficulty beginning the retelling, suggest beginning with "Once upon a time," or "Once there was . . .".
   b. If the child stops retelling before the end of the story, encourage continuation by asking, "What comes next?" or "Then what happened?"
   c. If the child stops retelling and cannot continue even with general prompts, ask a question that is relevant at the point in the story at which the child has paused. For example, "What was Jenny's problem in the story?"
3. When a child is unable to retell the story, or if the retelling lacks sequence and detail, prompt the retelling step by step. For example:
   a. "Once upon a time," or "Once there was . . .".
   b. "Who was the story about?"
   c. "When did the story happen?" (day, night, summer, winter?)
   d. "Where did the story happen?"
   e. "What was [the main character's] problem in the story?"
   f. "How did [he or she] try to solve the problem? What did [he or she] do first [second, next]?"
   g. "How was the problem solved?"
   h. "How did the story end?" (Morrow, 1985b, p. 659.)

In addition to its usefulness as a learning technique, retelling also allows adults to evaluate children's progress. If you plan to evaluate a retelling, let the child know during your introduction of the story you are about to read that he or she will be asked to retell it after the reading. During the evaluative retellings, do *not* offer prompts beyond such general ones as "Then what happened?" or "Can you think of anything else about the story?" Retellings commonly reveal a child's sense of story structure, focusing mostly on literal recall, but they also reflect the child's inferential and critical thinking ability. To assess the child's retelling for sense of story structure, the examiner should first parse (divide) the events of the story into four categories—*setting, theme, plot episodes,* and *resolution.* A guide sheet and the outline of the parsed text are then used to record the number of ideas and details the child includes within each category in the retelling, regardless of their order. *Do* credit a child for partial recall or for recounting the "gist" of a story event (Pellegrini & Galda, 1982; Thorndyke, 1977). Evaluate the child's sequencing ability by comparing the order of events in the child's retelling with the proper order of setting, theme, plot episodes, and resolution. The analysis indicates not only which elements a child includes or omits and how well a child sequences, but also where instruction might be focused. Comparing analyses of several retellings over a year will indicate a child's progress.

The following example uses a parsed outline of *Jenny Learns a Lesson* (Fujikawa, 1980). The story is about a little girl who likes to play "pretend games" with her friends. However, when her friends come to play, Jenny becomes bossy and tells everyone what to do, and her friends leave angry. After several such episodes, her friends leave and do not return. Jenny becomes lonesome and realizes her problem. She apologizes to her friends, invites them back to play, and promises not to boss them. They agree to play, and this time all do as they wish. The following parsed outline is accompanied by transcriptions of two children's retellings of the story. A retelling guidesheet follows with an analysis of the second transcription told by Beth (Morrow, 1985b).

Parsed Story
Setting
a. Once upon a time there was a girl who liked to play pretend.

b. Characters: Jenny (main character), Nicholas, Sam, Mei Su, and Shags, the dog.

Theme
Every time Jenny played with her friends, she bossed them.

Plot Episodes
First episode: Jenny decided to pretend to be a queen. She called her friends. They came to play. Jenny told them all what to do and was bossy. The friends became angry and left.

Second episode: Jenny decided to play dancer. She called her friends and they came to play. Jenny told them all what to do. The friends became angry and left.

Third episode: Jenny decided to play pirate. She called her friends and they came to play. Jenny told them all what to do. The friends became angry and left.

Fourth episode: Jenny decided to play duchess. She called her friends and they came to play. Jenny told them all what to do. The friends became angry and left.

Fifth episode: Jenny's friends refused to play with her beause she was so bossy. Jenny became lonely and apologized to them for being bossy.

Resolution
a. The friends all played together and each person did what he or she wanted to do.

b. They all had a wonderful day and were so tired that they fell asleep.

Verbatim Transcriptions

Beth (age five) Once upon a time there's a girl named Jenny and she called her friends over and they played queen and went to the palace. They had to . . . they had to do what she said and they didn't like it so then they went home and said that was boring. It's not fun playing queen and doing what she says you have to. So they didn't play with her for seven days and she had . . . she had a idea that she was being selfish, so she went to find her friends and said, I'm sorry I was so mean. And said, let's play pirate, and they played pirate and they went onto the ropes. Then they played that she was a fancy lady playing house. And they have tea. And they played what they wanted and they were happy. The end.

Sample Analysis

Story Retelling Evaluation Guide Sheet

Child's Name _____ Beth _____ Age ___ 5 ___
Title of Story _____ Jenny Learns a Lesson _____ Date _____

General directions: Give 1 point for each element included as well as for "gist." Give 1 point for each character named as well as for such words as *boy*, *girl*, or *dog*. Credit plurals (friends, for instance) with 2 points under characters.

Sense of story structure

Setting
  a. Begins story with an introduction   1
  b. Names main character   1
  c. Number of other characters named   2
  d. Actual number of other characters   4
  e. Score for "other characters" (c/d):   .5
  f. Includes statement about time or place   1

Theme
Refers to main character's primary goal
or problem to be solved   1

Plot Episodes
  a. Number of episodes recalled   4
  b. Number of episodes in story   5
  c. Score for "plot episodes" (a/b)   .8

Resolution
  a. Names problem solution/goal attainment   1
  b. Ends story   1

Sequence
Retells story in structural order: setting,
theme, plot episodes, resolution. (Score 2 for
proper, 1 for partial, 0 for no sequence evident.)   1
Highest score possible: ___ 10 ___ Child's score   8.3

Checks can be used instead of numbers to get a general sense of elements children include & progress over time. A quantitative analysis as shown above is optional. Retellings can be evaluated for interpretive critical comments as well.

Morrow, 1988b

FAVORITE STORYBOOK READINGS

To study emergent reading behaviors Sulzby (1985) observed children from ages two to six attempt to read favorite storybooks. Although they were not yet readers in the conventional sense, the children were asked, "Read me your book." Sulzby found that in their "reading" the children produced speech that could indeed be categorized as a first act of reading; that the speech they used as they "read" was clearly different in structure and intonation from their typical conversation; and that different developmental levels could be observed in these "oral readings." Sulzby's Simplified Classification Scheme for Children's Emergent Reading of Favorite Storybooks follows (Sulzby 1987; adapted by permission):

1. *Attending to pictures but not forming stories.* The child "reads" by labeling and commenting on the pictures in the book, but does not "weave a story" across the pages.

2. *Attending to pictures and forming oral stories.* The child "reads" by following the pictures, but weaves a story across the pages through wording and intonation like those of someone telling a story. Often, however, the listener too must see the pictures in order to understand the story the child is "reading."

3. *Attending to a mix of pictures, reading, and storytelling.* The child "reads" by looking at the pictures. The majority of the child's "reading" fluctuates between the oral intonation of a storyteller and that of a reader.

4. *Attending to pictures but forming written stories.* The child "reads" by looking at the pictures. The child's speech sounds like reading, both in wording and intonation. The listener rarely needs to see the pictures in order to understand the story. With his or her eyes closed, the listener would think the child was reading print. The "reading" is similar to the story in print, and sometimes follows it verbatim.

5. *Attending to print.* This category has four divisions: (a) exploring the print, as evident in such strategies as refusing to read for print-related reasons; (b) using only some of the aspects of print; (c) reading with imbalanced strategies; and (d) reading independently, or "real" reading.

From children's attempts at storybook reading, then, we can determine stages of development. Since the activity is developmental and leads to literacy, teachers should ask children to participate in it, either to evaluate their ability or simply to encourage their emergent literacy.

ASSESSING CHILDREN'S CONCEPTS ABOUT BOOKS AND COMPREHENSION OF STORY

Children's concepts of books and their comprehension of story can be developed and assessed by a broad range of techniques and in various contexts. To determine how much children know about books—such as their front, back, top, and bottom; which is print and which are pictures; how pages are turned; where reading begins; and what titles, authors, and illustrators are—one can observe regularly how youngsters handle books; hold one-to-one interviews with children; question and otherwise encourage response in whole-group, small-group, or individual interaction; or use any of the several other techniques described in this chapter. Children's responses can be literal, interpretive, or critical. They can reflect simple recall, detail, sequence, association, prediction, judgment, and evaluation. Children's comprehension of story can be demonstrated and evaluated through their story retelling, attempted reading of favorite storybooks, role playing, picture sequencing, use of puppets or felt-boards to reenact stories, and their questions and comments during storybook reading.

The techniques described in this chapter are designed to develop concepts about books and comprehension of story through the use of children's literature.

ACTIVITIES

1. Ask a two-, a four-, and a six-year-old to read their favorite story using a storybook. Describe the reading behaviors they attempt. Are developmental differences evident among their performances?

2. Select a child between the ages of three and seven. Meet with the child five times, each time to let the child practice retelling a story. Tape and transcribe each session. Using the guidesheet provided in this chapter, analyze the tapes for the elements of story structure, details, sequence, and so on, that the child includes in retelling. Are there developmental changes in the child's performance from session to session?

3. Prepare two different directed listening–thinking activities, including pre- and post-discussions. Select different objectives for each DLTA. Use your plans with small groups of chlidren. On the basis of the children's responses, evaluate how well your objectives are met.

7

Developing Reading Through Concepts About Print

CHAPTER OVERVIEW

- Mastery of certain characteristics of print is necessary for literacy development.
- Environmental print is an excellent source for developing a child's concepts about print.
- The Language Experience Approach to the teaching of reading can help in the development of concepts about print.
- Emergent literacy is assessed best by using several different measures frequently.

First words must have an intense meaning.
First words must be already part of the dynamic life.
First books must be made of the stuff of the child himself, whatever and wherever the child.

SYLVIA ASHTON-WARNER
Teacher

A child's development of print awareness involves objectives that are more traditional to instructional programs than most of those presented so far in this book. Objectives concerning the development of concepts about print assume the child:

1. knows that print is read from left to right;
2. knows that oral language can be written down and then read;
3. knows what a letter is and can point one out on a printed page;
4. knows what a word is and can point one out on a printed page;
5. is aware of environmental print and can read at least some signs and logos;
6. recognizes some words by sight in the context of other print;
7. can identify letters by name;
8. associates at least some letters with their corresponding sounds;
9. asks questions about names of letters, sounds, and words;
10. attempts reading by attending to pictures;
11. attempts reading by attending to the print;
12. begins to use story context, syntax, and semantics to identify words.

Some of these capabilities involve the familiar reading readiness skills that have dominated so many early literacy programs. Some early childhood educators are concerned about such a taxonomy since it may overemphasize practice with isolated skills to early literacy instruction. Nevertheless, children do need to learn letters and sound symbol associations, and there is research to substantiate the importance of that learning in developing the ability to read. The question is how do we introduce these concepts to children? How much time should be spent dealing with them in the total program? What other experiences should youngsters be provided in a *complete* emergent literacy program?

Instructional activities designed to help youngsters learn about the function, form, structure, and conventions of print should, again, involve socially interactive and emulative behavior; provide experiences that are meaningful and connected with real life; and incorporate what children already know. If children see a need or usefulness attached to a reading skill, that skill will probably be learned without difficulty.

ENVIRONMENTAL PRINT

Several researchers have found that children as young as two can read familiar environmental print (Goodman, 1980; Harste, Woodward, & Burke, 1984; Hiebert, 1978). Others, however, have shown that a child is often reading the sign rather than its print; when the print is separated from its familiar environmental context, the young child sometimes can no longer identify it (Dewitz & Stammer, 1980; Mason, 1980). Even so, when very young children associate the McDonald's logo with the word *McDonald's* and try to read it, they are learning that a group of letters make up a word that can be read and thus provide information. Reading environmental print also carries with it a sense of accomplishment and usually elicits positive reinforcement of the child's achievement by caring adults.

As noted earlier, parents can make children aware of environmental print from the first year of life. During daily routines, parents need to point out and read words and labels on food boxes, road signs, stores, and restaurants. The world is filled with environmental print.

School, however, is not. With the exception of *Exit, Boys, Girls,* and special names such as *Library* and *Office,* few familiar words appear in the typical school building. Thus, environmental print needs to be brought into school from outside, and classroom teachers need to label items within the walls of their own day-care centers, nursery schools, kindergartens, and first grades. Such print, once familiar, becomes part of a child's sight vocabulary.

The environmental print that children tend to know best appears on food containers, especially those for cereal, soup, milk, and cookies, and on detergent boxes and bottles. Among common signs, they recognize fast-food logos, road signs, traffic signals, names of popular store chains, supermarkets, and service stations. Collect such logos and trade names and make them available in your classroom. Most firms distribute various printed materials free, complete with logos. Photograph examples of environmental print yourself to bring to your classroom. Suggest that children read such words and copy them, if they wish.

Fill your room with its own environmental print. Start at the beginning of a school year with only a few signs, such as children's names on their cubbies, and the word *block center* to identify that area of the room. Make labels with five-by-eight index cards and dark felt-tip markers. Begin each word with a capital letter and continue with lowercase manuscript, thus providing youngsters with configuration clues. Hang labels at heights easy for children to see. Point out the labels to the children, and suggest that they read them to friends and, if they wish, copy them. As the school year progresses and things you are learning about are added to the classroom, label these items as well. Refer to the labels as part of your normal routine so that they are used and will then add to the child's sight vocabulary. Label

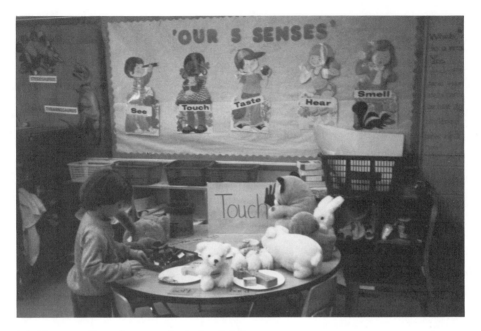

Label the room with words representing topics of study.

items because they are of interest to the class and serve a function such as identifying important classroom materials and learning centers. use labels for relating messages such as **Wash Your Hands Before Snack.** Refer to the labels often so the children identify them as useful and functional.

Label items related to content area topics. If you are studying dinosaurs—a very popular topic in early childhood years—display toy dinosaurs and label each with its name. Even long, difficult words such as *brontosaurus* and *tyrannosaurus* immediately become sight words for many preschoolers and kindergarteners. It is not at all uncommon to observe preschool, kindergarten and first grade children reading labels to themselves or to each other. I observed a preschool room shortly after the teacher had put up two new labels in the science center, which featured a lesson on the sense of touch and focused on items that were hard and soft. I watched Josh take Jennifer by the hand and heard him say, "See, Jen. See this. This bunny is soft. This word says 'soft.' " Josh continued, "See this, Jen. This is a rock and this word says 'hard.' Touch it. It is hard." The two children stroked the bunny, pointed to the label, and said in unison, "soft"; they then touched the rock, pointed to the label, and said, "hard." They repeated the sequence several times.

Another way to make print part of the classroom environment is to communicate through print, even with children as young as two. Every day have messages and assignments for children. Select a permanent spot on the chalkboard. Use rebus or picture writing along with print to help children make sense of the message. For example:

Happy Birthday, Tyrone!

Happy Valentine's Day!

Read a book to a friend.

We are going on a trip to the town library today.

This routine will have children automatically looking at the chalkboard each day for a special message. They will learn that print carries meaning that is interesting and useful. Some teachers refer to this practice as the *Morning Message* and have formalized it into a lesson when the school day commences (Stewart, Benjamin, & Mason, 1987). Continue to communicate in print throughout the day whenever the opportunity occurs. Write at least some of the message with the children watching, so that you provide a writing model for them. Use the message to develop various concepts about print. Emphasize specific words or letters, pursue questions about meaning, or let children add sentences to the original message.

Computers are a newer part of our print environment. They are now present in many of our homes and schools. Computer literacy is almost a must, and early childhood is the time to expose children to computers. Early exposure makes the computer a part of the child's life rather than a threat. Many adults are intimidated by computers, especially since their

In our technological world computers must become a part of literacy development, just as books, pencils, and paper are. Computers should be a part of early childhood equipment and provide a source for literacy development.

introduction came after they were set in their ways. Many avoid using them or approach them with trepidation, but today's children must be made as comfortable with computers as their parents and grandparents have been with typewriters. Children as young as a year can sit on an adult's lap and use a keyboard. The computer places letters of the alphabet before the child and instant left-to-right progression on the screen as keys are pressed.

Many computer programs teach children literacy skills, some better than others. It is important to be selective when choosing software, since some of it is no more creative than the skills-oriented workbooks that have been criticized for years. Other programs, however, encourage active, creative participation rather than simply questions and answers. Selected computer software for children is listed in Appendix E.

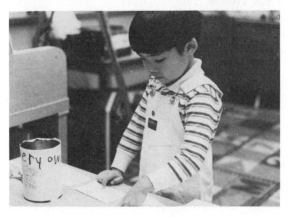

Very Own Words provide a source for a personal sight vocabulary. Teachers provide new Very Own Words and encourage children to copy, write stories with, and read them.

VERY OWN WORDS FOR DEVELOPING SIGHT VOCABULARY

In *Teacher* (1963), Sylvia Ashton-Warner described Very Own Words as a method for developing sight vocabulary. She encouraged children to write their favorite words from a story or content area lesson on three-by-five cards, each word on a separate card. Very Own Words are often from a child's home life—*Mommy, Daddy, Grandpa, Grandma, birthday*—they also reflect emotional feelings—*naughty, nice, good, no, punish*. After Very Own Words are recorded on index cards, they are stored in a child's file box, in a coffee can, or on a loose-leaf ring hung on a bulletin board. Teachers have devised many other methods for storing Very Own Words.

Helping children start their collections of Very Own Words is an exciting experience in school. Before an activity or exercise, let them know that at its completion you will ask them to name their favorite words from the activity. The activity should be a pleasant one that produces interesting language, perhaps popping corn or making play dough. It can also be a favorite word in a story book. Soon children will request their Very Own Words without being asked.

Encourage children to do things with their words—to read them to friends or to themselves, copy them, dictate them to the teacher, and use them in sentences or stories. Because they are based on a child's expressed interests in situations at home and in school, the collection of Very Own Words is a powerful technique for developing sight vocabulary.

THE LANGUAGE EXPERIENCE APPROACH

The Language Experience Approach (LEA) has been used for many years in beginning reading instruction. Already tried and true for many teachers, it encompasses in its techniques and suggestions the newer theories of emergent literacy. It can help children associate oral language with written language, teaching them specifically that what is said can be written down and read. It illustrates the left-to-right progression of our written language. In practice, it demonstrates the formation of letters plus their combination into words, it helps build sight vocabulary, it is a source of meaningful teaching of letter sounds, and it is based on the child's interest and experiences.

Many educators have been associated with developing and articulating the Language Experience Approach, among them R. V. Allen (1976), M. A. Hall (1976), and J. Veatch et al. (1973). The LEA is based on the following premises, all from the learner's point of view:

What I think is important.
What I think, I can say.
What I say can be written down by me or by others.
What is written down can be read by me and by others.

The interests and experiences on which the LEA builds come from children's lives both at home and at school. Home experiences, of course, tend to be spontaneous. In school, the teacher needs to plan experiences—for example, class trips, cooking projects, use of puppets, guest speakers, class pets, plants, holiday events, or the study of topics that are exciting to young children, such as dinosaurs, outer space, and other cultures. The language experience lesson is usually carried out with an entire class, but it can also take place with a small group or an individual child.

An LEA lesson begins with oral language. A discussion is usually generated from an interesting or exciting class experience—a recent trip to the zoo, for instance, Halloween costumes, or the pet gerbil's new litter. To begin the discussion, ask open-ended questions that will encourage descriptive responses rather than yes/no answers. For example, if the topic is a trip to the zoo, ask children to name their favorite animal. Why was it their favorite animal? What did the animal look like? What did the animal do while the child was watching it at the zoo? It is important to accept all of the children's responses. Accept nonstandard English without correction, but provide a language model by using standard English to paraphrase what the child has said.

After a discussion has generated several ideas, write them down. With a large group of children, write the ideas on a large sheet of paper (approximately twenty-four by thirty-six inches), which becomes an experience chart. It can be taped to the wall or mounted on an easel. Print with a dark felt-tip marker of medium thickness, allowing ample spacing between words and between lines so that the chart is very readable. Use manuscript in upper- and lowercase letters, following the conventions of regular print and thus giving configuration to words that the use of uppercase alone cannot give. Word configuration aids children in word identification.

In recording language on experience charts, teachers should write quickly and legibly, providing good manuscript samples for children to read and copy. Not only is rewriting a chart time-consuming, but a rewritten chart is typically more difficult for children to read because they have not witnessed the writing of the chart firsthand. As you write what children dictate, use their language unless it is difficult for others to understand. When dictation is difficult to understand, ask a child to restate an idea or, if necessary, help the child restate it. It is important to include the comments of as many children as possible. When creating a new chart, try to remember which children have not contributed in the past, and encourage them to contribute to the new chart. It is a good idea to identify who said what. The chart is more interesting to youngsters whose names are included. For example: "John said, "I liked the gorilla at the zoo. He jumped around and made funny faces." Jordanna said, "I liked the baby deer. They had big, bright, black eyes, wet black noses, and shiny brown fur." Try to accompany each sentence with an illustration; this will help children be able to read the charts.

•   Experience charts should not be very long. Charts dictated by two- and three-year-olds can simply be lists of words, such as names of animals with illustrations next to them. Used occasionally, lists of words make appropriate charts for older children as well. They are a quick way to record and reinforce vocabulary associated with topics being studied. Small-group and individual dictations of experiences can be made into books by the teacher or the child. While writing a chart, take the opportunity to point out concepts about print: "Now I am writing the word 'gorilla'— g-o-r-i-l-l-a. See, it begins here with a 'g' and ends here with an 'a.' " Mentally note which letters or sounds interest children. Ask children to point out on the chart where you should begin to write. Like the Directed Listening (or reading)–Thinking Activity and the Morning Message, the LEA lesson can have a specific skill objective.

The last step in the LEA lesson is to read the chart back to the class. Use a pointer to emphasize left-to-right progression. Let the class read the chart in unison, or ask individual children who contributed different sentences to read them. Leave the chart in a visible spot in the room and encourage the children to read it and copy parts of it, copy words they like, or add to their Very Own Word collection from the chart. Vocabulary charts and experience charts representing the different topics discussed in school can be left hanging in the room as long as space permits, then made into big books for children to look at throughout the school year. If a laminating machine is available, it is wise to preserve charts. They can also be covered with clear contact paper to withstand handling by the children. Children's dictated stories can also be placed in the class library for others to read, as can books made by the entire class. Those made by the class often become the most popular books in the room. Class books can be made by having each child draw and write directly onto a duplicating master. This method allows easy production of multiple copies, one for each child.

Although the Language Experience Approach has been used for many years, it has often been seen only as a program supplement. Skill drills and standard workbooks on letters and sounds have too often been given instructional priority. Yet, the LEA incorporates all the constructs found to be sound principles in nurturing emergent literacy. LEA materials are inexpensive and easy to use. They include chart paper, markers, colored construction paper, white paper, index cards, scissors, staplers,

The Language Experience Approach provides experiences that interest children, who in turn can write about, develop vocabulary from, and read about them. Experience charts, dictated by the children and written by the teacher, develop language and encourage reading and writing.

pencils, and crayons. With directions from the teacher, these simple classroom materials record the precious words and pictures created by children from their own meaningful, real-life experiences. The LEA (Language Experience Approach) should be central, not supplemental, to literacy instruction in early reading programs.

USING CONTEXT AND PICTURES TO DEVELOP READING

Experiences with literature can lead children to use contextual print and illustrations to recognize that words have meaning and to help them decode words written on the printed page. Again, those experiences can take place in whole-class, small-group, or one-to-one settings and through such techniques as directed listening–thinking activities, shared book experiences, and repeated readings of stories. For example, select a story that is predictable, in which the text and illustrations are very closely related. Ask children to look at the pictures on a page before reading it to them. Ask them what they think the words will say. Then read the page to demonstrate that print and illustration are closely related and that the pictures provide information that can help the children as they read the story.

The syntax and semantics of a sentence (its grammatical structure and meaning) also help children to identify words. Encourage children to use these elements of written language by stopping your oral reading at predictable points in a story and asking them to fill in words. For example, when reading *The Little Engine That Could* (Piper, 1954), first read the repetitive phrase "I think I can" through, the second time say, "I think I ———," the next time "I think ———," and last "I ———." This technique is most effective with a Big Book because you can point to the words as the children say them. As the children begin to understand the concept of filling in words, choose more difficult passages for your pauses. Children unconsciously use their prior knowledge of syntax and context in predicting words. They assimilate and use the strategy when they begin to read themselves.

IDENTIFYING LETTERS OF THE ALPHABET

Many children who cannot yet identify individual letters of the alphabet are able to read. As we have seen, they read sight words from environmental print, from classroom labels, and from Very Own Words lists. They learn other sight words from repeated readings and shared book experiences. It is obviously not necessary to be able to identify and name the letters of the alphabet in order to develop an initial sight-reading vocabulary. It is actually more desirable and easier for a young child *initially* to learn whole words already familiar through oral language, rather than learn abstract letters. Familiar words carry meaning for them whereas isolated letters do not.

Children do, however, need to learn the alphabet to eventually become independently fluent readers and writers. There is no evidence that alphabet identification ought to be treated as the first skill in early literacy; it makes more sense for children to learn to identify letters after they have learned a number of sight words. Traditionally, learning the alphabet has often been the first thing parents try to teach their children at home, and it is usually high on any list of reading readiness skills in preschool and kindergarten curricula. Because it is hard to depart from deeply rooted tradition, learning the alphabet will probably always be prominent in emergent literacy programs. The main concern is that it not be overemphasized in experiences provided for learning, in our expectations for the children's performance, and in terms of the time given to it.

Allow children to explore letters by using manipulative materials available in the literacy center. Be sure to have on hand alphabet puzzles, magnetic upper- and lowercase letters with an accompanying magnetic board, a set of wooden upper- and lowercase letters, tactile letters made of sandpaper, alphabet games, felt letters and an accompanying felt-board, letter stencils, alphabet flash cards, and a long alphabet chart posted along the wall of the classroom at the eye level of the children. In addition to these materials, a large supply of alphabet books and taped songs about the alphabet should be in the classroom library. Encourage children to explore these materials, first through play. Later, they will begin to identify the letters they are playing with, and teach letters they know to other children. Provide chalk and a chalkboard so they can make letters themselves. Children also enjoy finger-painting letters, painting them on easels, shaping them out of clay, and eating them in alphabet soup or as cookies or pretzels.

Systematic teaching of the alphabet, one letter per week, is not as successful as teaching children letters that are meaningful to them. Many teachers lead children to identify the letters in their own names first. When they have learned to identify several different letters, ask them to look for the same letters in other contexts, such as magazines, newspapers, and books. Check children individually by using flash cards to determine just which letters they know and which they do not know. Ask children which letters they would like to learn next from their Very Own Words or other sources that allow them to decide for themselves. Give children flash cards of the letters they choose to learn and encourage them to use those letters in all of the activities just mentioned.

A prepared environment rich with alphabet materials to be explored and experienced will help children learn the letters of the alphabet. (Alphabet books are listed in Appendix A.)

ASSOCIATING LETTERS AND SOUNDS

We do have research that supports the importance of learning sound-symbol relationships, and there is no research that suggests we should ignore it in the development of emergent literacy. The newer research *does* suggest, however, that traditional early reading instruction ignores many important strategies and practices while abstracting discrete skills from the total act of reading. It suggests that the teaching of letter–sound association has dominated early childhood programs to the point of excluding other practices. As with teaching the alphabet, caution is proposed in the instructional strategies, time allocation, and performance expectations we bring to sound–symbol relationships in the early child-hood classroom. Children who have already had substantial experience with books, who are firmly familiar with the structures and uses of lan-guage, and who have already acquired large sight vocabularies are per-haps ready to deal with sound–symbol relationships in preschool and kindergarten; children without those backgrounds are not. Like the let-ters of the alphabet, sound–symbol relationships are abstract and lack intrinsic meaning for children. Only a child who has already assimilated certain concepts about books and print and who has acquired a sight vocabulary begins to show an interest in trying to decode unknown words independently, and is thus ready to learn initial consonant sounds. Usually children ask about letters and sounds themselves when they see a need for these skills. Studies have demonstrated that children who are taught phonics as part of initial reading instruction do achieve better in the early grades than children who have not (Chall, Conrad, & Harris-Sharples, 1983; Williams, 1985). It must be remembered, however, that the goal of phonics is not to teach a set of rules, but to get across the alphabetic principle that there are systematic relationships between let-ters and sounds.

If you do introduce kindergarten children to sound–symbol relation-ships, deal only with initial consonants, then initial digraphs, and then vowels. Although there does not seem to be a particularly appropriate sequence for teaching specific sounds, it does seem as if the letters used more often should be more familiar to children and therefore easier for them to learn—letters such as initial *s, t, p,* and *m*. After initial consonants, introduce the more familiar beginning digraphs, such as *sh, ch, th,* and *ph*. Then introduce vowels. Teach sounds in meaningful contexts rather than by isolating sounds from words. Using meaningful context tends to avoid the pedagogical distortion of sounds. Rather than asking a child, "Can you think of words that begin with the 'buh' sound?" ask the child to think of words that begin with the letter *b,* such as *baby*. Feature different letters and provide many experiences with the sound–symbol relationship of each letter.

Children need continual practice in order to learn sound–symbol relationships; rarely is a single lesson sufficient. Therefore, provide several experiences with each letter and review frequently, even after proceeding to new letter sounds. Incorporate experiences with sound–symbol associ-ation in all content areas whenever possible, and in situations that are meaningful to the child.

How might children be helped to recognize the sound–symbol rela-tionships of consonants—the letter *p* as an initial consonant, for example?

1. Make pop corn and eat it.
2. Read stories that use the letter *p* prominently, such as *Peter Pan* (Carey, 1972).
3. Collect objects that begin with the letter *p*, such as pins, pots, plates, pencils, pens, and paper, and place them in a box labeled *p*.
4. Read a poem that features the letter *p*, such as "Peter, Peter, Pumpkin Eater" (Dean, 1977).
5. List all the words the children can think of that begin with *p*.
6. Make a book of *p* words drawn by children or cut from magazines.
7. Read the children a story that includes blanks where *p* words can be filled in orally.
8. Ask children to search their collections of Very Own Words for words that begin with *p*.
9. Provide sensory experiences that reinforce the sound of the letter *p*—for example, a stuffed animal *p*uppy to touch, a framed *p*icture to look at, a *p*iano to listen to, *p*erfume to smell, and a *p*each to taste.
10. Make a collage of items whose names begin with *p*—pink paper, popcorn, pipe cleaners, and pine needles.
11. Sing the song "Peter Cottontail."

These and similar activities can be carried out for any initial consonant. Whenever a letter being taught appears in a language experience

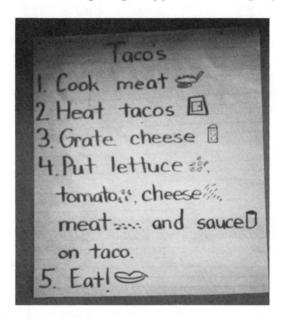

Manipulative learning materials should be available for children to explore as they learn sound–symbol relationships. To make the learning of sound–symbol relationships more meaningful, incorporate it into all content areas. For example if teaching the sound of *t*, cook tacos, read *Teeny Tiny Woman*, (Seuling, 1976) and so forth.

chart or a piece of children's literature, take the opportunity to point it out to the children. Alphabet books generally use sound–symbol relationships as they introduce each letter as can picture story books that use a particular letter prominently. (See Appendix A-18 for children's literature for building sound–symbol relationships.) For additional practice and individual exploration, include in the literacy center among the language arts manipulatives any materials that help children associate sounds and their symbols—materials in Lotto or Bingo formats, puzzles that require children to match pictures with initial consonants, felt pictures and letters, and boxes of objects representing initial consonant sounds.

When we read, we use several skills concurrently to decode and derive meaning from the printed page. We therefore need to encourage children to use multiple rather than isolated skills in their approach to reading. Children should be taught to use context clues and phonic clues simultaneously. One strategy that accomplishes this goal has already been suggested—reading a sentence in which you pause and leave a "blank" to be filled in by the child. For example, say, "The b——— flew up to the tree and landed on a branch." Supplying the initial consonant for the word, either by sound or by sight, draws on a child's skills with phonics, context, syntax, and semantics.

It must be emphasized that many preschool, kindergarten, and first grade children are not likely to associate the identification of sound–symbol relationships with reading. Many of them do seem to be able to name words beginning with specific consonants, but they will probably not relate that ability to reading until they approach the end of first grade. Very little time should be spent on such skills before then, and more time spent with the many other strategies suggested already. Although many more phonic rules have been identified, such as those involving final consonants, long and short vowels, and blends, early childhood classrooms should deal only with the sound–symbol relationships of initial consonants and digraphs and perhaps rudimentarily with the most obvious vowel sounds.

As suggested, a section of the classroom literacy center should be set aside for general language arts manipulatives. This section will include the multipurpose materials preschools, kindergartens, and first grades characteristically use to develop eye–hand coordination and sharpen visual and auditory discrimination and memory. Such manipulatives include puzzles; pegboards; sewing cards; beads and string; materials that lace, button, or snap; construction toys such as Legos and Tinker Toys; picture collections for holidays and unit topics; materials for sorting and identification; games such as Concentration, Bingo, Lotto, and Candyland; and card games that involve such skills as use of the alphabet, rhyme, and letter–sound association.

Many of the materials for developing the skills just mentioned can be purchased from school supply companies. Teacher-made items increase the inventory and often suit children's needs better than purchased materials. They also add warmth and help personalize the classroom. Older children, parents, aides, and teachers can all contribute to the classroom inventory by making materials. (School supply companies that offer materials and resource books for making materials are listed in Appendix F.)

USING PUBLISHED MATERIALS

As recently as the mid 1960s commercially prepared instructional materials for the development of early literacy were rare. Nursery schools and kindergartens, still very much directed by the doctrines of Pestalozzi and Froebel, used manipulative materials and real-life settings for the child's development. But the burgeoning concept of reading readiness brought with it commercial materials for developing those skills believed to be prerequisite to learning to read. Generally, the reading readiness materials were developed by the same publishers that had produced basal readers for primary grades. What they offered did not look very much like what had been used with children in preschool and kindergarten in the past. Rather, the materials were similar to those used by first, second, and third graders. They consisted mostly of workbooks accompanied by teacher's manuals.

Such materials are quite common and will probably continue to be, since they provide a complete package of materials for instruction and are revised to include new findings in early literacy development. Some general rules need to be applied to the selection and use of materials:

- Be sure to study the objectives for the published program and determine if they include those that incorporate the latest findings on strategies for nurturing emergent literacy.
- Be sure that the materials suit the needs of the children you teach. Urban and rural children may need materials different from those needed by children raised in suburban settings.
- Examine the materials for clarity, appeal to children, and durability.
- Analyze the teacher's manual for clarity of objectives, descriptions of plans, suitability of lesson content, and flexibility given to teachers in using the material.
- You, the teacher, should determine how the materials are to be used; materials should not dictate their use to you.
- Select sequences that seem most appropriate. You need not start at the beginning of a book and follow it page by page to the end.

- Eliminate units that you feel are inappropriate for your children. On the other hand, material can be repeated if it is particularly good or if children have not grasped its content.

Remember at all times that you are the teacher and that you need to make critical decisions about your instructional program. Published materials are tools to be used by you. Often they are best used for reinforcing concepts. Published materials can also provide independent work for students when you need to work with individuals or small groups.

It is extremely important to realize that published materials are only one part of a program of emergent literacy development. What has been described thus far in this book is all but devoid of such programs except for children's literature, which is different from basal reading and reading readiness materials. Many school districts require the use of published readiness and basal materials and many teachers depend on them as organizational tools. When they are used, select them carefully for quality of content; use them as you see fit, and remember that they do not provide a complete literacy program. As the teacher you must be a decision maker about the design of your literacy program, the materials you use, and how you use them.

ASSESSING CHILDREN'S CONCEPTS ABOUT PRINT

Children's knowledge about print and the skills they have mastered in recognizing and using it can be evaluated best through running records of their behavior in frequent individual observation, collection of work samples, and personal interviews. Frequent checking and rechecking are required because young children are constantly learning and occasionally they also forget. Standardized tests also measure some of the print concepts covered in this chapter. Because they are used to assess "readiness for reading" in most kindergartens and some preschools in the United States, those tests raise issues that need to be addressed.

There are a number of problems associated with standardized tests. First, we must recognize that they represent only one form of assessment; their use must be coordinated with that of other assessment measures. Second, some standardized tests for early literacy test only reading readiness skills. These tests evaluate children on skills different from those identified in this book as characteristic of emergent literacy. For the most part, they deal with skills abstracted from the reading process and then designated as precursors of reading. Those skills include such things as auditory memory, rhyme, letter recognition, visual matching, school language, and listening. By contrast, practices that nurture emergent literacy emphasize children's prior knowledge, book concepts, attitudes about reading, association of meaning with print, and characteristics of printed materials. One child might pass all portions of a standardized reading readiness test yet not be able to begin to read, whereas a second child might not pass any portion of the test but already be reading.

Reading readiness training was a major emphasis in my first year of teaching. Imagine my surprise, then, when I saw some of my kindergarteners reading during free-choice time. I had no idea that any of them could read. The results of their reading readiness tests certainly gave no indication of this. I was so busy getting them ready to read that I never stopped to ask them if they could read or if they would read to me.

Some standardized tests may not match the instructional practices suggested by the latest research and theory on emerging literacy. This leads to a third problem. Unfortunately, because school districts are often evaluated on how well children perform on the standardized tests, teachers may feel pressured to teach for the test. Teachers who succumb to this temptation are likely to be using inappropriate strategies for teaching young children. In addition, such teachers spent an enormous amount of kindergarten time preparing children for standardized tests by drilling them on sample tests similar to the real tests. The sample tests are graded, and instruction geared to remedy student weaknesses indicated by the test. If teachers do not prepare children for the test with practice sessions, and do not teach to the test, their children may not score well. Thus, teachers may feel they are putting their own jobs on the line if they refuse to teach to standardized tests. It is a frightening dilemma.

A fourth problem with standardized tests is that the results of such tests given in kindergarten are commonly used in placing children in first-grade classrooms and reading groups. Once placed, a child is seldom shifted to a different group. Yet, the standardized tests on which placement decisions are based can yield information that is inaccurate. Note the following graph, which illustrates the subscores and overall percentile ranks of three kindergarten children on a typical standardized reading readiness test. (See p. 139.)

Child A scored well in auditory and visual discrimination skills, and poorly in language skills. The child's overall score is at the fiftieth percentile. Child B has good auditory skills, poor visual skills, and good language skills and also scored overall at the fiftieth percentile. Child C scored fairly consistently across visual, auditory, and language skills and likewise scored overall at the fiftieth percentile. All three children will go to the first grade and could be placed in the same reading group, even though child A, for example, has a possible language deficit and is missing one of the most important ingredients for reading success—a strong language base. These three children are quite different in ability yet have scored at the same overall percentile on a standardized test. It is very unlikely that the three

Readiness Test

Hypothesized subtest profiles on three (3) kindergarten children achieving about the same Test Performance Rating

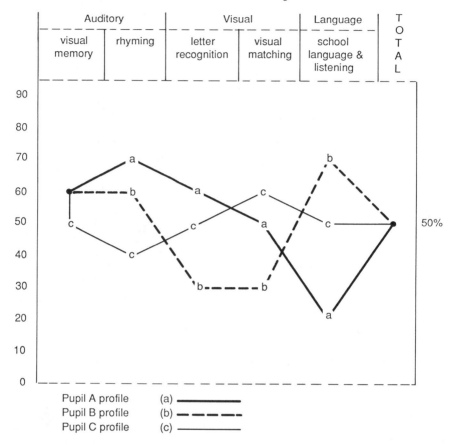

Pupil A profile   (a) ──────────
Pupil B profile   (b) ── ── ── ──
Pupil C profile   (c) ──────────

will achieve similar success in reading, although they might be expected to on the basis of their test scores.

Yet another problem with standardized tests is bias. For example, standardized test scores are less reliable with younger children than with older children. Furthermore, some standardized tests are still biased in favor of white, middle-class children despite genuine attempts to alleviate the problem. Their use tends to place rural, black, and bilingual youngsters at a disadvantage. Prior knowledge plays a large role in how well children will do on the test. Children from white, middle-class homes tend to have more of the experiences that lead to better achievement on the tests. In addition, following test directions such as "Put your finger on the star" or "Circle the goat that is behind the tree" is often a problem for the young child. Children who have never seen a goat may not circle anything, since the animal on the page might look to them like a dog.

The policy statement of the International Reading Association on *Literacy Development and Pre–First Grade* (IRA, 1985) suggests that evaluative procedures used with young children be developmentally and culturally appropriate and that the selection of evaluative measures be based on the objectives of an instructional program and consider each child's total development and its effect on reading performance. Various steps can be taken to remedy the abuse of standardized testing in early childhood education. First, administrators and teachers must understand the shortcomings of standardized tests. Second, the use of multiple assessment tools given frequently throughout the school year would tend to prevent undue emphasis on standardized test results. Third, tests that measure demonstrated characteristics of emergent literacy should be developed and used.

Finding suitable tests is a difficult task. However, some test makers are becoming aware of the discrepancies between new instructional strategies and the design of the present tests. There are tools for assessing many aspects of early literacy that acknowledge the newer theories and research findings and reflect the instructional strategies suggested in this book, specifically Marie Clay's Concept about Print Test (1979) and the Early Reading Test (Mason, Stewart, & Dunning, 1986). The Early Reading Test examines such things as children's ability to read environmental print, their attempts to read predictable books, and their awareness of how they are learning to read. In addition to any standardized test informal assessment measures such as interviews, anecdotal records, collection of work samples, and others described throughout the book should be used frequently.

ACTIVITIES

1. Select five kindergarten children whose scores on standardized reading readiness tests are available. Observe each child for oral language ability and knowledge of concepts about print, books, and meaning. Compare what you observe of the child's literacy ability with his or her test results.

2. Observe the environmental print in a nursery or kindergarten classroom. Note what you think could be added to it, both from within the classroom and from the outside world.

3. Write an experience chart dictated to you by preschool, kindergarten, or first grade children. Critique the appearance of your chart and note problems you encountered while writing it. Use them as suggestions for improvement.

4. Select five children at random from a kindergarten or first grade room in which children have collected Very Own Words. List all of the words in the children's collections. Compare the list with the words found in a preprimer from a basal series. How closely do the preprimer's words and the children's Very Own Words match each other?

5. Select three initial consonants other than *p*. Design classroom experiences that will illustrate and reinforce the sound–symbol relationships of each.

8

Writing as a Vehicle for Developing Literacy

Robert P. Parker
with Lesley Mandel Morrow

CHAPTER OVERVIEW

- Writing is related to both oral language and reading development.
- Theories of early writing development and of how writing is acquired are important to knowledge concerning early literacy.
- Well-planned teaching strategies assist children in their writing development.

Children want to write. They want to write the first day they attend ⌐
school. This is no accident. Before they went to school they marked up
walls, pavements, newspapers with crayons, chalk, pens or pencils . . .
anything that makes a mark. The child's marks say, "I am."

DONALD GRAVES,
WRITING: TEACHERS AND CHILDREN AT WORK

Children love to play. Through play they develop socially and intellectually in fundamental ways. Especially in literate societies, children's play
can take the form of making marks on paper. Children enjoy the act of
making the marks, the social relationships they develop in the process, the
sense of accomplishment mark making brings, and the products of the
action. By writing messages, children achieve a sense of identity in their
own eyes and in the eyes of others. The movement from playing with
drawing and writing to communicating through written messages is a con-
tinuum that reflects the basic theories of emergent literacy (Dyson, 1985;
Halliday, 1975; Parker, 1983; Sulzby, 1986a).

RELATIONSHIPS BETWEEN READING AND WRITING

Some scholars view writing and reading as identical; others consider them
unrelated. As Birnbaum and Emig (1983, p.87) assert, "Both ultimate
positions can be swiftly dismissed." In either process, they point out, readers and writers transform their experiences through verbal symbols. Writers reconstruct meanings by constructing texts; readers reconstruct texts by
constructing anticipated meanings.

The parallels between writing and reading are more obvious for young
children than for older children and adults. For example, children teach
themselves to write in much the same way that they teach themselves to read:
experimentally. Through personally motivated and personally directed trial
and error—a necessary condition of their literacy development—they try
out various aspects of the writing process. They invent and decorate letters,
symbols, and words; they mix drawing and writing; they invent messages in
various forms and shapes; and they often continue to use invented forms of
writing after they have begun to master conventional ones (see Figure 8–1).

More specifically, by experimenting with writing, children construct
and refine the kind of knowledge about written language that makes reading possible. In Marie Clay's words:

> The child who engages in creative writing is manipulating the units of written
> language—letters, words, sentence types—and is likely to be gaining some
> awareness of how these can be combined to convey unspoken messages. The

142

child is having to perform within the directional constraints that we use in written English. The child is probably learning to generate sentences in a deliberate way, word by word. He makes up sentences which fit both his range of ideas and his written language skills. Fluent oral language may permit the young reader to depend almost entirely on meaning and the eye may overlook the need for discriminating details of letters and words. Creative writing demands that the child pay attention to the details of print. To put his message down in print, he is forced to construct words, letter by letter, so he becomes aware of letter features and letter sequences, particularly for the vocabulary which he uses in writing again and again. (1979, p. 2)

In other words, as children write they integrate knowledge of reading with knowledge of writing. They need relatively little direct instruction to do so—just active models, supportive talk about writing and reading, and praise for their efforts.

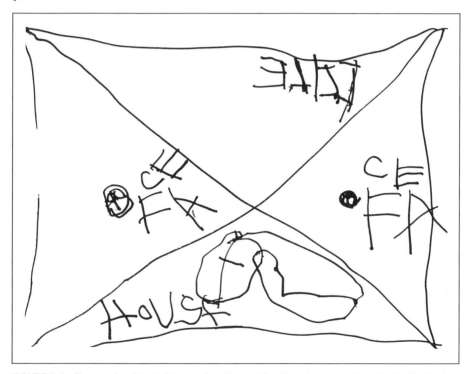

FIGURE 8–1 The sample written by Max, age five. He uses his writing almost as a decoration for the drawing.

HOW EARLY WRITING IS ACQUIRED

Children's early literacy experiences are embedded in the familiar situations and real-life experiences of family and community membership (Gundlach et al., 1985). In fact, ethnographers have discovered that because these literacy events are so natural, most parents simply do not know about many of their own children's writing and reading experiences until researchers point them out (Taylor, 1983). Many things that family members do, including the ways they relate to each other, involve literacy. They write each other notes, lists, holiday greetings, complaints, and directions. As Anderson and Stokes (1984) discovered in a study of working-class white, black, and Latino families, early literacy experiences and learning are not confined to middle- and upper-class families, even though such experiences may differ greatly from one another. "Literacy," they concluded, "is influenced largely by social institutions and not cultural membership" (p. 35).

As a process, early writing development is characterized by children's moving from playfully making marks on paper, through communicating message on paper, to making texts as artifacts. Like Giti (Baghban, 1984), children are at first unconcerned about the products of their "writing"; they lose interest in them almost immediately. However, once Giti began to understand that the marks she made on paper "could be meaningful and [that] she enjoyed producing them, she was determined to learn how to write" (pp. 89–90). The description parallels Yetta Goodman's (1986) conclusions on children's earliest learning about writing and reading.

Children learn the uses of written language before they learn the forms (Gundlach et al., 1985; Rosen & Rosen, 1973; Taylor, 1983). In observing children scribbling and inventing primitive "texts," researchers have observed that children seem to know what writing is *for* before they know much about how to write in correct forms. The letters to friends or relatives, the greeting cards, and the signs they produce hardly resemble conventional forms. Yet, the children seem impelled by an understanding of the function of written texts. Teale (1986) draws a similar conclusion: "The functions of literacy are as much a part of learning to read and write as are the formal aspects of written language" (p. 9). (See Figure 8–2.)

Children's writing develops through constant invention and reinvention of the forms of written language (Dyson, 1986; Parker, 1983). Children invent ways of making letters, words, and texts, moving from primitive forms through successively closer approximations of conventional forms. As they reconstruct their abilities to produce messages and texts, they simultaneously reconstruct their knowledge about written language (Bissex, 1980; Read, 1975). Parents of preschool children who show great interest in writing typically accept and support their youngsters' production of the primitive forms, offering little or no criticism or correction. Just as children's early forms of oral language are sometimes called *proto-language*, their invented writing might be called *proto-writing*. No one teaches them the forms; they invent them from their observations of environmental print and their observing, modeling, and interacting with more literate individuals who write in their presence.

Children's involvement in written language, though typically embedded in social situations and interactions, is essentially self-initiated and self-directed. Most of the time, young children choose when to write, what to write, and how

FIGURE 8–2 Jay's early attempts at functional writing. When Jay, age five, was asked to write a letter, he chose to write to his friend Peter.

to do it. Parents, other adults, or siblings may encourage them to write, and certain situations (such as playing restaurant or waitress) may demand it, but most young children seldom write as the result of a direct order or as part of anything resembling an assignment. Tracing, copying, drilling—all such activities do not work well when given as external assignments. However, if a child voluntarily chooses to participate in such tasks, they can contribute to their writing development. Researchers such as Harste, Woodward, & Burke (1984) and Newman (1984) emphasize the importance of intent in children's early writing and learning. Children learn to expect written language to be meaningful, and they relate best to those situations in which writing occurs in that manner.

In writing, as in talking, story making is a primary impulse and activity. As humans, we share a deep and fundamental need to turn our experiences into stories (Hardy, 1968). Story making is a fundamental means by which we learn and by which we shape our intellectual development. Making and telling stories plays a central role in the development of literacy and the growth of children's minds. Children often surprise us with the things they can do with written language and with what they know about it (Britton, 1982b). They seem to grasp important aspects of its functions and forms, using this imaginative awareness to produce primitive but extraordinary manifestations of language because they want to.

Children learn about writing by observing more skilled others and by participating with them in literacy events. People who are more proficient writers play an important modeling role in children's writing development (Birnbaum, 1981). Children need to observe adults participating in writing and they must write having the guidance and support of the adult.

Children need to work independently on the functions and forms of writing that they have experienced through interactions with literate others. Teale (1986) calls these activities *explorations* and claims they make it possible for children's literacy to come to "complete fruition." They may involve practicing or rehearsing aspects of writing—letter formation and differentiation; similarities or differences between drawing and writing; spelling; punctuation; and so forth. They are apparently linked to children's evolving knowledge *about* language—their *metalinguistic knowledge.* When children explore their emergent knowledge and their skill in writing independently, they become more conscious of what they know and more explicit. They may even develop language to talk about it (Goodman, 1986). The more they make their knowledge about language explicit, the more children are able to use that explicit knowledge to direct and control their own attempts at writing, and thus the forms and functions of writing.

Two points are important here. First, children practice what they learn about writing, but such practice is most helpful when self-initiated. Second, self-initiated practice contributes to what children learn consciously

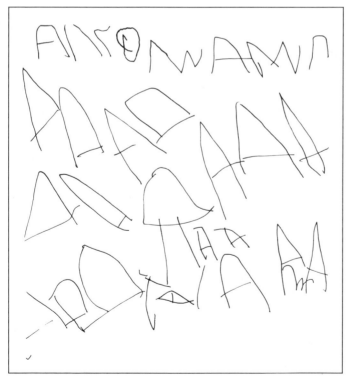

FIGURE 8–3 Jennifer, age three and a half, practices writing through the repetition of similar letter patterns from left to right across the page.

about writing, an evolving phenomenon that plays a fundamental role in the development of their writing abilities. (See Figures 8–3 and 8–4).

THEORY OF WRITING DEVELOPMENT

In the broadest sense, children's language development can be viewed as part of their process of learning to participate in sharing and making social meanings (Halliday, 1975). To achieve this participation, they learn to understand, use, and make various symbols. Though language is just one of the symbol systems used, it is the most important and pervasive one. Thus, as part of their broad process of symbol development, children learn to listen, talk, write, and read; that is, they develop language in all four of its uses. Their language learning begins in the prespeech communication that parents and infants construct, and it builds through listening to talking, to gesturing, to playing symbolically, to drawing, and from there to

FIGURE 8–4 Three-year-old Robert separates his writing from his drawing by enclosing each in a circle during self-initiated practice.

writing and reading (Vygotsky, 1978). Children's main resource for literacy learning is their knowledge of ways to symbolize experience and to communicate through those symbols in pre- and postspeech interactions.

This overall theoretical framework can be summarized as follows:

1. Literacy development is part of language development.
2. Language development is part of symbol development.
3. Symbol development is part of the development of social and cultural meanings.

For most children, the process is unitary. There are no sharp gaps or transitions from one aspect to another. Under normal circumstances, children's literacy development begins with the continual process of learning to communicate—first nonverbally, then by talking, next with symbolic play, and finally by drawing. Each new phase is rooted in earlier phases and forms a new network of communication resources and potential.

Further, this literacy learning occurs naturally in the interactions of family and community life. In the process, children move from playing

FIGURE 8–5 Scribble writing by Justin (age four) that goes from left to right across the page. An illustration accompanies the writing, and the child explained to the teacher what the writing said about the picture. The child understands that writing represents language.

with written language to using it to communicate. They invent and reinvent forms. When children first begin making marks on paper, most do so with no knowledge of the alphabetic nature of the written language's symbol system. Initially, they do not conceive of writing as a means of encoding speech (Dyson, 1985; Ferreiro, 1978; Ferreiro and Teberosky, 1982). Shortly thereafter, they view letters as referring to actual people or things, though they still believe that writing, like drawing, only encodes or reflects specific objects, not "filler" words such as articles or adjectives. Only later do they realize that writing represents language. (See Figure 8–5.)

THE DEVELOPMENT OF WRITING ABILITY

Researchers have arrived at various descriptions of what can be viewed as developmental stages of writing in early childhood (Clay, 1975; Dyson, 1985; Sulzby, 1986b; Teale, 1986; Vukelich & Golden, 1984). Most agree, though, that if there are indeed stages, they are not rigorously defined or necessarily sequential. Dyson (1986) describes children's writing development as having two broad phases. From birth to about age three, children begin to explore the form of writing by scribbling. Then, as children progress from three to six their "controlled scribbling gradually develops into recognizable objects which they name, and similarly, the scribbling gradually acquires the characteristics of print, including linearity, horizontal orientation, and the arrangement of letter-like forms . . ." (p. 118). In fact, as we have noted, children may initially attempt to encode objects directly, as in drawing, and only later attempt to encode language.

Sulzby (1985) identified six broad categories of writing in a sample of twenty-four kindergarten children, cautioning that these should not be considered a reflection of developmental ordering. They do describe, however, children's early attempts at writing. (Results from a longer study are reported in Sulzby, Barnhart, and Hieshima, forthcoming).

1. **Writing via drawing.** The child will use drawing to stand for writing. The child is working out the relationship between drawing and writing, not confusing the two. The child sees drawing/writing as communication of a specific and purposeful message. Children who participate in writing via drawing will read their drawings as if there is writing on them. (See Figure 8–6.)
2. **Writing via scribbling.** The child scribbles but intends it as writing. Often the child appears to be writing and scribbles from left to right. The child moves the pencil as an adult does, and the pencil makes writing-like sounds. The scribble resembles writing. (See Figure 8–7.)
3. **Writing via making letterlike forms.** At a quick glance, shapes in the child's writing resemble letters. However, close observation reveals that they only

FIGURE 8–6   Writing through drawing: When asked to write something, Brad (age four) drew a picture. The same request over time yielded the same response, a drawing for writing.

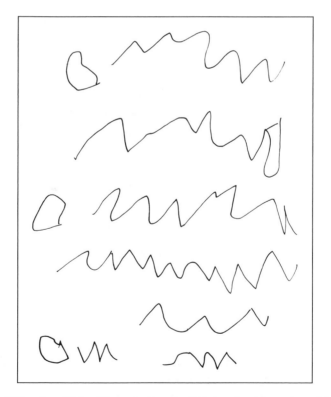

FIGURE 8–7   Writing via scribbling: When asked to write, Katie (age three) began by scribbling randomly on the page. She eventually progressed to a left-to-right scribble and then purposeful marks that began to look like letter forms.

FIGURE 8–8 Writing via making letterlike forms: Very carefully written by Olivia (age four), these letterlike forms go from left to right across the page.

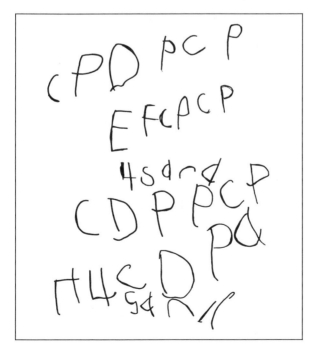

FIGURE 8–9 Writing via reproducing well-learned units: These random letters written by Brian (age four) go from left to right across the page.

look like letters. They are not just poorly formed letters, though, they are creations. (See Figure 8–8.)

4. **Writing via reproducing well-learned units.** The child uses letter sequences learned from such sources as his or her own name. The child sometimes changes the order of the letters, writing the same ones many different ways, or reproduces letters in long strings or in random order. (See Figure 8–9.)

5. **Writing via invented spelling.** Many varieties and levels of invented spelling are demonstrated by children. Basically, children create their own spelling for words when they do not know the conventional spellings. In invented spelling, one letter may represent an entire syllable and words sometimes overlap and are not properly spaced. As the child's writing matures, the words look more like conventional writing, with perhaps only one letter invented or left out. (See Figure 8–10.)

6. **Writing via conventional spelling.** The child's writing resembles adult writing.

Sulzby's general description of early writing is most helpful for parents and teachers when they are observing and describing children's writing. As we have noted, however, Sulzby emphasizes that these categories are not necessarily developmental or sequentially invariant.

FIGURE 8–10 Writing via invented spelling: "One day I went to the country. The country is nice. The end." This story was written by a kindergarten child.

STRATEGIES FOR PROMOTING WRITING DEVELOPMENT

Parents and teachers can use various strategies to encourage and respond to children's self-initiated writing efforts. They can create situations that will engage children in producing and learning about written language. These situations reflect our growing understanding that children's literacy develops within the context of family and community events that involve writing and reading, but for which literacy instruction is only infrequently an immediate goal.

Of all the new ideas, theories, and strategies concerning emergent literacy, the way in which we think about writing represents the most obvious break with tradition. We have allowed children to use crayons and paper to encourage development of motor coordination in preparation for writing, but we never thought of writing to convey meaning as being an integral part of an early literacy program for children as young as two. From now on, we will be suggesting the integration of strategies for writing into the daily routines of babies, toddlers, preschoolers, kindergarteners, and first graders. We will consider even the youngest child's marks on paper as early attempts at writing, rather than random marks. This perception is indeed a new element in programs for early literacy development.

OBJECTIVES IN PROMOTING WRITING DEVELOPMENT

The following objectives are posed from the perspective that children learn language, including writing and reading, by using it purposefully in social situations (for example, in playing or communicating), not by practicing isolated or abstracted skills. Generally, the best way to assist children in language and literacy development is to create situations for meaningful use rather than offering direct but parceled language instruction. This principle applies equally in the home, day-care center, nursery, kindergarten or first grade.

1. Children will be provided with an environment in which they are regularly exposed to many kinds of print.
2. Children will experience print as a source of pleasure and enjoyment.
3. Children will regularly observe adults writing, both for work and for leisure.
4. Children will be given opportunities and materials for writing themselves.
5. Children will be assisted in deciding what to write about, but left alone to make such decisions.
6. Children will be supported in constructing invented forms of letters, words, and messages.
7. Children's efforts at writing, however crude or primitive, will be responded to as meaningful communication.

8.   Children will be encouraged to use writing for a wide range of individual and social purposes, such as making lists, cards, letters, signs, announcements, stories, and books.
9.   Children will be read stories in a variety of styles, which may serve as eventual models for their writing.
10. The use of writing will be integrated throughout the curriculum.

STRATEGIES FOR WRITING DEVELOPMENT FROM BIRTH TO TWO

Earlier chapters have described strategies that parents can use in helping children with oral language development and early reading. Some of those strategies can be applied directly to children's early writing development; others can be adapted. Some strategies are helpful specifically with writing development. It is crucial to remember, though, that speaking, reading, and writing are dynamically linked in children's development. When we help children with oral language, we also contribute indirectly to their literacy development by increasing their language experience. Similarly, reading development contributes to speaking and writing, and writing to speaking and reading. This understanding forms the basis for the *whole-language* approaches used in some elementary schools (Newman, 1985).

In a detailed case study, Baghban (1984) describes observations of her daughter Giti's writing development from eighteen months, when Giti first began marking on paper, to twenty-four months. When Giti began scribbling, her productions sprawled all over the page. By nineteen months she had begun to make dots and her sprawl was noticeably less extreme. By twenty months she had added circles and wavy lines to her repertoire. When she wrote after watching one of her parents write, her productions "more closely resembled English script" (p. 48). At twenty-three months she averaged ten minutes per writing session, and at twenty-four months she began babbling over her own writing. She also attempted to write her first letter, *M* for *McDonald's* and for *Marcia,* her mother's first name. Throughout the period, and later as well, Giti's parents followed her literacy experiences and efforts attentively. Such attentiveness is something we urge all parents and primary care-givers to adopt.

As suggested in earlier chapters, another important way that we can support children's writing development is to become more aware of their experiences with environmental print, including print they see on television, in religious environments, on food cans and boxes, on signs, and in stores. Not only can we become more aware of the variety and frequency of children's experiences with environmental print, we can talk with them about these experiences, commenting, asking questions, and encouraging them to identify and remember signs, letters, and bits of print out of their normal contexts (for instance, *M* used somewhere other than in a

McDonald's sign). If we so interact with children, especially from their second year on, we are ready to support them when, as a part of their scribble writing, they try to write one or more of these environmentally learned letters. In fact, some children may make their first attempts to do this between eighteen and twenty-four months, though most children will not begin until twenty-four to thirty-six months.

We can also assist children in their first attempts to make marks on paper. Often, when children begin scribbling (some at eighteen months), they bang on the paper with their writing implements. Only a bit later do they begin using smoother, more deliberate, more coordinated movements to make their marks. When children are in their first, primitive stages of scribbling, we can show them how to hold markers or crayons. We can guide their hands to paper, not making marks for them but helping them understand that the paper is the place for writing.

Our responses to children's early scribbling are important. It is better not to urge children to write particular things. They should make marks spontaneously and decide for themselves when these marks are intended to represent something. It is important not to press them to tell us what their marks mean or represent. It is better to say, "I like that," than to ask, "What is it?" "Can you write some more?" is also a helpful response, but do not insist if the child says no. Expressing genuine pleasure in children's early markings, whether they resemble writing or not, and seeing them as an important step in a long developmental process are positive responses that will encourage children to continue. By continuing their "writing," they will incorporate in it what they are learning about print from the literacy events that fill their lives.

Beyond responding supportively to children, we can model writing for them by writing in their presence. As we have seen, we can let them see us writing letters, lists, and notes and filling out forms and bills, and we can interact with them about what we are doing. For example: "I'm writing a letter to Grandma and Grandpa. I'm telling them that we miss them. Do you want to tell them something? Do you want to write something on the paper to them?" When writing, invite the youngsters to sit with you, watch you, ask questions, and to try their own hand at writing. This gives children opportunities to see how we go about writing and to begin to understand that the marks we make convey meaning.

Junk mail is a form of environmental print that can arouse interest in writing. Children enjoy writing or making marks on flyers, brochures, ads, announcements, and forms. They will write over the print and in the blank spaces. Apparently, the look and arrangement of the print gives them the model and inspiration to make their own marks.

Repeating rhymes and singing songs can also contribute to children's early writing. So can using hand puppets and playing with toys and games, such as puzzles that can be taken apart and put back together. Manipulative toys that require dexterity help with the motor development needed to shape letters. Playing with clay or play dough, finger painting, using chalk-boards, and painting on easels helps build motor coordination as well. Birnbaum (1981) found that involvement in such activities was associated with learning to write and read easily and naturally. Of course, reading to children not only develops oral language and promotes early reading attempts, as discussed earlier, it can motivate children to emulate the writing or to make their own books, no matter how crude the first attempts. Parents and care-givers in day-care centers can display children's early writings on walls, doors, and appliances, to be enjoyed and not judged or corrected.

Homes as well as day-care centers should provide environments for writing—comfortable spots with rugs and child-size tables and chairs—and storage for writing materials. The latter should include felt-tip markers, pencils, crayons and chalk. There should be ample supplies and varied sizes of large unlined paper (newsprint works well) and a chalkboard. Materials should be stored consistently in the place provided for writing so that the child can learn how to select materials and put them away independently (Glazer, 1980).

STRATEGIES FOR WRITING DEVELOPMENT IN EARLY CHILDHOOD CLASSROOMS

Parents and teachers can expect to see rapid development in writing in children from two to six years of age. As we have seen, it is during this period that most children move from scribbling to producing random letters, to writing letters, to writing words with invented spellings, to beginning to use standard orthography. They may even space properly between words and use some marks of punctuation. They tend to write longer pieces, and their productions often represent wider ranges of functions and forms. In short, this is a time when children show intense bursts of writing activity, perhaps alternating these with intense bursts of reading activity (Bissex, 1980). It is important, therefore, that teachers have a sense of children's writing needs and interests at this time and know how to interact with them in order to support their efforts, learning, and growth.

Like even younger children, preschoolers and kindergarteners for the most part take more pleasure in the *process* of writing than in its *products*. The act of writing is their center of interest. Gradually they do develop some concern for the products. When they play waiter or waitress, for example, and take an "order," they may be concerned that others can "read" it. The same thing might happen with notes or greeting cards sent to relatives or friends. Children begin to evidence concern that recipients be able to read their messages—perhaps so they can write back. Children who have had little experience pretending to write might be reluctant to make marks on paper even by kindergarten age, possibly because they have become aware that their marks are not conventional writing and thus might not be accepted. It is important to let them know that writing that is not conventional will be accepted. Some children may request conventional spellings and will not write unless they know it is correct. They should be given the help they request.

Children in societies such as ours have experienced literacy widely by preschool and kindergarten, and they have constructed useful though usually asystematic knowledge about writing and reading. Some may also have begun to write and read on their own, though in primitive and invented forms. Therefore, it is inappropriate to think of these youngsters as preliterate. The challenge for schools is to provide experiences that complement children's prior experiences and to recognize individual differences in development among youngsters (Clark, 1984). It is important that adults observe the signs and pace of growth of children's understanding of writing, of their use of writing for a widening range of purposes, and of their ability to control various writing conventions in less primitive, more adultlike ways. Observing children's early writing development creates a context for the planned learning events and spontaneous interactions through which adults can contribute so fundamentally to children's emergent literacy.

Adults should take children's early writing seriously as interesting evidence of the kinds of experiments with writing that contribute centrally to their literacy development. Children's early writings are to be enjoyed, valued, and understood. At the same time, they should usually not be made the occasion for the hunting and correction of errors or for excessive direct teaching. The latter should follow only from children's questions and expressed needs, and should thus be individualized. Direct teaching should also be given in proportion to the magnitude of the request. Often, adults respond to children's requests with information and explanations that are appropriate and helpful but too long or detailed.

We must realize that what young children write about and how they approach writing is more important than their mechanics of writing (spelling, penmanship, punctuation, and spacing). Mechanical skills *are* related to writing, but not writing as we are concerned with it in early childhood literacy development. Learning to write involves learning to compose texts that convey meaning. As children gain experience with writing, they will learn the peripheral skills and mechanics of writing through practice and instruction when the need arises and by asking for the information.

No distinctions by importance should be made among the kinds of writing young children undertake. A list of words is as important as a creative story. For young children, the functions of writing are more important than the form or content. They choose to write if a situation has meaning for them. If we impose upon them our selection of what they should write about, we are not likely to see positive results. With these basic ideas in mind, we can create strategies and appropriate environments for helping children write naturally.

The Writing Center

The literacy area in the classroom should include a place designated for writing. It should be easily accessible, attractive, and inviting. It should be furnished with a table and chairs, plus a rug for youngsters who want to stretch out and write on the floor. Writing implements should include plenty of colored felt-tip marking pens, large and small crayons, large and small pencils (both regular and colored), chalk and a chalkboard. Various types of paper should be available, most of it unlined plain white or newsprint, ranging from eight and a half by eleven inches to twenty-four by thirty-six inches. Do not, however, use manuscript practice paper that is lined with different colored and dotted lines specifically to encourage proper size of letters and spacing between lines. Most preschoolers and kindergartners are not ready for such extrinsic discipline of form.

Index cards for recording Very Own Words should be stored in the writing area, as should the children's collections of Very Own Words. Each child should have a writing folder in which to collect written productions over the course of the school year. If available, a typewriter is useful, as is a computer for word processing. Materials for making books should also be available, including colored construction paper for covers, plain white paper for inside pages, a stapler, and scissors. Teachers can prepare blank books, keyed to special occasions, for children to use. For example, a blank Valentine's Day book shaped like a heart and made of red construction paper with five or six sheets of plain white paper stapled inside provides

The computer allows very young children to communicate thoughts they do not yet have the manual dexterity to write on paper. Early introduction to the computer will make it part of the child's everyday life.

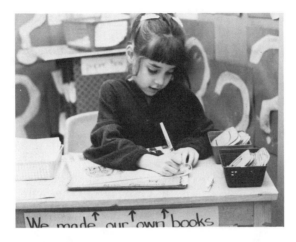

Allison adds her page to the class book at the writing table in the writing center.

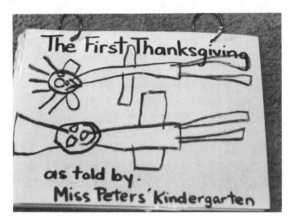

inviting space that children can fill with their written greetings. (See Figures 8–13, 8–14, and 8–15 on preparing blank books.) Stock *bare books* (books with hard covers but no print inside) for special projects. Keep a supply of interesting pictures, posters, magazines, and newspapers; these can stimulate, decorate, or illustrate children's writing.

An alphabet chart in easy view helps children identify and shape letters they may need while writing. Tactile plastic, magnetic, wooden, and felt letters should be among the language arts manipulatives. These help develop motor dexterity for the act of writing and aid in letter recognition and formation. A bulletin board should display children's writing and contain a space for posting notices or sending and receiving messages. "Mailboxes" for youngsters' incoming and outgoing "mail" can be placed in the writing center. The mailboxes are for a pen pal program discussed later.

Basic implements and supplies for writing should be stocked in every other learning center in the room as well. A child might want to copy the words to a song in the music center, write down a "phone number" during dramatic play, record the outside temperature on a chart in the science center, protect a construction of blocks with a "Do Not Touch" sign, or copy a Very Own Word in the social studies or science area. A group might decide to turn the dramatic-play corner into a dentist's office, including in it an appointment book for recording dates, times, and patients' names, appointment cards, patients' records, and a prescription pad for medication.

In all such situations, children should write independently according to function and interest. The teacher has prepared the environment in which such writing can occur and has introduced the materials and made suggestions to the children. With such preparation, children look naturally to writing as a means of communication.

Functional Writing

Children need to see purpose before they write. Class writing projects that are particularly purposeful include **greeting cards** for all occasions to parents, grandparents, sisters, brothers, friends, and relatives. Don't forget birthdays and holidays. Write **thank-you notes** to guest speakers who come to class, to mothers or other adults who help on class trips, to the director of the zoo you visited, or to the librarian who spent time with the class at the public library. Prepare **lists** of things to remember to do in preparing a party, a special program, or a class trip. Make **address and telephone books** with entries from class members. Write notes to parents about activities in school. Encourage individual children to write to their parents about specific things they are doing in school.

Collecting and using Very Own Words offer opportunities for writing and copying and so does using classroom environmental print in one's own writing. Some preschools and kindergartens, as well as elementary classrooms, have established **mail service** and **pen pal** programs (Green, 1985; Martinez & Teale, 1987; Mason, 1986). Children are offered pen pals to write to regularly (once a week is reasonable). Teachers or aides may have to help children write their letters or take dictation. Encourage children to use what writing capabilities they have, even if they cannot produce conventional writing. Teachers may have to read the incoming letters to students who cannot yet read.

A **notice board** for exchanging messages also motivates functional writing (Newman, 1984). Children can tack up pictures for each other as beginning messages. The teacher needs to provide a model by leaving messages for individuals and for the entire class. Notices about school or class events are appropriate. It is important to draw attention to the board when posting a class message or when leaving messages for individuals, so

While participating in dramatic play, Melissa writes her phone number in the class address book, found in the dramatic-play center.

that children get into the habit of looking for messages and leaving them themselves.

Journal writing can be carried out successfully in kindergartens, with entries made daily or at least several times a week. Children are encouraged to write anything they want in their journals and to write at their own developmental levels. Thus, some children's journals might include only

Teachers may need to take dictation for journal writing and for writing to pen pals. Eventually children should be encouraged to do their own writing.

pictures, only scribble writing, only random letters, or only invented spelling. The teacher models journal writing, perhaps with a personal message such as, "I'm very excited today. My daughter is going to be in a play tonight, and I'm going to watch her." By example the child is given an idea about the kinds of entries that are appropriate. Some children draw or write stories in their journals as well as personal experiences (Hipple, 1985). From time to time the journal can also take on dialogue form, the teacher responding to a child's journal entry with a comment. If the child writes, "I had a picnic," the teacher might respond, "That sounds like fun. What did you eat?" The length and fluency of children's journal entries show great gains when the activity is continued regularly throughout a school year (Newman, 1984).

Children's literature is as natural a medium for encouraging writing as it is for encouraging oral language and reading. Reading several books by the same author or illustrator can prompt a class letter asking the author how he or she gets ideas to write or asking the illustrator what kind of art materials he or she uses. It is best to identify authors or illustrators who are likely to respond, for it is important to receive a response, even if it comes from a publisher's representative. Series books—those that use the same character in several different books, such as *Madeline* (Bemelmans, 1939), *Curious George* (Rey, 1941), and *Harold and the Purple Crayon* (Johnson, 1955)—can motivate children to write their own books or a class book about the character. Books such as *Swimmy* (Lionni, 1963) and *Alexander and the Terrible, Horrible, No Good, Very Bad Day* (Viorst, 1972) involve the main character in a series of adventures or incidents as the story proceeds. Children can be asked to write still another episode or adventure for the character. Some stories, such as *Alexander and the Terrible, Horrible, No Good, Very Bad Day*, lend themselves to writing about personal experiences.

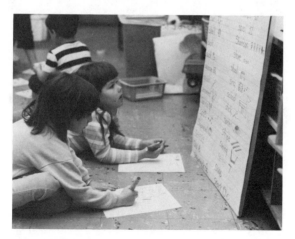

Print in the classroom provides an opportunity for children to copy writing. This is a task enjoyed by 4, 5, and 6-year-olds and encourages independent writing.

(Figure 8–11 illustrates one child's response to this task.) Shared book experiences, directed listening–thinking activities, one-to-one and small-group story readings (described in Chapter 6) can all lead to writing experiences. Predictable books provide patterns that children can imitate in their own writing: through cumulative patterns, as in *I Know an Old Lady* (Westcott, 1980); repetitive language, as in *Are You My Mother?* (Eastman, 1960); familiar sequences, as in *The Very Hungry Caterpillar* (Carle, 1970); or catch-phrases, as in *Horton Hatches the Egg* (Seuss, 1940). (See Appendix A for a list of such books.)

   Children need to share their writing. When they know they will be doing this they will write for an audience and have a greater purpose for writing. At a designated time during the day, usually at the end when the class gets together to review the day's happenings, a child can be selected as Author of the Day to share something that he or she has written (Graves & Hansen, 1983). More than one piece can be read and more than one child can be Author of the Day. Those authors who read their writings in a particular week should display them on a bulletin board in the writing center along with photographs of themselves. When sharing work, the child can sit in a chair marked "Author's chair." This is a permanent fixture in the room for all to use at some particular time. Children in the audience should be encouraged to comment about their friends' work with such statements as "I like what you wrote" or "I fell and cut my knee once, too." Because at first the children will not comment readily, the teacher needs to

FIGURE 8–11

John reads one of the books published by his kindergarten class. They tend to be very popular among the children.

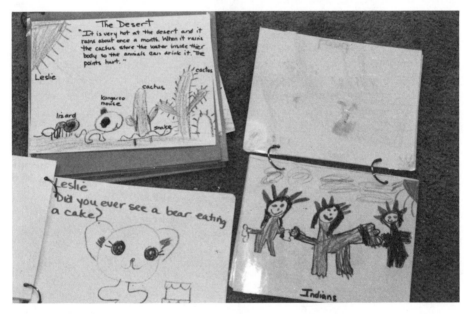

model comments for the audience, whose young members will soon emulate the behavior.

Children's work should be published. "Why publish?" almost answers the question "Why write?" "Writing is a public act, meant to be shared with many audiences" (Graves, 1983, p. 54). When children know their work will be published, they write for a defined purpose. When work is to be published it becomes special; it needs to be done carefully and refined. Children can publish their work in many ways. The most

These two children are publishing a story they have written by creating a roll movie that they will tell to the class or a friend.

Stephanie puts the finishing touches on the cover of a book she has written.

popular is to bind writings into books, which are placed in the library corner and featured on open bookshelves for others to read. Other means of publishing include creating felt-board stories or roll movies, telling stories to classmates, role-playing what has been written, or presenting the story in a puppet show. A computer can be used to type and store or print original material.

For rather experienced early writers, publishing can be the motivation for beginning the *process approach* to writing. Typical steps in this approach include prewriting, writing, rewriting, and editing (Calkins, 1986). If the work is to be published, some prewriting should be required—for kindergartners, for example, a discussion about what the topic will be and what ideas the child will write about. The initial writing step is then completed and shared with the teacher. The teacher asks the child if he or she can think of any changes to be made or other ideas to be added. This is the rewriting step. The final task is editing, which in the kindergarten means, at most, copying the work over into a bound book. (Three ways of making a book are illustrated in Figures 8–12 to 8–14.)

The process approach should be used with caution in preschools and kindergartens. The prewriting step may be accomplished appropriately through discussion or with word lists, but children are likely to be frustrated by editing, particularly by having to copy their work over. Be selective in choosing the youngsters with whom to use the process approach. Involve only those who seem capable of handling it.

Writing conferences between a teacher and a child are times to discuss what the child has written, to encourage the child in writing, and to assess progress by observing and reviewing the writing products gathered in the child's folder. During the conference the teacher can take dictation or help the child with a word, a caption, a picture, or a publishing activity. This is an especially good time to work with those students capable of dealing with any of the steps in process writing and to encourage reluctant writers.

Writing requires dexterity. Although it is unnecessary and often unwise to bog down preschoolers and kindergarteners with the particulars of proper letter formation, they can be encouraged to use manipulatives that strengthen their fine motor coordination such as puzzles and sewing cards.

Writing programs in early childhood should be initiated at the beginning of the school year. Teachers should refer to children as authors and writers so that they perceive themselves as such. Teachers need to model writing through messages on the message board, notes to parents, thank-you notes to children, and experience charts dictated by the class. They must be supportive when working with young writers. Reluctant writers need to be encouraged to write in "their very own way" (Martinez & Teale, 1987; Sulzby, 1986b). Youngsters need to know that their work does not have to look like adult writing. Showing them samples of other children's writing, including drawing, scribble writing, and random letters, helps them to see that they can do the same thing. Adults need to facilitate young writers' attempts by taking dictation if children cannot or will not write themselves, spelling words, showing children how to form letters when asked, and answering questions that arise during writing. Like other areas of literacy, writing requires social interaction if it is to promote development. Therefore, teachers need to offer young writers feedback, encouragement, and positive reinforcement.

ASSESSING CHILDREN'S WRITING DEVELOPMENT

As in other areas of literacy, assessment of a child's writing should take place from the beginning to the end of the school year. That way the teacher can determine a child's level of development, monitor progress, and plan programs accordingly. The following checklist on page 169 is one means of assessment.

The assessment checklist is used, of course, to analyze individual writing samples collected through the year. In addition to a child's own writing folder, the teacher should maintain a folder for each child that includes notes on observations, samples of their writing, notes from conferences with the child or his or her parents, and completed checklists. The folder can be used during parent conferences and can accompany a child to his or her next teacher. Assessment should be kept as informal as possible and be based on children's self-initiated activities and on teachers' observations of and interactions with them. There should be no formal evaluation of individual writing, no marking or correcting of children's work. The purpose of assessment is to enhance the teacher's understanding of children's writing ability and aid in program planning.

Writing Development Checklist

Child's name_____ Date_____

	Always	Sometimes	Never
Observations			
Independently explores with writing materials			
Attempts writing in order to convey meaning, regardless of writing stage			
Dictates stories or sentences he or she wants written down			
Copies letters or words			
Forms identifiable letters			
Writes from left to right			

Check(✔) the stage or stages at which the child seems to be writing:

_____ uses drawing for writing and drawing
_____ differentiates between writing and drawing
_____ scribbles for writing
_____ uses letterlike forms for writing
_____ uses learned letters in random fashion for writing
_____ uses invented spelling for writing
_____ uses conventional spelling for writing

ACTIVITIES

1. Ask each of three preschool children to write for you. Take notes on their behavior during writing and analyze samples of their writing, to determine the child's writing developmental level.

2. Observe a kindergarten child for several months. Meet with the child individually once a week. At each session ask the child to write something for you. Collect and date the writing samples. Evaluate them to determine the child's development in writing.

3. Select a social studies or science topic, such as plants, the five senses, or good health. Collect materials that will encourage functional writing on the topic.

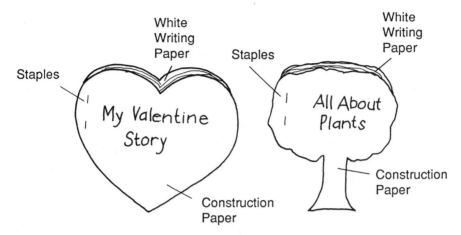

FIGURE 8–12 Stapled book: Cut colored construction paper and white writing paper into a desired shape. Staple at the side.

FIGURE 8–13 Sewn book: Punch holes into oaktag and white writing paper. Sew together with yarn.

a. Sew a running stitch down the center of eight to ten sheets of eight-and-a-half-by-eleven plain white writing paper backed with a piece of nine-by-twelve colored construction paper.

b. Place an eleven-by-fourteen piece of contact paper or wallpaper face down. Paste two pieces of six-by-nine oaktag or cardboard on the peeled contact paper a quarter inch apart, leaving about a one-inch border. Fold each corner of the contact paper onto the oaktag to form a triangle (glue if using wallpaper).

c. Fold the edges of the contact paper onto the oaktag (paste down if using wallpaper). Place a twelve-inch piece of Mystic Tape down the center of the contact paper and over its edges. Put glue on the two exposed pieces of oaktag and on the quarter-inch space between them.

d. Place the folded and stitched edge of the construction paper and plain white paper in the quarter-inch glued space. Paste the construction paper onto the oaktag and over the contact-paper border to make the inside covers.

FIGURE 8–14   Folded, stitched, and glued book:

9

Preparing and Organizing the Environment: A Vehicle for Literacy Development at School

CHAPTER OVERVIEW

- A literacy-rich classroom environment needs to be designed; it does not just happen.
- Literacy skills can and should be integrated throughout the curriculum.
- Appropriate grouping practices help educators attend to the needs of individual students.
- A school day must be planned so that it nurtures emergent literacy.

"What is honored in a country will be cultivated there." In classrooms in which teachers honor literacy development, it will be cultivated as an integral part of the school curriculum.

PLATO

The success of any program depends to a large extent on how it is organized, designed, and managed. Even creative and knowledgeable teachers fail without careful planning, preparation of the environment, organization of lessons, and management of daily routines. This chapter ties together all the prerequisites for successful implementation of all the ideas described earlier in this book. Specifically, it focuses on (1) preparation of the physical environment, including selection of materials and their placement in the classroom; (2) integration of literacy activities throughout the school day; (3) grouping practices to meet individual needs, and (4) a suggested outline for a school day that provides literacy experiences throughout.

This chapter is concerned with the teaching of youngsters from two and a half to seven—preschoolers and kindergarteners with implications for first grade. (Chapter 2 addressed home literacy environments and daily routines appropriate for infants and toddlers. Day-care centers for children of that age need to organize rich literacy environments, routines, programs, and activities similar to those described for homes.)

PREPARATION OF THE PHYSICAL ENVIRONMENT

The physical design of a classroom has been found to affect the choices children make among activities (Bumsted, 1981; Morrow & Weinstein, 1982, 1986; Phyfe-Perkins, 1979; Sutfin, 1980; Weinstein, 1977). The design of the room should accommodate the organization and strategies of the teaching that goes on there. Programs that nourish emergent literacy require a literacy-rich environment, an interdisciplinary approach to the development of literacy, and recognition of individual differences and levels of development.

Classrooms that accommodate those characteristics are arranged in centers dedicated to particular activities or content areas. Centers contain both materials specific to topics currently under study and general supplies, materials, and resources. The materials are usually manipulative and activity-oriented. They are also designed so that children can use them independently or in small groups. Centers are partially separated from each other by furniture that houses their materials. Center materials can be stored on tables, on shelves, or in boxes. Centers often include bulletin boards. Areas are accessible and labeled. Each piece of equipment in a center should have its own designated spot so that teachers can direct children to it and children can find and return it easily. Early in a school year, a center need hold only a small number of items; new materials are gradually added as the year progresses. The teacher should introduce the purpose, use, and placement of each item added.

The literacy center, which includes the library corner, writing area, oral language area, and additional language arts materials, is the focal point of the room (Stauffer, 1970). It is situated so that it is immediately visible when one enters the classroom. It is visually attractive and physically accessible (Morrow, 1982, 1983). Placement and size of materials, shelves, chairs, and tables are appropriate for young children, and all posters are at the child's eye level. According to Coody (1973) and Huck (1976), the effort of creating an inviting atmosphere for a classroom library corner is rewarded by the increased interest of children in participating in the activities offered there. The specific design of a library corner is described in Chapter 5, an oral language area in Chapter 3, a writing center in Chapter 8, and materials for developing concepts about print in Chapter 7. Although they have been described separately in this book, these areas should be placed together, forming one center for literacy development.

The literacy center can occupy at least one quarter of the wall space in a classroom. This says to the child that the use of reading, writing, and oral language is a valued and important part of the classroom. The materials range in difficulty so that they can meet individual needs and the different developmental levels of the children. Each set of materials has its own place, is to be respected, and is designed for independent use (Morrison, 1984).

Because the environment, organization, and strategies incorporate an interdisciplinary approach to literacy development, the rest of the room is set up in additional centers, including those for content areas, as shown in the accompanying floor plan. (See Figure 9–1.) The art center is placed by the sink for easy access to water. In this same area are children's cubbies for storage of individual work. Since the working needs of early childhood classrooms are better met by table surfaces than by desks, children must be provided with these storage areas. The contents of the various centers diagramed in the figure have been described in Chapter 3. In addition to all the materials available in them, it is important that each have books and writing materials. The music center, for example, can include picture storybooks adapted from songs, such as Ezra Jack Keats's *Over in the Meadow* (1971). In addition to looking at the book, children may choose to copy words from the story. Certainly social studies and science centers should hold informational books and children's literature that relate to the topic at hand. The art center might have books with craft ideas, including directions and diagrams. Books are appropriate as well in the dramatic-play area. If the class is discussing Halloween, the area should have a book of Halloween stories for pretend mothers and fathers to read to their "babies," or a Halloween recipe book. The block center can contain books that help develop ideas for building. Books that contain maps or plans of communities might motivate children to create such communities in their block play.

Each content area center is a source for literacy development: each contains things to listen to and read, write, and talk about. These materials create excitement and interest, a wealth of new vocabulary and concepts, and a reason for participating in literacy activities. With each new unit of instruction, additional books, posters, artifacts, music, art projects, dramatic-

FIGURE 9–1 Classroom Floor Plan

play materials, and scientific objects can be added to create new interest.

In addition to generating a rich literacy atmosphere and an interdisciplinary approach, the room is designed to cater to different teaching methods, organizational strategies, and grouping procedures so that the differences among the children can be accommodated. The centers provide space for independent or social learning, exploration, and self-direction. The tables illustrated in the diagram provide a place for whole-class instruction, as does the open area in the music-center with the rug where children can sit. The teacher's conference table is a place for individual learning or small-group lessons. All furniture is, of course, movable so that any other needed teaching arrangement may be accommodated. The centers are located so as to create both quiet, relatively academic areas and places for more active play. The literacy center, for example, which houses the library corner, writing and oral language areas, and language arts manipulatives, is next to the math center. These areas generally house activities that require relative quiet and are therefore in close proximity. On the other hand, dramatic play, woodworking, and block play tend to be noisier activities and so are placed at the opposite end of the room from the quiet areas. The art center can also be a noisy area and is set aside from the quieter sections of the room. The teacher's conference table is situated in a quiet area yet allows the teacher a view of the rest of the classroom. While the teacher is involved as he or she usually is, in small-group or individualized instruction at the conference table, the rest of the class is working independently. The table's location allows the teacher to see all the children even while working with just a few.

The classroom should be filled with functional print—labels on classroom items and areas; signs communicating functional information and directions, such as Please Clean Up Now and Quiet, Please; and charts labeled *Helpers, Daily Routines,* and *Attendance* (Schickedanz, 1986). The outdoor environment should also accommodate literacy development. In addition to the usual playground equipment, new materials that reflect unit instruction add to the interest of outdoor play. Where climates are seasonal, for example, flowers should be planted in the spring; rakes provided in the fall for leaf gathering; and pails, shovels, and other digging and building equipment provided in winter for snow play. Creative materials such as crates, boxes, plastic containers, boards, ropes, and balls give children incentives to play creatively. The materials generate language during play, discussions in class, and information for writing experience charts and class books.

INTEGRATION OF LITERACY ACTIVITIES

The concept of the integrated school day, an interdisciplinary approach to teaching, emerged from the work of Pestalozzi, Froebel, Piaget, and

Functional print in the classroom, such as helper charts and charts designating activities for Center Time, encourage reading for a purpose.

Dewey. These theorists suggested that learning is based on the interests of the child. Instruction, therefore, should be active, manipulative, and sense-oriented. They believed that children need time to explore, experiment, and play with interesting materials in order to learn. Dewey stressed the importance of a child's real-life experiences to learning. As children pursue their interests and experiences, their skill development is integrated functionally (Dewey, 1966). Open education and the British Primary School movement, which also draw from the theorists just mentioned, strongly emphasize learning and teaching through the integration of content areas. Instead of studying separate lessons on particular skills, children study topics of interest to them and learn skills in the process. If, for example, the topic is dinosaurs, the class discusses dinosaurs, reads, writes, and sings about them, counts them, and carries out other activities and projects about them. Interest in the topic motivates and leads to skill development.

Integration of content and emergent literacy skills includes concern for children's interests and individual differences. It provides socially interactive settings and behaviors for modeling and emulation. It focuses on real-life experiences, has purpose, and is functional. Characteristics of the integrated school day, while drawing upon ideas described by earlier theorists, include the findings of more recent research on how literacy is acquired (Goodman & Altwerger, 1981; Heath, 1980; Mason, 1980). Many literacy activities can be integrated into the school day. Several are described here so that you can see how some of the strategies discussed in previous chapters can be taught in other areas of the curriculum.

Art experiences allow children to explore and experiment with such interesting materials and activities as finger paints, watercolors, print painting, string painting, sponge painting, colored pencils, felt-tip markers, crayons, colored construction paper, tissue paper, foil, transparent wrap, paste, scissors, yarn, fabric scraps, pipe cleaners, clay, and play dough. If children are encouraged to discuss such materials as they use them, language development flourishes. Preschoolers and kindergartners immersed in finger painting, for instance, use such words as *mushy, smushy, gushy,* and *squiggle.* Playing with dough or clay elicits *pound, squeeze, roll, press,* and *fold.* Watercolors stimulate such comments as "Oooh, it's drippy," "The paint is running down the page like a stream of water," "Look how the colors all run together. The red is making the blue turn purple," and "My picture looks like a rainbow of colors across the sky." The teacher can take the opportunity to make word lists from the language generated in art activities and to encourage the children to share and talk about what they are doing. The words that individual children generate are a source of Very Own Words.

Children are often eager to show their creations and have other youngsters look. This habit is likely to result in children asking each other how they made their projects. The resulting description provides an excellent opportunity for language development. Children sometimes ask to dictate sentences or stories about their artwork, or write about it themselves. Individual works of art on similar subjects can be bound together in books that include captions, titles, or stories. Art activities can appropriately highlight concepts such as the letter *p,* for example, through the use of purple and pink paint, paper, and play dough.

Music provides ample means for literacy development. Children find new words in songs, thus increasing vocabulary. Songs emphasize syllabic patterns in words, which should be brought to the attention of the children. Songs can be written on charts and sung, the teacher pointing to the individual words. Picture storybooks adapted from songs, such as *Old Mac-Donald Had a Farm* (Quackenbush, 1972), provide predictable reading material for young children. Listening to classical music often creates images and is a rich source for descriptive language. Children can create stories about the music, describe their feelings, or describe the sounds of various instruments.

Dramatic play provides endless possibilities for development of oral and written language and reading. The materials and activities typical of a dramatic-play area stimulate considerable language, and occasional addition of new props and materials ensures continued opportunity for growth. Dramatic play provides especially realistic settings and functional reasons for using print. New units in social studies and science trigger opportunities to add print materials that stimulate reading and writing as well as speech. A unit on community helpers—a topic familiar to early childhood teachers—invariably leads to a discussion of fire fighters, police officers, supermarket clerks, doctors, nurses, mail carriers, and office workers. The mention of any of these community helpers is an opportunity to add literacy materials to the dramatic-play area.

Role-playing supermarket, for instance, is aided by the addition of food and detergent containers, a toy cash register, play money, note pads, a telephone and directory, store signs, a schedule of hours, advertisements, and posters for food and other products. Teachers or aides might visit a nearby supermarket not only to note and perhaps match for the classroom the print that abounds there, but to pick up outdated signs and posters. Store managers readily give away such materials when they no longer need them. Definitely include, among materials for dramatic play about supermarkets, a bookshelf full of magazines and books "for sale." All these materials help children engage in conversation as they role-play a store manager, clerk, or shopper. They read posters, books, signs, and magazines and write shopping lists, orders, and new signs when they are needed.

Many other topics lend themselves to dramatic play that incorporates literacy materials. A study of health-care personnel can lead to the creation of a doctor's office. A waiting room can be set up with magazines for the patients to read and pamphlets about good health. There can be a No Smoking sign, a notice containing the doctor's hours, and posters on the wall concerning good health habits. There should be an appointment book for the nurse and a pad for writing down appointment reminders for patients to take with them, a pad for writing prescriptions, patient folders containing forms to be filled out, and a patient address and phone book.

Creative play in the dramatic-play center encourages social interaction and vibrant discussion.

When studying transportation, the class can create a travel agency. Here there would be maps, travel posters, pamphlets about places to visit, and tickets to be issued for planes and trains.

The possibilities are numerous. The materials are easy to obtain, and they encourage functional reading and writing. Dramatic play involves children in literacy that relates to real life. The children enjoy role playing in these situations because the activity includes meaningful experiences. In dramatic play, children are voluntarily participating in reading and writing.

Science and social studies are the two content areas that provide perhaps the greatest opportunities for literacy development. Their contents typically generate enthusiasm, meaning, and a purpose for using emergent literacy strategies. A unit on the farm can lead to oral language development through discussions about farm work, different types of farms, and farm animals. Word lists of farm animals, crops, and jobs on the farm can be made. Pictures of farm scenes, a trip to a farm, or a visit by a farmer generates discussion, reading, and writing. To encourage positive attitudes toward books, the teacher can carefully select good pieces of children's literature about farms to read to the class. The *Petunia* series (Duvoisin, 1950) deals delightfully with a goose who lives on a farm. *The Little Red Hen* (Galdone, 1973), *The Tale of Peter Rabbit* (Potter, 1902), *The Little Farm* (Lenski, 1965), and *Charlie Needs a Clock* (DePaola, 1973) are just a few examples of good children's literature that relate to the farm and that will motivate youngsters to pick up the books on their own, retell the stories, role-play them, or otherwise share them. A farm visit can be retold in stories or drawings bound into class books, recaptured in a language experience chart, or reflected in Very Own Words. The teacher can associate letters and sounds in farm words with those in children's names or in environmental print.

Science experiments and food preparation offer opportunities for more discussion, generation of interesting word lists, reading and writing of recipes, directions, and results. The block center, too, can stimulate literacy activities. For instance, when introducing a unit on transportation the teacher can add toy trucks, trains, cars, boats, and airplanes to the block corner, along with travel tickets, luggage and freight tags, maps, travel guides, tour brochures, travel posters, and signs common to airports, train stations, and bus depots, such as gate numbers, names of carriers, and arrival and departure signs.

When literacy skills are developed in an integrated fashion, as in such practices and approaches as these, children see purposes and reasons for becoming literate. When we teach literacy skills that do not reflect real-life experience and lack content, children perceive no usefulness in those skills. When taught in an integrated, interdisciplinary fashion, children ask for the skills they find they need in order to participate fully in experiences that interest them during their work and play at school and at home. During a unit on transportation in a kindergarten class of my own, children asked for even more materials than I had already made available in the several centers. Books on transportation led to requests for books on space travel, and various maps of places not already represented in the center. Many children added to their Very Own Words. Children asked for help in preparing signs representing places they wanted to visit and highway signs indicating mileage to various destinations. Some dictated travel directions. The need for literacy information was created by the preparation of an environment that reflected interesting, real-life experiences. In such an environment, learning is to a great extent self-generated.

STRATEGIES FOR MEETING INDIVIDUAL NEEDS

There are, of course, a variety of strategies for organizing instruction. Children can be taught as a whole class, in small groups, and individually. Children can be grouped homogeneously or heterogeneously by ability, interests, or skills, or they can be divided into peer groups for cooperative learning. The use of a variety of organizational strategies is important, since some children benefit more in one setting than in another. The use of several different grouping schemes within the same classroom also tends to eliminate the stigmas attached to a single grouping system. Variable grouping makes it likely that children will interact with all others in one group or another. Finally, using varied organizational strategies provides children with a more interesting and broader educational experience.

Whole-group lessons are inappropriate until the children are almost three. Children younger than three lack the ability to concentrate or to sit and listen. Whole-group lessons are appropriate when the subject needs to be introduced to all the children and the presentation can be understood by all the children. In early childhood literacy development, story readings by an adult, group singing, and class discussions are appropriate whole-group activities.

Small groups are effective for instruction in specific skills and other more intricate lessons that require careful supervision or close interaction with children. Appropriate literacy activities in small groups include directed listening–thinking activities that involve interpretive or critical thinking, cooperative projects such as creating pictures for a class book on a particular topic, and assignments in a specific center or area (since whole groups cannot fit into these areas at the same time). Teachers often prefer a small, homogeneous group for skill development, since this organizational arrangement allows the teacher the opportunity to work closely with a few children who seem to be at a similar literacy level and have similar needs at the same time. Grouping should be flexible; for example, when members of a small group have mastered a particular skill, the group can be disbanded and new groups formed when necessary.

This flexible arrangement for grouping allows children to work with many others and eliminates the stigmas often attached to fixed homogeneous grouping that assigns general ability labels to groups. When children as young as four are organized for instruction into fixed high, middle, and low groupings, they become as aware of their group placement as children in third or fourth grade.

In addition to teacher-organized groups, children should be given opportunities to select groups they might like to be in because of interest and friendships.

Working with children on a one-to-one basis and allowing them to work independently are both forms of individualized instruction. Although children need to work cooperatively with peers and interact socially with both peers and adults, one-to-one instruction offers personal attention and an opportunity for the teacher to learn a great deal about the child. Literacy activities particularly appropriate for one-to-one instruction include (1) story retellings, (2) attempted readings of favorite storybooks, (3) helping children with specific skill needs, such as letters of the alphabet or color identification, (4) assessing a child's ability or knowledge in a particular literary area, (5) reading stories, with prompts for questions and comments, and (6) taking dictation of original stories or helping children to write themselves.

Regular one-to-one sessions can be extremely productive. A teacher

Children need to experience literacy learning in many contexts. The teacher should arrange for whole-class experiences, small-group learning (pictured here), one-to-one conferences, and activities in which children learn from other children.

can establish twenty minutes of conference time each day, thus allowing a one-to-one session with each child for at least a few minutes each week. During conferences, teachers can assess a child's needs, record accomplishments, offer instruction, and assign tasks or suggest goals. Conference time lets the teacher accommodate both the child who is already reading and the child who cannot yet differentiate print from pictures. Conference time with one child might best be used for reading a story and encouraging responses, with another child helping record Very Own Words.

At the end of each conference period, the teacher announces which children will be seen the next day, writing their names on the board in place of those of the children just seen. The agenda for each conference with each child is determined by the needs, interests, and abilities of that child at that time. Although children can participate in conferences from age three, their maturity determines exactly how a conference is carried out. The typical conference lasts about five minutes, but can be as short as two minutes or as long as fifteen. The atmosphere is informal and the session is usually a very special time for both teacher and child.

The value of meeting children one-to-one was made quite apparent to me early in my teaching career. A mother told me that her child liked to be absent from school. I was horrified, assuming immediately that he liked being absent because he was unhappy in my class. The mother, however, went on to say that her son liked being absent because when he returned to school he was given "private time with the teacher." I had made a practice of meeting "privately" with absentees on their return to school to share work we had accomplished during their absence.

On another occasion, I noticed several children reading on their own during free-choice time—an ability I was unable to recognize in them during my whole-class instruction in reading readiness skills. I began to work with children one-to-one, discovering what they knew, wanted to know, and needed to know. One-to-one instruction can be more easily and accurately designed to meet children's individual interests and needs. Assignments or suggestions can involve specific materials at a particular center or area of the room. Such targeted instruction not only gives children practice they specifically need but instills in them a sense of responsibility in accomplishing assigned tasks.

To make an assignment "official" and to help the child remember it, the teacher can draw up a contract or assignment sheet. Since most preschoolers and kindergartners cannot read conventional print, their contracts are composed of both pictures and words. The teacher and child check off the areas in which the child is to work. At the next conference they read over the contract together to check what the child has done. A typical assignment might be to read a book in the library corner, to read over one's Very Own Words, to copy words from a new word list, or to make a book of pictures about a particular topic. Assignments are based on the needs, interests, and ability levels of individual learners. A sample contract is illustrated here. (See Figure 9–2.)

During a one-to-one conference, the teacher takes notes and records anecdotes of the child's behavior. These notes, collected in one folder for each child, become part of the running records on the child's progress and prescriptions for future work. The folder also holds periodic samples of the child's drawings, writing, and dictated stories. It is helpful for the teacher to include in each folder copies of the various checklists and sets of objectives described throughout this book as an aid in observing and nurturing a child's development. The checklist beginning on page 184 is a guide to the assessment of early literacy development. The list is a compilation of the objectives and assessment information that appears in chapters throughout the book.

FIGURE 9–2

Contract		
Name	Date	
To Do	**Specific Activity**	**Done**
	Reading	
	Writing	
	Oral Language	
	Language Arts Manipulatives	
	Listening Station	
	Math Manipulatives $1 + 2 = 3$	

Checklist for Assessing Early Literacy Development

Child's Name_____

Date_____

	Always	Sometimes	Never
Language Development			
Makes phoneme sounds			
Speaks in one-word sentences			
Speaks in two-word sentences			
Identifies familiar sounds			
Differentiates similar sounds			
Understands the language of others when spoken to			
Follows verbal directions			
Speaks to others freely			
Pronounces words correctly			
Has appropriate vocabulary for level of maturity			
Speaks in complete sentences			
Uses varied syntactic structures			
Can be understood by others			

The items on this checklist correspond to the stages of language development from birth to 6.

	Always	Sometimes	Never
Reading Attitudes and Voluntary Reading Behavior			
Voluntarily looks at books			
Asks to be read to			
Listens attentively while being read to			
Responds with questions and comments to stories read to him or her			

	Always	Sometimes	Never
Concepts about Books			
Knows that a book is for reading			
Can identify the front, back, top, and bottom of a book			
Can turn the pages of a book properly			
Knows the difference between print and pictures			

	Always	Sometimes	Never
Knows that the pictures on a page are related to what the print says			
Knows where one begins reading on a page			
Knows what a title of a book is			
Knows what an author is			
Knows what an illustrator is			

	Always	Sometimes	Never
Comprehension of Story			
Retells familiar stories using the pictures in the book to help recall the details			
Retells a story without the help of the book and demonstrates knowledge of details			
Retells stories with readinglike intonation			
Includes elements of story structure in story retellings: setting (beginning, time, place, characters) theme (problem or goal of the main character) plot episodes (events leading toward the solution of the main character's problem or the attainment of his or her goal) resolution (problem solved, goal achieved, story ended)			
Responds to story readings with literal, inferential, and critical questions and comments			
Responds to story readings with inferential and critical questions and comments			
Participates in story-reading behavior by reciting or narrating stories as the teacher is reading them			
When read to, fills in words of a story according to knowledge of syntax and context			

	Always	Sometimes	Never
Concepts about Print			
Knows that print is read from left to right			
Knows that oral language can be written down, then read			
Knows what a letter is and can point to one on a printed page			

	Always	Sometimes	Never
Knows what a word is and can point one out on a printed page			
Is aware of environmental print and can read some signs and logos			
Recognizes some words by sight in book print			
Can identify letters by name			
Associates some sounds with letters			
Asks questions about letter names, words, and sounds			
Attempts reading by attending to pictures			
Attempts reading by attending to print			
Begins to use story context, syntax, and semantics to identify words			

	Always	Sometimes	Never
Writing Development			
Independently explores with writing materials			
Attempts writing in order to convey meaning, regardless of writing stage			
Dictates stories or sentences he or she wants written down			
Copies letters or words			
Forms identifiable letters			
Writes from left to right			
Check (✔) the category or categories at which the child seems to be writing:			
_____ uses drawing for writing and drawing			
_____ differentiates between drawing and writing			
_____ scribbles for writing			
_____ uses letterlike forms for writing			
_____ uses learned letters in random fashion for writing			
_____ uses invented spelling for writing			
_____ uses conventional spelling for writing			

General Comments about the Child's Development:

Working individually or with a friend can also mean working inde-pendently. Children sometimes read alone during recreational reading periods. They enjoy working alone with their Very Own Words. They listen to books on headsets and work alone when creating a book. They need practice in working independently, especially while the teacher is holding individual conferences. Montessori schools tend to be very effec-tive in helping very young children to be independent, self-directive, and capable of working individually or in small groups without the need for teacher supervision.

Children working individually or in small groups use manipulative learning materials placed in centers on accessible shelves. Teachers illus-trate the use of all such materials before placing them on the shelves, each item in its own place. Children select new items only after they replace those they have been using. During conference periods, only relatively quiet materials may be used independently, perhaps assigned during a student's own conference time.

It is important that the teacher use a variety of organizational strat-egies to meet the individual learning styles and to make the school day more interesting. Teaching children in groups and on a one-to-one basis may not seem as if one is creating a literacy environment in which literacy can emerge naturally; rather, it seems somewhat structured. Yet, it is not realistic to rely totally on a child's initiative and expect learning to take place. The teacher must create the climate and conditions and plan the learning opportunities within which the reading process can be nurtured and developed.

THE DAILY SCHEDULE

Scheduling the daily routine in nursery school, kindergarten, and first grade must take into account the social, emotional, physical, and intellec-tual level of the children. It must also reflect the best from theorists' models of early childhood education, including those of Piaget, Froebel, Dewey, Montessori, the behaviorists, and Vygotsky. The environment should be prepared so that learning can take place naturally, but with the guidance and instruction that will help children achieve their fullest potential.

Young children cannot sit for long periods; their schedule must vary. Whole-class lessons that require sitting and listening must be few and short. Children need large blocks of time for exploring environments. They need play situations, manipulative materials, learning centers, and outdoor areas. Children need small-group and one-to-one instruction. Activities that require sitting and listening need to be followed by ones that allow movement. Quiet times must be followed by noisier times. To nurture emergent literacy, the teacher must allow for rich literacy experiences throughout the day, experiences in using and enjoying language in all its forms and functions.

The sample schedules that follow illustrate where and when specific opportunities to promote literacy can occur. The schedule provides a routine or structure for the day which seems to make children comfortable.

Day-Care Centers

Full-Day Program for Infants and Toddlers

8:00–9:45
Arrival, caring for infants' needs (diapering, feeding). When involved in these routine activities, care-givers talk to babies, sing nursery rhymes, recite poems, reinforce babies' responses.

Activity period consisting of play (in small groups or one-to-one) with blocks, manipulative toys, books, or paper and crayons. Teacher and aides provide language models by identifying materials and talking about their use, and provide positive reinforcement for such literacy activity as attempting oral language, looking at books, and using crayons on sheets of paper.

9:45–10:00
Snack for toddlers, accompanied by song or poetry. (Infants are fed whenever necessary.)

10:00–10:45
Rest or nap. Adults sing a napping song before children lie down.

10:45–11:15
Washing, diapering, caring for babies' needs in preparation for lunch. Adults interact with children verbally through conversation, song, or rhymes.

Activity time focuses on reading stories and looking at pictures, using taped stories, paper and crayons.

11:15–12:00
Lunch. Conversation involves the taste, smell and texture of the food. After lunch, babies are readied for nap time with washing, diapering, and caring for infant needs.

12:00–1:45
Naps, begun with a song and carried through with quiet background music.

1:45–2:00
As children wake, their needs are taken care of again and a small snack is provided.

2:00–3:30
Indoor and outdoor play. In either setting, adults work with small groups, reading stories, encouraging responses from children, pointing out print.

3:30–4:00
Teacher attempts a group session involving singing a song or reading a book aloud. The last ten minutes of the day are spent in preparing the children to leave—toileting, diapering, and general care.

As noted in the introduction to this chapter, the day-care center needs to emulate as much as possible homes with rich literacy environments if they are to ensure the natural development of literacy in infants and toddlers.

Preschools and Kindergartens

There is no one daily routine that has been established as the model for all preschool and kindergarten programs. There are, however, basic categories of activities that ought to be included. The daily routines for preschool and kindergarten do not vary much in the blocks of time allocated to specific activities. The tone, content, and means of what actually occurs in those time periods are far more important. Time allotments for activities should be flexible to accommodate spontaneous educational experiences. When activities are particularly productive, they should be continued beyond allotted time schedules.

Two sample schedules follow, one for a half-day program and one for a full day. Then a sample day presented in detail illustrates how literacy activities can be woven throughout the entire school day.

Half-Day Program for Preschool and Kindergarten

8:30–8:50
  Arrival at school, storage of outdoor clothing. Quiet activities.
8:50–9:20
  Morning get-together, opening exercises, discussion of unit topic, songs or musical movement activities related to unit topic, daily news, planning for the school day.
9:20–9:40
  Whole-class lesson in language arts, mathematics, social studies, or science, varying from day to day, with an assignment to complete that flows into the next period.
9:40–10:00
  Conference period or small-group work. The rest of the class completes work from the whole-class lesson, children work on individual contracts in small groups or at designated centers (literacy, social studies, science, or mathematics).
10:00–10:35
  Center time. All centers open, including art, music, blocks, dramatic play, literacy, science, and social studies. Special projects may be set up at different centers, such as art or science.
10:35–10:50
  Cleanup and snack.
10:50–11:10
  Independent reading and writing. Children use materials from the literacy center (library corner, oral language area, writing area).
11:10–11:30
  Outdoor play, if weather permits, or large-motor games in the gymnasium.
11:30–12:00
  Storybook reading with varied strategies, including shared book experiences, role playing, creative storytelling. Review of the school day. Dismissal.

Full-Day Program for Nursery School or Kindergarten

(It should be noted that full-day schedules allow for larger blocks of time and more time for learning through exploration and manipulation of materials.)

8:30–9:00

Arrival at school, storage of outdoor clothing. Quiet activities.

9:00–9:30

Morning get-together, opening exercises, discussion of unit topic, songs and musical movement activity related to the unit topic, daily news, planning for the school day.

9:30–9:50

Whole-class lesson, either in language arts or mathematics, varying from day to day, with an assignment to complete that flows into the next period.

9:50–10:15

Conference period or small-group work with emphasis on literacy development and math skills. The rest of the class completes work from the whole-class lesson or works on individual contracts from small groups or at centers designated for use during this quiet period (literacy center, math, social studies, science).

10:15–10:45

Free play. All centers open, including dramatic play, blocks, and woodworking. Special art or food-preparation projects are set up in the art center once each week for small groups.

10:45–11:00

Cleanup and snack.

11:00–11:30

Storybook reading, creative storytelling, repeated story readings, role playing, shared book readings, use of Big Books.

11:30–12:15

Independent reading and writing. Children use materials in the literacy center (library corner, writing area, oral language area, language arts manipulatives), including Very Own Words.

12:15–1:15

Lunch and outdoor play, if time and weather permit. Otherwise, large-motor activities in the gymnasium.

Afternoon Schedule for Kindergarten

1:15–1:45

Whole-group lesson in science or social studies incorporating language arts, music, or art.

1:45–2:15

Center time (literacy, mathematics, science, social studies). Special projects can be set up in any of these for small groups to rotate through in a given week. The teacher meets with small groups for instruction in math or literacy skills.

2:15–2:50

Circle time. Review of the day's activities, planning for the next day, sharing of items brought from home that are related to study units, story sharing by children, songs, and adult story reading.

2:50–3:00

Preparation for dismissal. Dismissal.

Afternoon Schedule for Preschool   The morning schedule would be the same for preschool and kindergarten. In preschool, however, the afternoon would differ somewhat and look more like this:

1:00–1:45
Rest period.
1:45–2:10
Center time. All centers open and special projects in one of the areas.
2:10–2:35
Outdoor play, large-motor play in gymnasium, or large-motor musical movement activities.
2:35–2:50
Circle time. Review of the day's activities, planning for the next day, sharing items brought from home that are related to the study unit, songs, story reading.
2:50–3:00
Preparation for dismissal. Dismissal.

Full-Day Program for Kindergarten   (Activities described here are applicable in preschool and first grade.) The detailed outline that follows illustrates how literacy development and content area instruction can be integrated throughout a full kindergarten day. Let us assume that the topic under study is animals.

8:30–9:00
Arrival and quiet activities. Books about animals are featured on the open-faced bookshelves in the library corner. The science and social studies table holds collections of pictures and figures of four different types of animals: farm, zoo, pet, woodland. Farm and woodland animals are particularly featured here, zoo and pet animals in the block and dramatic-play areas. Also in the classroom are one or more live animals, such as fish in an aquarium, gerbils, hamsters, guinea pigs, newts, hermit crabs, or rabbits. They are located near the dramatic-play area, which is designed as a veterinarian's office. Children are encouraged to look at the books, explore with the model animals, or play with the pet animals during this quiet activity period. Background pictures of toy barns, a silo, farm equipment, mountains and trees, and zoo scenes encourage interesting play and language use. Index cards are readily available for labeling animals or making signs such as Deer Crossing, No Hunting, or Endangered Species. A Morning Message on the chalkboard says, "We will be going on a trip to a farm."
9:00–9:30
Morning get-together. A child leads the opening exercises. Children are encouraged to tell news for the day, including things that have happened outside of school that they would like to share. The teacher writes on an experience chart what the children have to say—for example, "I got new red sneakers after school yesterday," or "My dad got a flat tire while we

were driving home. We had to use the little tire from the trunk until we got to the gas station to buy a new one."

The teacher asks if anyone can read the Morning Message. "We will be going on a trip to a farm." After children attempt to do so, she reads it with them, asking them to join in unison. To generate discussion and build anticipation she asks, "What do we need to think about before going to the farm?" She generates further discussion about the unit topic, asking the children to name all the farm animals they can think of and listing them as they are named. She then asks the function or purpose of each animal—for example, "Cows give milk for the farmer to sell." The group sings "Old MacDonald Had a Farm" and "The Farmer in the Dell."

The teacher and children discuss plans for the rest of the day and the work children will choose during their free times. The teacher reminds the children to look for messages on the notice board and to leave messages there for friends.

9:30–9:50

Whole-group language arts lesson. The class makes its fourth book about animals. Thus far they have completed one each for pet, zoo, and woodland animals; this one covers farm animals. The teacher asks each child which animal he or she will draw and tries to include as many animals as possible from the list just completed. The teacher asks the children to write sentences, stories, or simply names connected with their animals. Children who finish early can choose to write to pen pals, write messages for the notice board, copy from charts, or ask the teacher for help with their writing. Children who are hesitant to write are encouraged to dictate to the teacher, who provides a writing model for them.

9:50–10:45

Conference period or small-group work. The teacher reminds the children that most of them will work independently, alone or with friends, during conference time. Each child's individual folder holds a contract suggesting individual activities to complete. Children use the literacy, math, and science centers. They complete their page for the farm animal class book if they have not already done so.

The teacher meets with three or four children individually, tailoring work to their individual needs, interests, and abilities. For example:

Christopher has had little experience with books before coming to school. The teacher tries to provide him with experiences that many other children have already had at home. She continues a discussion begun at his last conference, encouraging him to differentiate print and pictures. She uses a book that is familiar to him, one she has read to him before. They talk about the book, pointing out its front and back. The teacher reads the story to Christopher, occasionally asking him to point out the print or the picture on a page, or where she should start to read on a new page. For his contract assignment, she asks Christopher to look at books and find their beginning and end, their print and pictures. Before Christopher leaves, she asks him if he would like a new word for his Very Own Word collection. If he does, she writes it for him on an index card.

Jim has had substantial experience with books. He is beginning to merge narrational reading and conventional reading. Jim has shown an interest in words and asks to have them identified. He likes to associate letters and sounds because it helps him become more independent in his reading. The teacher selects a familiar story, *Are You My Mother?* (Eastman, 1960) and asks Jim to read it. He uses the intonation of conventional reading and looks at the print as he narrates the story. In particularly predictable parts he attends to the print, a behavior the teacher encourages. She asks him to point out the words *Are you my mother?* wherever the main characters say them in the story. When Jim is finished reading the story the teacher asks, "If you were the baby bird, would you have looked for your mother or just waited for her?" and follows his response with "Why?" For his contract assignment, she asks Jim to read three familiar storybooks and write down all the words he recognizes in print. Before he leaves, she asks if he would like a new word for his Very Own Word collection.

Jennifer has had little experience with writing materials at home and is reluctant to try to write. The teacher initiates a discussion of the child's family. She knows a new baby has just arrived. The baby's name is Joseph. The teacher asks Jennifer if she would like to write something about her new brother. Jennifer responds that she can't write. The teacher explains that she doesn't have to write like a grownup but that children can write in their own ways. The teacher shows Jennifer samples of other children's writing, which include invented spelling, random letters, and scribble writing. Jennifer responds that she would like to write Joseph's name but she can't do it. Because of Jennifer's reluctance, the teacher writes the name *Joseph* on an index card and asks Jennifer if she can copy some of it. Jennifer copies the *J* and comments that it is the first letter of her name, too. As a contract activity, the teacher asks Jennifer to draw a picture of her new brother and to think of things she would like to say about him and try to write them in her own way. The word *Joseph* becomes Jennifer's new Very Own Word.

10:15–10:45

Free play. Children may select activities in any area in the room. This is the only time during the day that blocks, art, workbench, and dramatic-play areas are open. Items that incorporate the animal theme have been added to the areas. The dramatic-play area is set up as a veterinarian's office, with typical signs such as *No smoking* and *Doctor Is In [or Out]*. There are pictures of pets with their names, waiting room magazines, pamphlets on animal health, appointment pads, a telephone and directory, prescription pads, and health charts. The classroom pets and stuffed animals serve as patients; students role-play the doctor, nurse, secretary, and pet owner.

The block corner is set up as a zoo. It includes tickets for admission, posters of zoo animals with their names, pamphlets and brochures about a real zoo, and pamphlets on zoo animals. Children use figures of zoo animals as they construct a zoo from the blocks. Typical signs include the name of the zoo, *Don't Feed the Animals, I Bite, Petting Zoo, Pony Rides,* and signs identifying various animals.

The art center offers on a large chart a simple recipe for play dough, to be used for making animals. The ingredients and equipment are laid out. The teacher is there to offer assistance.

How to Make Play Dough

Put 2 cups of flour into a bowl.
Add 1 cup of water.
Add 1 tablespoon of salt.
Add 1 teaspoon of food coloring of your choice.
Mix together with your hands till it feels like play dough.
If it is too sticky, add more salt.
If it is too dry, add 1 tablespoon of water.
If it is too wet, add 1 tablespoon of flour.

Each child in the art center who makes a piece of play dough then shapes it into an animal of his or her choice. Conversation is encouraged as the children follow the recipe, discuss textures, and create their animals. It is advisable that an adult be available for supervision.

The social studies center is set up with materials that focus on farm and woodland animals. It includes a store for selling farm products such as eggs, milk, vegetables, and wool. Also included are signs (Fresh Farm Products, Open, Closed), a cash register, order pads, shopping lists, name and price tags for various products, food posters, bags for groceries, play money, and markers for pricing food.
10:45–11:00

Cleanup and snack. Children receive animal crackers with juice, and conversation is encouraged.
11:00–11:30

Storybook reading. The teacher has selected *The Little Red Hen* for a shared book reading. She tells the story, using felt figures on a felt-board, and asks the children to participate every time the animal characters say, "Not I." After telling the story she uses a Big Book to review the pages and points out the words *Not I*. She asks the children if they think the little red hen is right in not sharing her bread with the other animals, and why. She asks if there are other ideas for ending the story. She then leads the children into an independent reading and writing period and says that the Big Book and the felt figures for the story will be in the library corner for those who want to use them.

11:30–12:15

Independent reading and writing. Featured on the open-faced bookshelves are books dealing with farm, zoo, pet, and woodland animals. Animal puppets are available, as are taped stories about animals. The writing area includes animal pictures and word lists, plus all the usual materials needed for drawing and writing. The language arts manipulatives include animal puzzles, labeled pictures of animals that can be alphabetized, animal Lotto, animal dominoes, a concentration card game on animals, and animal sewing cards. Although children may participate in any activities in the literacy center during this period, they are encouraged to use books during the period and to write a few times a week. The special writing project this week is making a book about animals, either a book about one of the four types under study or a book about all four. Children are encouraged to use their Very Own Words during this period and to ask for new ones.

12:15–1:15

Lunch and outdoor play. Part of the outside play area has been turned into a farm where seeds can be planted and vegetables grown. Markers identify plantings, and other signs say *Careful* and *Don't Step on the Plants*.

1:15–1:45

Whole-group lesson in science or social studies. The class discusses its upcoming trip to a farm. With the teacher using an experience chart, the class lists things to remember for the trip: behavior reminders, safety rules, spending money and lunch, animals of particular interest, things they would like to see or do at the farm, questions to ask the farmer. Each child is encouraged to think of a question accompanied by a picture that will be sent to the farmer in advance so he will know what to discuss when the class visits.

1:45–2:15

Center time. The literacy, science, social studies, and math centers are open. At the science center a special project has been set up for churning butter. If possible, have cream and a churn available. If not, five or six children with an adult supervisor can make butter by following a simple recipe posted on a large chart; materials and ingredients should be at hand. Each day, five or six other children can be assigned to the center for this activity.

Recipe for Making Butter

Two children work together.
Take one baby food jar.
Fill it halfway with whipping cream.
Place the lid on the jar tightly.
Take turns shaking the jar briskly for a total of five minutes.
Let it stand for a few minutes and pour off the liquid.
Run cold water over the butter and pour off the water.
Add a little salt, spread on a cracker, and eat.

The teacher may meet with small groups or individuals to help with particular needs or projects, or read to small groups during this time.
2:15–2:50

Circle time and review of the day. Several children share items from home that are related to farm, pet, zoo, or woodland animals. They are encouraged to speak in sentences. Other children share on other days. The teacher displays work that students have prepared earlier in the day for the class book on animals. With an alphabet chart visible, she suggests that the book be assembled in alphabetical order and leads the children as they do so in a whole-group activity. Student Authors of the Day are asked to share their part of the letter that will go to the farmer before the class visit to the farm. With a few children sharing each day, over the course of a week each child will have shared some writing. Children also take turns telling about good books they have read. The day's activities are reviewed, with children commenting on things they liked or did not like and things they accomplished or still have to do. As a large-motor musical activity, children listen to music, decide which animals the music brings to mind, then act out how those animals might move, walking like elephants, jumping like kangaroos, waddling like ducks, and so forth. The class sings "Go Tell Aunt Rhody." The words to the song have been posted on a chart, and the teacher points to each word as it is sung. She then reads and displays a book version of the song to end the day.
2:50–3:00

Preparation for dismissal. Dismissal.

ACTIVITIES

1. Select a unit topic other than animals for social studies or science. Prepare a room environment with materials that promote literacy in different content area centers based on the topic. Specifically address what will be available in the dramatic-play and block areas.

2. Outline a preschool or kindergarten day different from the one described in the chapter, but include activities that encourage oral language, reading, and writing development.
3. Outline a unit of study on Thanksgiving. List activities to carry out in all content areas—social studies, science, math, music, and art. Be sure that each activity includes practice in or motivation for the use of reading, writing, or oral language.

Afterword

This volume has presented a theory- and research-based program for developing emergent literacy in early childhood. It has emphasized the importance of literacy-rich environments; social interaction; peer interaction; and whole-class, small-group, and individual learning with adult guidance. The activities suggested underscore the concurrent, integrated nature of learning how to use oral language, reading, and writing. The volume has outlined education that is functional and related to real-life experiences and is thus meaningful and interesting to the child. It has provided for the integration of literacy activities and content areas, which adds enthusiasm, motivation, and meaning. It has suggested careful monitoring of individual growth through direct instruction and frequent assessment using multiple measures and allowing ample space for children to learn through play, manipulation, and exploration.

The program described in this volume is meant to be enjoyable for both teachers and children. Enjoyment allows the teacher to work with vigor and enthusiasm. Enjoyment allows the child to associate literacy with a school environment that is natural, pleasurable, positive, and imbued with success. Such an environment ensures a lifelong desire to refine and use literacy skills. The program is designed to help this generation "reignite our romance with the written word" (Spielberg, 1987).

BIBLIOGRAPHY

ALLEN, R. V. (1976). *Language experience in communication.* Boston: Houghton Mifflin.

ALTWERGER, A., DIEHL-FAXON, J., and DOCKSTADER-ANDERSON K. (1985). Reading aloud events as meaning construction. *Language Arts, 62,* 476–484.

ANDERSON, A., and STOKES, S. (1984). Social and institutional influences on the development and practice of literacy. In H. Goelman, A. Oberg, and F. Smith, (eds.), *Awakening to literacy.* Exeter, N.H.: Heinemann Educational Books.

ANDERSON, R. C., HIEBERT, E. H., SCOTT, J.A., and WILKINSON, I. A. G. (1985). *Becoming a nation of readers.* Washington, D.C.: National Institute of Education.

ANDERSON, R. C., MASON, J., and SHIRLEY, L. (1984). The reading group: An experimental investigation of a labyrinth. *Reading Research Quarterly, 20,* 6–38.

ANDERSON, R. C., WILSON, P. T., and FIELDING, L. G. (1985, December). A new focus on free-reading. Symposium presentation at the National Reading Conference, San Diego.

APPLEBEE, A. N., and LANGER, J. A. (1983). Instructional scaffolding: Reading and writing as natural language activities. *Language Arts, 60,* 168–175.

ARBUTHNOT, M. H., and SUTHERLAND, Z. (1977). *Children and books* (5th ed.). Glenview, Ill.: Scott, Foresman.

ASHTON-WARNER, S. (1959). *Spinster.* New York: Simon & Schuster.

ASHTON-WARNER, S. (1963). *Teacher.* New York: Bantam.

ATHEY, I. (1971). Synthesis of papers on language development and reading. *Reading Research Quarterly, 7,* 9–16.

BADEN, M. J. P. (1981). A comparison of composition scores of third grade children with reading skills, pre-kindergarten verbal ability, self-concept, and sex. *Dissertation Abstracts International, 42,* 1517A.

BAGHBAN, M. (1984). *Our daughter learns to read and write.* Newark, Del.: International Reading Association.

BAUMANN, J. F. (1984). The effectiveness of a direct instruction paradigm for teaching main idea comprehension. *Reading Research Quarterly, 20,* 93–115.

BECKMAN, D. (1972). Interior space: The things of education. *National Elementary Principal, 52,* 45–49.

BEMELMANS, L. (1939). *Madeline.* New York: Viking.

BEMELMANS, L. (1953). *Madeline's rescue.* New York: Viking.

BIEHLER, R. F. (1976). *Child development: An introduction.* Boston: Houghton Mifflin.

BIPPUS, A. C. (1977). The relationship of the quality of students' written and reading comprehension in grades four and six. *Dissertation Abstracts International, 38,* 3993A.

BIRNBAUM, J. (1981). A study of reading and writing behaviors of selected fourth grade and seventh grade students. Doctoral dissertation, Rutgers University.

BIRNBAUM, J., and EMIG, J. (1983). Creating minds: Created texts. In R. Parker and F. Davis, (eds.), *Developing literacy: Young children's use of language.* Newark, Del.: International Reading Association.

BISSETT, D. (1969). The amount and effect of recreational reading in selected fifth grade classes. Doctoral dissertation, Syracuse University.

BISSETT, D. (1970). The usefulness of children's books in the reading program. In J. Catterson (ed.), *Children and literature.* Newark, Del.: International Reading Association.

BISSEX, G. (1980). *GNYS at work: A child learns to write and read.* Cambridge, Mass.: Harvard University Press.

BLOOM, B. (1964). *Stability and change in human characteristics.* New York: John Wiley.

BLOOM, B. (1972) *Language development: Form and function in emerging grammars.* Cambridge, Mass.: MIT Press.

Book Industry Study Group. (1984). *The 1983 consumer research study on reading and book publishing.* New York.

BOORSTIN, D. (1984). Letter of transmittal. In *Books in our future: A report from the Librarian of Congress to the Congress.* Washington, D.C.: U. S. Congress, Joint Committee on the Library.

BRENNER, B. (1972). *The three little pigs.* New York: Random House.

BRIGGS, C., and ELKIND, D. (1973). Cognitive development in early readers. *Developmental Psychology, 9,* 279–280.

BRITTON, J. (1982). *Retrospect and prospect.* Upper Montclair, N.J.: Boynton/Cook. (a)

BRITTON, J. (1982). The spectator role and the beginnings of writing. In M. Nystrand (ed.),

What writers know: The language, process and structure of written discourse. New York: Academic Press. (b)

BRITTON, J. (1983). Writing and the story world. In B. Kroll and G. Wells (eds.), *Explorations in the development of writing: Theory, research and practice.* Chichester, England: John Wiley.

BROWN, A. (1975). Recognition, reconstruction and recall of narrative sequences of preoperational children. *Child Development, 46,* 155–166.

BROWN, M. (1939). *The noisy book.* New York: Harper.

BROWN, M. (1957). *The three billy goats gruff.* New York: Harcourt, Brace.

BROWN, R. (1973). *A first language: The early stages.* Cambridge, Mass.: Harvard University Press.

BROWN, R., and BELLUGI, U. (1964). Three processes in the child's acquisition of syntax. *Harvard Educational Review, 34,* 133–151.

BROWN, R., CAZDEN, C., and BELLUGI-KLIMA, U. (1968). The child's grammar from one to three. In J. P. Hill (ed.), *Minnesota symposium on child development.* Minneapolis: University of Minnesota Press.

BRUNNER, J. (1975). The ontogenesis of speech acts. *Journal of Child Language, 3,* 1–19.

BUMSTED, L. A. (1981). Influencing the frequency of children's cooperative and learning task-related behavior through change in the design and management of the classroom. Master's thesis, Cornell University.

BURTON, V. L. (1943). *Katy and the big snow.* Boston: Houghton Mifflin.

BUSHNER, D. E. (1979). The relationship between the reading comprehension ability of seventh grade subjects and the syntactic complexity of their written language. *Dissertation Abstracts International, 40,* 4978A.

CALKINS, L. M. (1983). *Lessons from a child: On the teaching and learning of writing.* Exeter, N.H.: Heinemann Educational Books.

CALKINS, L. M. (1986). *The art of teaching writing.* Exeter, N.H.: Heinemann Educational Books.

CAMBOURNE, B. (1984). "Language, learning and literacy," in *Towards a Reading-Writing Classroom* by A. Butler and J. Turbill. Primary Teaching Association. Exeter, N.H.: Heineman Educational Books.

CAREY, M. (1972). *Peter Pan.* New York: Random House.

CARLE, E. (1969). *The very hungry caterpillar.* New York: Philomel.

CARROLL, LEWIS, pseud. (Charles L. Dodgon) Alice's adventues in wonderland, N.Y.: Macmillan, 1963 (1865).

CAZDEN, C. (1972). *Child language and education.* New York: Holt, Rinehart & Winston.

CHALL, J. S., CONRAD, S. S., and HARRIS-SHARPLES, S. H. (1983). *Textbooks and challenges: An inquiry into textbook difficulty, reading achievement, and knowledge acquisition.* Final Report to the Spencer Foundation. Chicago Ill.

CHOMSKY, C. (1965). *Aspects of a theory of syntax.* Cambridge, Mass.: MIT Press.

CHOMSKY, C. (1969). *The acquisition of syntax in children from five to ten.* Cambridge, Mass.: MIT Press.

CHOMSKY, C. (1972). Stages in language development and reading. *Harvard Educational Review, 42,* 1–33.

CHUKOVSKY, K. (1963). *From two to five.* Berkeley: University of California Press.

CLARK, M. M. (1976). *Young fluent readers.* London: Heinemann Educational Books.

CLARK, M. M. (1984). Literacy at home and at school: Insights from a study of young fluent readers. In H. Goelman, A. Oberg, and F. Smith (eds.), *Awakening to literacy.* Exeter, N.H.: Heinemann Educational Books.

CLAY, M. M. (1966). *Emergent reading behavior.* Doctoral dissertation, University of Auckland.

CLAY, M. M. (1972). *Reading: The patterning of complex behavior.* Auckland: Heinemann Educational Books.

CLAY, M. M. (1975). *What did I write?* Auckland: Heinemann Educational Books.

CLAY, M. M. (1979). *Reading: The patterning of complex behavior* (2nd ed.). Auckland: Heinemann Educational Books. (a)

CLAY, M. M. (1979). *The early detection of reading difficulties: A diagnostic survey with recovery procedures.* Auckland: Heinemann Educational Books. (b)

COCHRAN-SMITH, M. (1984). *The making of a reader.* Norwood, N.J.: Ablex Publishing Corp.

COHEN, D. (1968). The effects of literature on vocabulary and reading achievement. *Elementary English, 45,* 209–213, 217.

COODY, B. (1973). *Using literature with young children.* Dubuque, Iowa: Wm. C. Brown.

CULLINAN, B. E. (1977). Books in the life of a young child. In B. Cullinan and C. Carmichael (eds.), *Literature and young children.* Urbana, Ill.: National Council of Teachers of English.

CULLINAN, B. E. (Ed.) (1987). *Children's Literature in the Reading Program.* Newark, Del: International Reading Association.

CULLINAN, B. E. (1989). *Literature and the child* (2nd ed.) New York: Harcourt, Brace, Jovanovich, Inc.

DANFORD, H. (1973). The effects of purposeful reading upon comprehension of and interest in social studies materials. Doctoral dissertation, Temple University.

DEAN, J. (1977). Peter, Peter, pumpkin eater. In *Dean's Mother Goose book of rhymes.* London: Dean & Son.

DEPAOLA, T. (1973). *Charlie needs a clock.* Englewood Cliffs, N.J.: Prentice-Hall.

DEWEY, J. (1966). *Democracy and education.* New York: Free Press.

DEWITZ, P., and STAMMER, J. (1980). The development of linguistic awareness in young children from label reading to world reading. Paper presented at the Annual Meeting of the National Reading Conference, San Diego.

DOWNING, J. (1970). The development of linguistic concepts in children's thinking. *Research in the Teaching of English, 4,* 5–19.

DURKIN, D. (1966). *Children who read early.* New York: Teachers College Press.

DUVOISIN, R. (1950). *Petunia.* New York: Knopf.

DYSON, A. H. (1983). The role of oral language in early writing processes. *Research in the Teaching of English, 17,* 1–30.

DYSON, A. H. (1985). Individual differences in emerging writing. In M. Farr (ed.), *Advances in writing research: Vol. 1: Children's early writing development.* Norwood, N.J.: Ablex Publishing Corp.

DYSON, A. H. (1986). Children's early interpretations of writing: Expanding research perspectives. In D. Yoden and S. Templeton (eds.), *Metalinguistic awareness and beginning literacy.* Exeter, N.H.: Heinemann Educational Books.

EASTMAN, P. D. (1960). *Are you my mother?* New York: Random House.

EHRI, L. C. (1979). Linguistic insight: Threshold of reading acquisition. In T. G. Waller and G. E. MacKinnon (eds.), *Reading research: Advances in theory and practice* (Vol. 1). New York: Academic Press.

EMBERLEY, B. (1967). *Drummer Hoff.* Englewood Cliffs, N.J.: Prentice-Hall.

EVANECHKO, P., OLLILA, L., and ARMSTRONG, R. (1974). An investigation of the relationships between children's performance in written language and their reading ability. *Research in the Teaching of English, 8,* 315–326.

FERREIRO, E. (1978). What is written in a written sentence? *Journal of Education, 160,* 24–39.

FERREIRO, E., and TEBEROSKY, A. (1982). *Literacy before schooling.* Exeter, N.H.: Heinemann Educational Books.

FLACK, M. (1932). *Ask Mr. Bear.* New York: Macmillan.

FLOOD, J. (1977). Parental styles in reading episodes with young children. *Reading Teacher, 30,* 864–867.

FOSTER, C. R. (1982). Diffusing the issues in bilingualism and bilingual education. *Phi Delta Kappan, 63,* 338–345.

FROEBEL, F. (1974). *The education of man.* Clifton, N.J.: Augustus M. Kelly.

FUJIKAWA, A. (1980). *Jenny learns a lesson.* New York: Grosset & Dunlap.

GALDONE, P. (1973). *The little red hen.* Boston: Houghton Mifflin.

GAMBRELL, L., PFEIFFER, W., and WILSON, R. (1985). The effect of retelling upon comprehension and recall of text information. *Journal of Educational Research, 78,* 216–220.

GENISHI, C., and DYSON, A. (1984). *Language assessment in the early years.* Norwood, N.J.: Ablex Publishing Corp.

GESELL, A. (1925). *The mental growth of the preschool child.* New York: Macmillan.

GIBSON, E., and LEVIN, H. (1975). *The psychology of reading.* Cambridge, Mass.: MIT Press.

GILLIAN, Strickland. (1936). The Reading Mother. in *Best Loved Poems of American People* Ed. H. Felleman, N.Y.: Doubleday.

GLAZER, S. M. (1980). *Getting Ready to Read: Creating readers from birth through six.* Englewood Cliffs, N. J.: Prentice-Hall.

GLAZER, S. M., and SEARFOSS, L. (1988). *Reading diagnosis and instruction: A C–A–L–M approach.* Englewood Cliffs, N.J.: Prentice-Hall.

GONZALES-MENA, J. (1976). English as a second language for preschool children. *Young Children, 32,* 14–20.

GOODMAN, K. S. (1967). Reading: A psycholinguistic guessing game. *Journal of the Reading Specialist, 4,* 126–135.

GOODMAN, Y. (1980). The roots of literacy. In M. Douglas (ed.), *Claremont Reading Conference forty-fourth yearbook.* Claremont, Calif.: Claremont Reading Conference.

GOODMAN, Y. (1984). The development of initial literacy. In H. Goelman, A. Oberg, and F. Smith (eds.), *Awakening to literacy.* Exeter, N.H.: Heinemann Educational Books.

GOODMAN, Y. (1986). Children coming to know literacy. In W. H. Teale and E. Sulzby (eds.), *Emergent literacy: Writing and reading.* Norwood, N.J.: Ablex Publishing Corp.

GOODMAN, Y., and ALTWERGER, B. (1981). *Print awareness in preschool children: A study of the development of literacy in preschool children* (Occasional Paper 4). Tucson: University of Arizona, College of Education, Arizona Center for Research and Development, Program in Language and Literacy.

GRAVES, D., and HANSEN, J. (1983). The author's chair. *Language Arts, 60,* 176–183.

GRAVES, D. H. (1983). *Writing: Teachers and children at work.* Exeter N.H.: Heinemann Educational Books.

GREANEY, V. (1980). Factors related to amount and type of leisure reading. *Reading Research Quarterly, 15,* 337–357.

GREEN, J. (1985). Children's writing in an elementary school postal system. In M. Farr (ed.), *Advances in writing research: Vol. 1. Children's early writing development.* Norwood, N.J.: Ablex Publishing Corp.

GRIEVE, R., and HOOGENRAAD, R. (1979). First words. In M. Garmen (ed.), *Language acquisition: Studies in first language development.* Cambridge: Cambridge University Press.

GRIMMER, F. L. (1970). The effects of an experimental program in written composition on the writing of second-grade children. *Dissertation Abstracts International, 31,* 5666A.

GUNDLACH, R., McLANE, J., SCOTT, F., and McNAMEE, G. (1985). The social foundations of early writing development. In M. Farr (ed.), *Advances in writing research: Vol. 1. Children's early writing development.* Norwood, N.J.: Ablex Publishing Corp.

HALL, M. A.. (1976). *Teaching reading as a language experience.* Columbus, Ohio: Chas. E. Merrill.

HALLIDAY, M. A. K. (1975). *Learning how to mean: Exploration in the development of language.* London: Edward Arnold.

HANSEN, J. S. (1969). The impact of the home literacy environment on reading attitude. *Elementary English, 46,* 17–24.

HARDY, B. (1968). Toward a poetics of fiction: An approach through narrative. In *The novel: A forum on fiction.* Providence: Brown University Press.

HARRIS, L., and SMITH, L. (1980). *Reading instruction and diagnostic teaching in the classroom* (3rd ed.). New York: Holt, Rinehart & Winston.

HARSTE, J., WOODWARD, V., and BURKE, C. (1984). *Language stories and literacy lessons.* Exeter, N.H.: Heinemann Educational Books.

HEATH, S. B. (1980). The function and uses of literacy. *Journal of Communication, 30,* 123–133.

HEATH, S. B. (1982). What no bedtime story means. *Language in Society, 11,* 49–76.

HEATH, S. B. (1983). *Ways with words.* New York: Oxford University Press.

HIEBERT, E. H. (1978). Preschool children's understanding of written language. *Child Development, 49,* 1231–1234.

HIEBERT, E. H. (1981). Developmental patterns and interrelationships of preschool children's print awareness. *Reading Research Quarterly, 16,* 236–260.

HIEBERT, E. (1986). Using environmental print in beginning reading instruction. In M. R. Sampson (ed.), *The pursuit of literacy: Early reading and writing.* Dubuque, Iowa: Kendall/Hunt.

HIPPLE, M. (1985). Journal writing in kindergarten. *Language Arts, 62,* 255–261.

HITTLEMAN, D. (1983). *Developmental reading: A psycholinguistic perspective.* Chicago: Rand McNally.

HOBAN, R. (1960). *Bedtime for Frances.* New York: Harper & Row Publishers.
HOBAN, R (1964). *Bread and jam for Frances.* New York: Harper & Row Publishers.
HOLDAWAY, D. (1979). *The foundations of literacy.* Sydney: Ashton Scholastic.
HOLDAWAY, D.(1986). The structure of natural learning as a basis for literacy instruction. In M. Sampson (ed.), *The pursuit of literacy: Early reading and writing.* Dubuque, Iowa: Kendall/Hunt.
HOLDSWORTH, W. (1968). *The Gingerbread Boy.* New York: Farrar, Straus & Giroux.
HUCK, C. (1976). *Children's literature in the elementary school* (3rd ed.). New York: Holt, Rinehart & Winston.
HUNT, K. W. (1970). *Syntactic maturity in children and adults.* Monograph of the Society for Research in Child Development (Vol. 25). Chicago: University of Chicago Press.
IRA (International Reading Association). (1985). *Literacy development and pre–first grade.* Newark, Del.
IRVING, A. (1980). *Promoting voluntary reading for children and young people.* Paris: UNESCO.
IZAWA, T. (1968). *Goldilocks and the three bears.* New York: Grosset & Dunlap. (a).
IZAWA, T. (1968). *The little red hen.* New York: Grosset & Dunlap. (b).
JAGGER, A. (1985). Allowing for language differences. In G. S. Pinnell (ed.) *Discovering language with children.* Urbana, Ill.: National Council of Teachers of English.
JEWELL, M., and ZINTZ, M. (1986). *Learning to read naturally.* Dubuque, Iowa: Kendall/Hunt.
JOHNSON, C. (1955). *Harold and the purple crayon.* New York: Harper & Row Publishers.
KEATS, E. (1962). *The snowy day.* New York: Viking.
KEATS, E. (1966). *Jenny's hat.* New York: Harper & Row Publishers.
KEATS, E. (1967). *Peter's chair.* New York: Harper & Row Publishers.
KEATS, E. (1971). *Over in the meadow.* New York: Scholastic Book Services.
KING, E. M., and FRIESEN, D. T. (1972). Children who read in kindergarten. *Alberta Journal of Educational Research, 18,* 147–161.
KOCH, A., and PEDEN, W. (eds.). (1974). *The life and selected writings of Thomas Jefferson.* New York: Random House.
KRESS, G. (1982). *Learning to write.* Sydney: Oxford University Press.
KRIPPNER, S. (1963). The boy who read at eighteen months. *Exceptional Child, 30,* 105–109.
LAMME, L. (1981). *Learning to love literature: Preschool through grade 3.* Urbana, Ill.: National Council of Teachers of English.
LEICHTER, H. P. (1984). Families as environments for literacy. In H. Goelman, A. Oberg, and F. Smith (eds.), *Awakening to literacy.* Exeter, N.H.: Heinemann Educational Books.
LENNENBERG, E. (1967). *Biological foundations of language.* New York: John Wiley.
LENNENBERG, E., and KAPLAN, E. (1970). Grammatical structures and reading. In H. Levin and J. Williams (eds.), *Basic studies in reading.* New York: Basic Books.
LENSKI, L. (1965). *The little farm.* New York: Henry Z. Walek.
LESIEG, T. (1961). *Ten apples up on top.* New York: Random House.
LINDEN, M., and WITTROCK, M. C. (1981). The teaching of reading comprehension according to the model of generative learning. *Reading Research Quarterly, 17,* 44–57.
LIONNI, L. (1963). *Swimmy.* New York: Pantheon.
LOBAN, W. (1976). *Language development: Kindergarten through grade twelve.* Urbana, Ill.: National Council of Teachers of English.
MCCLOSKEY, R. (1948). *Blueberries for Sal.* New York: Viking.
MCCORMICK, C., and MASON, J. (1981). What happens to kindergarten children's knowledge about reading after summer vacation? *Reading Teacher, 35,* 164–172.
MCCRACKEN, M., and MCCRACKEN, J. (1972). *Reading is only the tiger's tail.* San Rafael, Calif.: Leswing Press.
MCGOVERN, A. (1967). *Too much noise.* Boston: Houghton Mifflin.
MCGRAW, B., and GROTELEUSCHEN, A. (1972). Direction of the effect of questions in prose materials. *Journal of Educational Psychology, 63,* 580–588.
MCNEIL, D. (1970). *The acquisition of language: The study of developmental psycholinguistics.* New York: Harper & Row Publishers.
MANDLER, J., and JOHNSON, N. (1977). Remembrance of things parsed: Story structure and recall. *Cognitive Psychology, 9,* 111–151.
MARTINEZ, M., and TEALE, W. (1988). Reading in a kindergarten classroom library. *Reading Teacher, 41,* 6, 568–572.

MARTINEZ, M., and TEALE, W. (1987). The ins and outs of a kindergarten writing program. *Reading Teacher, 40,* 444–451.

MASON, J. (1977). *Reading readiness: A definition and skills hierarchy from preschoolers' developing conceptions of print* (Technical Report 59). Urbana: University of Illinois, Center for the Study of Reading.

MASON, J. (1980). When do children begin to read: An exploration of four year old children's letter and word reading competencies. *Reading Research Quarterly, 15,* 203–227.

MASON, J. (1982). Acquisition of knowledge about reading. Paper presented at the Annual Meeting of the American Educational Research Association, New York.

MASON, J. (1984). Early reading from a developmental perspective. In P. D. Pearson (ed.), *Handbook of reading research.* New York: Longman.

MASON, J. (1986). *Reading instruction for today.* Glenview, Ill.: Scott, Foresman.

MASON, J., and McCORMICK, C. (1981). *An investigation of pre-reading instruction: A developmental perspective* (Technical Report 224). Urbana: University of Illinois, Center for the Study of Reading.

MASON, J., STEWART, J., and DUNNING, D. (1986). *Testing kindergarten children's knowledge about reading* (Technical Report 368). Urbana: University of Illinois, Center for the Study of Reading.

MENYUK, P. (1977). *Language and maturation.* Cambridge, Mass.: MIT Press.

MITCHELL, J. N. (1984). Advantages and disadvantages of retelling for reading assessment. Presentation at the International Reading Association Conference, Atlanta.

MONTESSORI, M. (1965). *Spontaneous activity in education.* New York: Schocken Books.

MORPHETT, M. V., and WASHBURNE, C. (1931). When should children begin to read? *Elementary School Journal, 31,* 496–508.

MORRISON, G. S. (1984). *Early childhood education today* (3rd ed.). Columbus, Ohio: Chas. E. Merrill.

MORROW, L. M. (1978). Analysis of syntax in the language of six-, seven-, and eight-year-olds. *Research in the Teaching of English, 12,* 143–148.

MORROW, L. M. (1980). The parent corner. *Home ideas for reading. New Jersey Reading Association Newsletter.* Volume 2, 3–4.

MORROW, L. M. (1981). *Supertips for storytelling.* New York: Harcourt Brace Jovanovich, Inc. Instructor Books.

MORROW, L. M. (1982). Relationships between literature programs, library corner designs and children's use of literature. *Journal of Educational Research, 75,* 339–344.

MORROW, L. M. (1983). Home and school correlates of early interest in literature. *Journal of Educational Research, 76,* 221–230.

MORROW, L. M. (1984). Reading stories to young children: Effects of story structure and traditional questioning strategies on comprehension. *Journal of Reading Behavior, 16,* 273–288.

MORROW, L. M. (1985). *Promoting voluntary reading in school and home.* Bloomington, Ind.: Phi Delta Kappa Educational Foundation. (a)

MORROW, L. M. (1985). Retelling stories: A strategy for improving children's comprehension, concept of story structure and oral language complexity. *Elementary School Journal, 85,* 647–661. (b)

MORROW, L. M. (1986). Promoting responses to literature: Children's sense of story structure. Paper presented at the National Reading Conference, Austin, Tx. (a)

MORROW, L. M. (1986). *Promoting voluntary reading: A curriculum guide for reading rainbow program.* New York: WNET/13; Public Broadcasting Corporation. (b)

MORROW, L. M. (1987). The effects of one-to-one story readings on children's questions and comments. In S. Baldwin and J. Readance (eds.), *Thirty-sixth Yearbook of the National Reading Conference.* Rochester, N.Y. (a)

MORROW, L. M. (1987). Promoting voluntary reading: The effects of an inner city program in summer day care centers. *The Reading Teacher, 41,* 266–274. (b)

MORROW, L. M. (1988a). Young children's responses to one-to-one story readings in school settings. *Reading Research Quarterly, 23,* 1, 89–107.

MORROW, L. M. (1988b). Retelling as a diagnostic tool. In S. M. Glazer, L. W. Searfoss &

L. Gentile, (eds.). *Re-examining reading diagnosis: New trends and procedures in classrooms and clinics.* Newark, Del.: International Reading Association.

MORROW, L. M., and WEINSTEIN, C. S. (1982). Increasing children's use of literature through program and physical design changes. *Elementary School Journal, 83,* 131–137.

MORROW, L. M., and WEINSTEIN, C. S. (1986). Encouraging voluntary reading: The impact of a literature program on children's use of library centers. *Reading Research Quarterly, 21,* 330–346.

NEWMAN, J. (1984). *The craft of children's writing.* Exeter, N.H.: Heinemann Educational Books.

NEWMAN, J. (ed.) (1985). *Whole language: Theory in use.* Exeter, N.H.: Heinemann Educational Books.

NINIO, A. (1980). Picture book reading in mother–infant dyads belonging to two subgroups in Israel. *Child Development, 51,* 587–590.

NINIO, A., and BRUNNER, J. (1978). The achievement and antecedents of labeling. *Journal of Child Language, 5,* 1–15.

PARKER, R. (1983). Language development and learning to write. In R. Parker and F. Davis (eds.), *Developing literacy: Young children's use of language.* Newark, Del.: International Reading Association.

PEARSON, P. D., HANSON, J., and GORDON, C. (1979). Effects of background knowledge on young children's comprehension of explicit and implicit information. *Journal of Reading Behavior, 11,* 201–209.

PELLEGRINI, A., and GALDA, L. (1982). The effects of thematic fantasy play training on the development of children's story comprehension. *American Educational Research Journal, 19,* 443–452.

PFLAUM, S. (1986). *The development of language and literacy in young children* (3rd ed.). Columbus, Ohio: Chas. E. Merrill.

PHYFE-PERKINS, E. (1979). Application of the behavior–person–environment paradigm to the analysis and evaluation of early childhood education programs. Doctoral dissertation, University of Massachusetts.

PIAGET, J., and INHELDER, B. (1969). *The psychology of the child.* New York: Basic Books.

PIPER, W. (1954). *The little engine that could.* New York: Platt & Munk.

PLESSAS, G. P., and OAKES, C. R. (1964). Prereading experiences of selected early readers. *Reading Teacher, 17,* 241–245.

POTTER, B. (1902). *The tale of Peter Rabbit.* New York: Scholastic Book Services.

PRESCOTT, O. (1965). *A father reads to his child: An anthology of prose and poetry.* New York: Dutton.

QUAKENBUSH, R. (1972). *Old MacDonald had a farm.* New York: Lippincott.

QUAKENBUSH, R. (1973). *Go tell Aunt Rhody.* New York: Lippincott.

READ, C. (1971). Pre-school children's knowledge of English phonology. *Harvard Educational Review, 41,* 1–34.

READ, C. (1975). *Children's categorization of speech sounds in English* (National Research Report 17). Urbana, Ill. National Council of Teachers of English.

REY, H. A. (1941). *Curious George.* Boston: Houghton Mifflin.

RICHARDS, J. (1979). Adjunct post questions in text: A critical review of methods and processes. *Review of Educational Research, 49,* 181–196.

ROBINSON, V., STRICKLAND, D., and CULLINAN, B. (1977). The child: Ready or not? In L. Ollila (ed.), *The kindergarten child and reading.* Newark, Del.: International Reading Association.

ROSEN, H., and ROSEN, C. (1973). *The language of primary school children.* London: Penguin Education.

ROSENTHAL, B. A. (1973). *An ecological study of free play in the nursery school.* Doctoral dissertation, Wayne State University.

ROSER, N., and MARTINEZ, M. (1985). Roles adults play in preschool responses to literature. *Language Arts, 62,* 485–490.

ROUSSEAU, J. (1962). *Emile.* ed. and trans. William Boyd. New York: Columbia University Teachers College.

RUDDELL, R. (1971). *Oral language and development of other language skills: Listening and speaking.* London: Macmillan.

RUSK, R., and SCOTLAND, J. (1979). *Doctrines of the great educators.* New York: St. Martin's Press.

SCHICKEDANZ, J. (1986). *More than ABC's: The early stages of reading and writing.* Washington, D.C.: National Association for the Education of Young Children.

SCHICKEDANZ, J. A. (1978). Please read that story again: Exploring relationships between story reading and learning to read. *Young Children, 33,* 48–55.

Scholastic Big Books. (1986). Toronto: Scholastic–TAB Publications.

SEEFELDT, C., and BARBOUR, N. (1986). *Early childhood education: An introduction.* Columbus, Ohio: Chas. E. Merrill.

SENDAK, M. (1962). *Chicken soup with rice.* New York: Harper & Row, Publishers.

SENDAK, M. (1963). *Where the wild things are.* New York: Harper & Row, Publishers.

SEUSS, DR. (1940). *Horton hatches the egg.* New York: Random House.

SEUSS, DR. (1957). *How the Grinch stole Christmas.* New York: Random House.

SEUSS, DR. (1960). *Green eggs with ham.* New York: Random House.

SEUSS, DR. (1970). *Mr. Brown can moo! can you?* New York: Random House.

SHURE, M. B. (1963). Psychological ecology of a nursery school. *Child Development, 34,* 979–992.

SKINNER, B. F. (1957). *Verbal behavior.* Boston: Appleton-Century-Crofts.

SLOBODKINA, E. (1947). *Caps for sale.* Reading, MA: Addison-Wesley.

SMITH, F. (1971). *Understanding reading.* New York: Holt, Rinehart & Winston.

SMITH, F. (1972). The learner and his language. In R. Hodges and E. H. Rudorf, (eds.) *Language and learning to read.* Boston: Houghton Mifflin.

SMITH, F. (1973). *Psycholinguistics and reading.* New York: Holt, Rinehart & Winston.

SMITH, F. (1978). *Understanding reading* (2nd ed.). New York: Holt, Rinehart & Winston.

SMITH, F. (1983). A metaphor for literacy: Creating words or shunting information? In F. Smith, *Essays into literacy.* Exeter, N.H.: Heinemann Educational Books.

SMITH, J. A., and PARKER, M. (1977). *Words music and word magic: Children's literature methods.* Newton, Mass.: Allyn & Bacon.

SNOW, C., and PERLMANN, R. (1985). Assessing children's knowledge about bookreading. In L. Galda and A. Pelligrini (eds.), *Play, language, and stories.* Norwood, N.J.: Ablex Publishing Corp.

SNOW, C. E. (1983). Literacy and language: Relationships during the preschool years. *Harvard Educational Review, 53,* 165–189.

SOUNDY, C. (1987). Effect of writing experiences in the expressive mode on children's reading comprehension and writing ability. Doctoral dissertation, Rutgers University.

SPIEGEL, D. L. (1981). *Reading for pleasure: Guidelines.* Newark, Del.: International Reading Association.

SPIELBERG, S. (1987). Acceptance speech at the Academy Award Ceremonies. Los Angeles.

STAUFFER, R. G. (1970). A reading teacher's dream come true. *Wilson Library Bulletin, 45,* 282–292.

STAUFFER, R. G. (1980). *The language-experience approach to the teaching of reading* (2nd ed.). New York: Harper & Row, Pub.

STEWART, J., BENJAMIN, L., and MASON, L. (1987). An early literacy program: Putting research into practice. Paper presented at the University of the Virgin Islands.

STEWIG, J. W. and SEBESTA, S. (eds.). (1978). *Using literature in the elementary classroom.* Urbana, Ill.: National Council of Teachers of English.

SULZBY, E. (1985). Children's emergent reading of favorite storybooks. *Reading Research Quarterly, 20,* 458–481.

SULZBY, E. (1986). Children's elicitation and use of metalinguistic knowledge about "word" during literacy interactions. In P. Yaden and S. Templeton, *Metalinguistic awareness and beginning literacy.* Exeter, N.H.: Heinemann Educational Books. (a)

SULZBY, E. (1986). Kindergarteners as writers and readers. In M. Farr (ed.), *Advances in writing research: Vol. 1. Children's early writing.* Norwood, N.J.: Ablex Publishing Corp. (b)

SULZBY, E. (1986). Writing and reading: Signs of oral and written language organization in the young child. In W. Teale and E. Sulzby (eds.), *Emergent literacy: Writing and reading.* Norwood, N.J.: Ablex Publishing Corp. (c)

SULZBY, E. (1987). Simplified Version of Sulzby's (1985) Classification Scheme for "Children's Emergent Reading of Favorite Storybooks." Paper presented at the International Reading Assocation Conference, Anaheim, Calif.

SULZBY, E., BARNHART, J., and HIESHIMA, J. Forms of writing and rereading from writing: A preliminary report. In J. Mason (ed.), *Reading/Writing Connections.* Boston: Allyn & Bacon, forthcoming.

SUTFIN, H. (1980). The effects on children's behavior of a change in the physical design of a kindergarten classroom. Doctoral dissertation, Boston University.

TAYLOR, D. (1983). *Family literacy.* Exeter, N.H.: Heinemann Educational Books.

TAYLOR, D. and STRICKLAND, D. (1986). *Family storybook reading.* Exeter, N.H.: Heinemann Educational Books.

TEALE, W. (1978). Positive environments for learning to read: What studies of early readers tell us. *Language Arts, 55,* 922–932.

TEALE, W. (1981). Parents reading to their children: What we know and need to know. *Language Arts, 58,* 902–911.

TEALE, W. (1982). Toward a theory of how children learn to read and write naturally. *Language Arts, 59,* 555–570.

TEALE, W. (1984). Reading to young children: Its significance for literacy development. In H. Goelman, A. Oberg, and F. Smith (eds.) *Awakening to literacy.* Exeter, N.H.: Heinemann Educational Books.

TEALE, W. (1986). The beginning of reading and writing: Written language development during the preschool and kindergarten years. In M. Sampson (ed.), *The pursuit of literacy: Early reading and writing.* Dubuque, Iowa: Kendall/Hunt.

TEALE, W. (1987). Emergent literacy: Reading and writing development in early childhood. In J. Readance and R. S. Baldwin (eds.), *Thirty-sxith Yearbook of the National Reading Conference.* Rochester, N.Y.

TEALE, W., HIEBERT, E., and CHITTENDEN, E. (1987). Assessing young children's literary development. *Reading Teacher, 40,* 772–778.

THORNDYKE, R. (1977). Cognitive structures in comprehension and memory of narrative discourse. *Cognitive Psychology, 9,* 77–110.

TOBIN, A. W. (1981). A multiple discriminant cross-validation of the factors associated with the development of precocious reading achievement. Doctoral dissertation, University of Delaware.

TORREY, J. (1969). Learning to read without a teacher. *Elementary English, 46,* 556–559.

TORVEY, D. R., and KERBER, J. E. (eds.). (1986). *Roles in literacy learning: A new perspective.* Newark, Del.: International Reading Association.

VEATCH, J., SAWICKI, F., ELLIOT, G., BARNETT, E., and BLACKEY, J. (1973). *Key words to reading: The language experience approach begins.* Columbus, Ohio: Chas. E. Merrill.

VIORST, J. (1972). *Alexander and the terrible, horrible, no good, very bad day.* New York: Atheneum.

VUKELICH, C., and GOLDEN, J. (1984). Early writing: Developmental teaching strategies. *Young Children, 38,* 3–5.

VYGOTSKY, L. S. (1978). *Mind in society: The development of psychological processes.* Cambridge, Mass.: Harvard University Press.

VYGOTSKY, L. S. (1981). The genesis of higher mental functions. In J. J. Wertsch (ed.), *The concept of activity.* White Plains, N.Y.: M. E. Sharpe.

WEINSTEIN, C. S. (1977). Modifying student behavior in an open classroom through changes in the physical design. *American Educational Research Journal, 14,* 249–262.

WELLS, G. (1986). *The meaning makers: Children learning language and using language to learn.* Exeter, N.H.: Heinemann Educational Books.

WESTCOTT, N. B. (1980). *I know an old lady.* Boston: Little, Brown.

WHITEHEAD, F., CAPEY, A. C., and MADDREN, W. (1975). *Children's reading interests.* London: Evans & Methuen.

WILLIAMS, J. P. (1985). The case for explicit decoding instruction. In J. Osborn, P. T. Wilson, and R. C. Anderson (eds.), *Reading education: Foundations for a literate America.* Lexington, Mass.: Heath, Lexington Books.

WISEMAN, D. E., and ROBECK, C. P. (1983). The written language behavior of two socio-economic groups of preschool children. *Reading Psychology, 4,* 349–363.

WITTROCK, M. C. (1974). Learning as a generative process. *Educational Psychologist, 11,* 87–95.

WITTROCK, M. C. (1981). Reading comprehension. In F. J. Pirozzolo and M. C. Wittrock (eds.), *Neuropsychological and cognitive processes in readings.* New York: Academic Press.

YADEN, D. (1985). Preschoolers' spontaneous inquiries about print and books. Paper presented at the Annual Meeting of the National Reading Conference, San Diego.

YLISTO, I. P. (1967). *An empirical investigation of early reading responses of young children.* Doctoral dissertation, University of Michigan.

ZOLOTOW, C. (1962). *Mr. Rabbit and the lovely present.* New York: Harper & Row, Pub.

Appendix A

Children's Literature

I am indebted to Mary Joyce Santoloci, a graduate student at Rutgers University, for preparing a major portion of the appendixes.

1. BOOKS FOR BABIES

a. Cardboard Concept Books
BOONE, E. (1986). *It's spring*. Peterkin, N.Y.: Random House.
DURRELL, J. (illus.). (1986). *The pudgy book of farm animals*. New York: Grosset & Dunlap.
DYER, J. (1986). *Moo, moo, peek-a-boo*. New York: Random House.
HANDS, H. (1985). *First-look nature books*. New York: Grosset & Dunlap.
HAUS, F. (1986) *Beep! Beep! I'm a jeep*. New York: Random House.
HAYES, G. (1986). *Patrick and his grandpa*. New York: Random House.
HILL, E. (1985). *Spot at play*. New York: Putnam's. (Other titles: *Spot at the fair* and *Spot on the farm*.)
LILLY, K. (1982). *Baby animal board books*. New York: Simon & Schuster.
MCCUE, L. (1986). *The little chick*. New York: Random House.
MILLER, J. P. (1986). *Yoo-hoo, little rabbit!* New York: Random House.
OXENBURY, H. (1986). *I can*. New York: Random House. (Other titles: *I hear; I see; I touch*.)
SCARRY, R. (1963). *I am a bunny*. Racine, Wis.: Western Publishing Co., Inc.

b. Cloth Books
ANGLUND, J. W. (1985). *Baby's first book*. New York: Random House.
ATTINELLO, L. (illus.). (1986). *Baby piggy's purse*. New York: Random House.
BEASLEY, R. (illus.). (1986). *Baby's cradle songs*. New York: Random House.
BRACKEN, C. (illus.). (1984). *Baby Strawberry Shortcake's playtime words*. New York: Random House.
COOK, T. (illus.). (1986). *In a popple's pocket*. New York: Random House.

GORBATY, N. (illus.). (1986). *Baby animals say hello.* New York: Random House.
MARKSBURY, T. (1986). *Nighty-night Teddy beddy bear.* New York: Random House.
PARR, J. (1979). *Baby's animal book.* New York: Random House.
SCARRY, R. (1979). *Richard Scarry's huckle's book.* New York: Random House.
SHORTALL, L. (1980). *Zoo animals.* New York: Random House.

c. Plastic Books

ANGLUND, J. (1986). *Tubtime for Thaddeus.* New York: Random House.
BERENSTAIN, S. and J. (1985). *The Berenstain bears bath book.* New York: Random House.
CHAUHAN, M. (1986). *Muppet babies take a bath.* New York: Random House.
DAVIS, J. (illus.). (1985). *Garfield's water fun.* New York: Random House.
HILL, E. (1984). *Spot goes splash.* New York: Putnam's.
MILLER, J. (1984). *The duck says quack book.* New York: Random House.
SCARRY, R. (1984). *Richard Scarry's lowly worm bath book.* New York: Random House.
SESAME STREET. (illus.). (1982). *Ernie's bath book.* New York: Random House.
SUSTENDAL, P. (illus.). (1986). *The Care Bear bath book.* New York: Random House.
WALT DISNEY PRODUCTIONS. (illus.). (1985). *How do you do, I'm Winnie The Pooh.* New York: Random House.

d. Touch-and-Feel Books

CARLE, E.(1972). *The secret birthday message.* New York: Thomas Y. Crowell.
GEORGE, G. (1986). *If you rub a wrinkle.* New York: Random House.
KUNHARDT, D. (1984). *Pat the cat.* Racine, Wis. Western Publishing Co., Inc.
KUNHARDT, (1984). *Pat the bunny.* Racine, Wis. Western Publishing Co., Inc.
LEWIS, S. (1976). *Zoo city.* New York: Greenwillow.
MUNARI, B. (1975). *The circus in the mist.* New York: Collins Publishers.
PENICK, E. and I. (1983). *The good morning book.* New York: Western Publishing Co., Inc.
PERRYMAN, J. (1984). *Where are all the kittens?* New York: Random House.
WHITE, E. and P. (1984). *The touch me book.* New York: Western Publishing Co., Inc.
WITTE, E. and P. (1976). *Who lives here?* New York: Greenwillow.

2. CONCEPT BOOKS

BERENSTAIN, S. and J. (1968). *Inside, outside, upside down.* New York: Random House.
BYRON, B. (1981). *Wheels.* New York: Thomas Y. Crowell.
CARTWRIGHT, S. (1973). *Water is wet.* New York: Coward, McCann & Geoghegan.
DOMANSKA, J. (1976). *Spring is.* New York: Greenwillow.
HOBAN, T. (1972). *Push, pull, empty, full.* New York: Macmillan.
HOBAN, T. (1973). *Over, under and through.* New York: Macmillan.
HOBAN, T. (1976). *Big ones, little ones.* New York: Greenwillow.
KESSLER, E. and L. (1966). *Are you square?* New York: Doubleday.
PIENKOWSKI, J. (1975). *Shapes.* New York: Harvey House.
PROVENSEN, A. and M. (1967). *What is color?* New York: Golden Press.
ROBBINS, K. (1983). *Tools.* New York: Four Winds Press.
ROUND, G. (illus.). (1976). *Top and bottom.* New York: Grosset & Dunlap.
SPIER, P. (1972). *Fast–slow, high–low: A book of opposites.* New York: Doubleday.
TAYLOR, T. and T. (1971). *The adventures of three colors.* New York: World Publishing.

3. ALPHABET BOOKS

ANNO, M. (1975). *Anno's alphabet: Adventure in imagination.* New York: Thomas Y. Crowell.
BASKIN, L. (1972). *Hosie's alphabet.* New York: Viking.

BOYNTON, S. (1983). *A is for angry: An animal and adjective alphabet.* New York: Workman Publishers.
BROWN, M. (1975). *All butterflies.* New York: Scribner's.
EICHENBERG, F. (1952). *Ape in a cape.* New York: Harcourt Brace Jovanovich, Inc.
FALLS, C. B. (1951). *ABC Book.* New York: Doubleday.
FEELINGS, M. (1974). *Jambo means hello: A Swahili alphabet book.* New York: Dial Press.
FIFE, D. (1971). *Adam's ABC.* New York: Coward, McCann & Geoghegan.
FUJIKAWA, G. (1974). *A to Z picture book.* New York: Grosset & Dunlap.
GAG, W. (1971). *The ABC bunny.* New York: Coward, McCann & Geoghegan.
GARTEN, J. (1964). *The alphabet tale.* New York: Random House.
HAGUE, K. (1983). *Alphabears.* New York: Holt, Rinehart & Winston.
KRAUS, R. (1972). *Good night little ABC.* New York: Scholastic.
LARRICK, N. (1965). *First ABC.* New York: Platt & Munk.
LEAR, E. (1983). *An Edward Lear alphabet.* Glenview Ill.: Scott, Foresman.
NOLAN, D. (1977). *Alphabrites.* Englewood Cliffs, N.J.: Prentice-Hall.
SCARRY, R. (1963). *Best word book ever.* New York: Random House.
SEUSS, DR. (1963). *Dr. Seuss's ABC.* New York: Random House.
WILDSMITH, B. (1963). *Brian Wildsmith's ABC.* New York: Franklin Watts, Inc.

4. NUMBER BOOKS.

ANNO, M. (1977). *Anno's counting book.* New York: Thomas Y. Crowell.
BAUM, A. and J. (1962). *One bright Monday morning.* New York: Random House.
BROWN, M. (1976). *One, two, three: An animal counting book.* Boston: Little, Brown.
CARLE, E. (1968). *1,2,3 to the zoo.* New York: William Collins.
CHWAST, S., and MOSKOF, M. S. (1971). *Still another number book.* New York: McGraw-Hill.
EHRLICH, A. (1977). *The everyday train.* New York: Dial Press.
FEELINGS, M. (1971). *Moja means one: A Swahili counting book.* New York: Dial Press.
FESCHET, B. (1973). *The ants go marching.* New York: Scribner's.
FUJIKAWA, G. (1977). *Can you count?* New York: Grosset & Dunlap.
HOBAN, T. (1972). *Count and see.* New York: Macmillan.
HOLL, A. (1976). *Let's count.* Reading, Mass.: Addison-Wesley.
KEATS, E. J. (1972). *Over in the meadow.* New York: Four Winds Press.
LIVERMORE, E. (1973). *One to ten, count again.* Boston: Houghton Mifflin.
MACK, S. (1974). *10 bears in my bed.* New York: Pantheon.
MOORE, L. (1956). *My first counting book.* New York: Simon & Schuster.
OXENBURY, H. (1968). *Numbers of things.* New York: Franklin Watts, Inc.
WILDSMITH, B. (1965). *Brian Wildsmith's 1,2,3.* New York: Franklin Watts, Inc.
YEOMAN, J. (1971). *Sixes and sevens.* New York: Macmillan.
YOLEN, J. (1976). *An invitation to the butterfly ball.* New York: Parents Magazine Press.
ZINER, F. (1962). *Counting carnival.* New York: Coward, McCann & Geoghegan.

5. NURSERY RHYMES

BATTAGLIA, A. (1973). *Mother Goose.* New York: Random House.
BRIGGS, R. (1966). *The Mother Goose treasury.* New York: Coward, McCann & Geoghegan.
DEANGELI, M. (1954). *The book of nursery and Mother Goose rhymes.* New York: Doubleday.
DEPAOLA, T. (1985). *Tomie dePaola's Mother Goose.* New York: Putnam's.
EMBERLEY, E. (1967). *London Bridge is falling down.* Boston: Little, Brown.
GALDONE, P. (1961). *Old Mother Hubbard and her dog.* New York: McGraw-Hill.
GALDONE, P. (1966). *The history of Simple Simon.* New York: McGraw-Hill.
JEFFERS, S. (1973). *Three jovial huntsmen: A Mother Goose rhyme.* New York: Bradbury Press.
LOBEL, A. (1986). *The Random House book of Mother Goose.* New York: Random House.

PIPER, W. (1972). *Mother Goose: A treasury of best loved rhymes.* New York: Platt & Munk.
RACKHAM, A. (1975). *Mother Goose nursery rhymes.* New York: Viking.
TUDOR, T. (1944). *Mother Goose.* New York: D. McKay.
WATSON, C. (1971). *Father Fox's penny rhymes.* New York: Thomas Y. Crowell.
WILDSMITH, B. (1964). *Brian Wildsmith's Mother Goose.* New York: Franklin Watts, Inc.
WRIGHT, B. F. (1965). *The real Mother Goose.* New York: Rand McNally.

6. PICTURE STORYBOOKS

The following books represent a careful selection of some distinguished authors and excellent children's literature not to be missed.

BARRETT, J. (1970). *Animals should definitely not wear clothing.* New York: Atheneum.
BEMELMANS, L. (1939). *Madeline.* New York: Viking.
BERENSTAIN, S. and J. (1966). *The bear's picnic.* New York: Random House.
BROWN, M. (1947). *Stone soup.* New York: Scribner's.
BROWN, M. W. (1957). *Goodnight moon.* New York: Harper & Row, Publishers.
CARLE, E. (1969). *The very hungry caterpillar.* New York: Philomel.
CARLE, E. (1971). *Do you want to be my friend?* New York: Thomas Y. Crowell.
DEPAOLA, T. (1975). *Strega nona: An old tale.* Englewood Cliffs, N.J.: Prentice-Hall.
EASTMAN, P. D. (1960). *Are you my mother?* New York: Random House.
FLACK, M. (1932). *Ask Mr. Bear.* New York: Macmillan.
GALDONE, P. (1975). *The little red hen.* New York: Scholastic.
HOBAN, R. (1960). *Bedtime for Frances.* New York: Harper & Row, Publishers.
HOBAN, R. (1969). *Best friends for Frances.* New York: Harper & Row, Publishers.
HUTCHINS, P. (1978). *Don't forget the bacon.* New York: Puffin Books.
JOHNSON, C. (1955). *Harold and the purple crayon.* New York: Harper Books.
KEATS, E. J. (1962). *The snowy day.* New York: Viking.
KEATS, E. J. (1967). *Peter's chair.* New York: Harper & Row, Publishers
KEATS, E. J. (1971). *Over in the meadow.* New York: Scholastic.
KELLOGG, S. (1971). *Can I keep him?* New York: Dial Press.
KRAUS, R. (1971). *Leo the late bloomer.* New York: Windmill.
LIONNI, L. (1966). *Frederick.* New York: Pantheon.
LIONNI, L. (1973). *Swimmy.* New York: Random House.
LOBEL, A. (1972). *Frog and toad together.* New York: Harper & Row, Publishers.
MAYER, M. (1967). *A bog, a dog and a frog.* New York: Dial Press.
MAYER, M. (1974). *One monster after another.* Racine, Wis.: Western Publishing Co., Inc.
McCLOSKEY, R. (1941). *Make way for ducklings.* New York: Viking.
McCLOSKEY, R. (1948). *Blueberries for Sal.* New York: Penguin.
PIPER, W. (1954). *The little engine that could.* New York: Platt & Munk.
POLUSHKIN, M. (1986). *Mother, mother I want another.* New York: Crown.
POTTER, B. (1902). *The tale of Peter Rabbit.* New York: Scholastic.
REY, H. A. (1952). *Curious George rides a bike.* Boston: Houghton Mifflin.
SENDAK, M. (1963). *Where the wild things are.* New York: Harper & Row, Publishers.
SENDAK, M. (1970). *In the night kitchen.* New York: Harper & Row, Publishers.
SEUSS, DR. (1940). *Horton hatches the egg.* New York: Random House.
SEUSS, DR. (1957). *The cat in the hat.* New York: Random House.
SHAW, C. (1947). *It looked like spilt milk.* New York: Harper.
SLOBODKINA, E. (1947). *Caps for sale.* Reading, Mass.: Addison-Wesley.
STEIG, W. (1969). *Sylvester and the magic pebble.* New York: Simon & Schuster.
VIORST, J. (1972). *Alexander and the terrible, horrible, no good, very bad day.* New York: Atheneum.
VIORST, J. (1978). *Alexander who used to be rich last Sunday.* New York: Atheneum.
WABER, B. (1975). *Ira sleeps over.* Boston: Houghton Mifflin.
ZOLOTOW, C. (1962). *Mr. Rabbit and the lovely present.* New York: Harper & Row, Publishers.
ZOLOTOW, C. (1966). *If it weren't for you.* New York: Harper & Row, Publishers.

7. TRADITIONAL LITERATURE (FAIRY TALES, FABLES, MYTHS, AND FOLKTALES)

ADAMS, A. (illus.). (1975). *Hansel and Gretel.* New York: Scribner's.
ASBOJORNSEN, P. C., and JORGEN, E. M. (1957). *The three Billy Goats Gruff.* New York: Harcourt Brace Jovanovich, Inc.
EHRLICH, A. (trans.). (1985). *The Random House book of fairy tales.* New York: Random House.
GALDONE, P. (1972). *The three bears.* New York: Scholastic.
GALDONE, P. (1975). *The gingerbread boy.* New York: Seabury Press.
GRIMM BROTHERS. (1968). *Grimm's fairy tales.* Chicago: Follett.
GRIMM BROTHERS. (1968). *Little red riding hood.* New York: Harcourt Brace Jovanovich, Inc.
HAVGAARD, E. (trans.). (1978). *Hans Christian Andersen: His classic fairy tales.* New York: Doubleday.
HAVILAND, V. (1980). *The fairy tale treasury.* New York: Dell Pub. Co., Inc.
HOGROGIAN, N. (1971). *One fine day.* New York: Collier Books.
KENT, J. (1974). *Fables and Aesop.* New York: Parents Magazine Press.
McDERMOTT, J. (1972). *Anansi the spider.* New York: Puffin Books.
PERRAULT, C. (1954). *Cinderella.* New York: Scribner's.
ROCKWELL, A. (1984). *The three bears and fifteen other stories.* New York: Harper & Row, Publishers.
SEGAL, L., and JARRELL, R. (trans.). (1973). *The juniper tree and other tales from Grimm.* New York: Farrar, Straus & Giroux.
STEVENS, J. (1971). *The tortoise and the hare.* New York: Holiday House.
STOBBS, W. (1970). *Rumpelstiltskin.* New York: Walck.
WILDSMITH, B. (1975). *Python party.* New York: Franklin Watts, Inc.

8. EASY-TO-READ BOOKS

BROWN, M. W. (1957). *Goodnight moon.* New York: Harper & Row, Publishers.
EASTMAN, P. D. (1960). *Are you my mother?* New York: Random House.
LESIEG, T. (1961). *Ten apples up on top.* New York: Random House.
LOBEL, A. (1972). *Frog and toad together.* New York: Harper & Row, Publishers.
LOBEL, A. (1979). *Frog and toad are friends.* New York: Harper & Row, Publishers.
MARTIN, B. (1967). *Brown bear, brown bear, what do you see?* New York: Holt, Rinehart & Winston.
PERKINS, A. (1968). *The ear book.* New York: Random House.
SEUSS, DR. (1957). *The cat in the hat.* New York: Random House.
SEUSS, DR. (1960). *Green eggs with ham.* New York: Random House.
SEUSS, DR. (1963). *Dr. Seuss's ABC.* New York: Random House.

9. BOOKS ABOUT REALISTIC ISSUES

ALEXANDER, M. (1971). *Nobody asked me if I wanted a baby sister.* New York: Dial Press.
ARDIZZONE, E. (1970). *The wrong side of the bed.* New York: Doubleday.
BEIM, L. and J. (1945). *Two is a team.* New York: Harcourt Brace Jovanovich, Inc.
FLACK, M. (1943). *The new pet.* New York: Harper & Row, Publishers.
HOBAN, R. (1960). *Bedtime for Frances.* New York: Harper & Row, Publishers.
LAPSLEY, S. (1975). *I am adopted.* New York: Bradbury Press .
McPHAIL, D. (1972). *The bear's toothache.* Boston: Little, Brown.
MAY, J. (1971). *Why people are different colors.* New York: Holiday House.
PRESTON, E. (1969). *The temper tantrum book.* New York: Viking.
SHERMAN, I. (1973). *I do not like it when my friend comes to visit.* New York: Harcourt Brace Jovanovich, Inc.

SONNEBORN, R. (1970). *Friday night is papa night.* New York: Viking.
SONNEBORN, R. (1971). *I love Gram.* New York: Viking.
VIORST, J. (1971). *The tenth good thing about Barney.* New Atheneum Press.
WALDE, G. (1971). *Tommy takes a bath.* Boston: Houghton Mifflin.
WEBER, A. (1969). *Elizabeth gets well.* New York: Thomas Y. Crowell.
ZOLOTOW, C. (1963). *The quarreling book.* New York: Harper & Row, Publishers.
ZOLOTOW, C. (1968). *The new friend.* Abelard-Schuman.

10. WORDLESS STORYBOOKS

ALEXANDER, M. (1968). *Out! Out! Out!* New York: Dial Press.
ALEXANDER, M. (1970). *Bobo's dream.* New York: Dial Press.
ARUEGO, J. (1971). *Look what I can do.* New York: Scribner's.
GOODALL, J. S. (1971). *Jacko.* New York: Harcourt Brace Jovanovich, Inc.
HUTCHINS, P. (1968). *Rosie's walk.* New York: Macmillan.
HUTCHINS, P. (1971). *Changes, changes.* New York: Macmillan.
KEATS, E. J. (1973). *Skates.* New York: Franklin Watts, Inc.
MAYER, M. (1967). *A boy, a dog, and a frog.* New York: Dial Press.
OXENBURY, H. (1982). *Good night, good morning.* New York: Dial Press.
WARD, L. (1973). *The silver pony.* Boston: Houghton Mifflin.
WEZEL, P. (1964). *The good bird.* New York: Harper & Row, Publishers.

11. POETRY BOOKS

ADOFF, A. (1973). *Black is brown is tan.* New York: Harper & Row, Publishers.
ADOFF, A. (1975). *Make a circle to keep us in.* New York: Delacorte.
AIKEN, C. (1965). *Cats and bats and things with wings.* New York: Atheneum.
BENNETT, J. (1981). *Roger was a razor fish and other poems.* New York: Lothrop.
CIARDI, J. (1961). *The man who sang the sillies.* New York: Lippincott.
COATSWORTH, E. (1966). *The sparrow bush.* New York: W. W. Norton & Co., Inc.
COLE, W. (1981). *Poem stew.* New York: Lippincott.
COLE, W. (ed.). (1972). *Pick me up: A book of short, short poems.* Boston: Little, Brown.
CRUISE, B. (1985). *My book of poems.* New York: Western Publishing Co., Inc.
FISHER, A. (1963). *Cricket in a thicket.* New York: Scribner's.
FRANK, J. (1968). *More poems to read to the very young.* New York: Random House.
GEISMER, B., and SITER, A. (1975). *Very young verses.* Boston: Houghton Mifflin.
HILLERT, M. (1975). *Come play with me.* Chicago: Follett.
HOPKINS, L. B. (1979). *Go to bed: A book of bedtime poems.* New York: Knopf.
HYMES, J., and HYMES, L. (1965). *Hooray for chocolate.* New York: Wm. R. Scott.
KNIGHT, H. (1983). *The owl and the pussy-cat.* New York: Macmillan.
KUSKIN, K. (1980). *Dogs and dragons, trees and dreams.* New York: Harper & Row, Publishers.
LARRICK, N. (1968). *On city streets.* New York: M. Evans.
LARRICK, N. (1972). *The wheels on the bug go round and round.* New York: Golden Gate.
LEWIS, R. (1965). *In a spring garden.* New York: Dial Press.
McCORD, D. (1977). *One at a time: Collected poems for the young.* Boston: Little, Brown.
MERRIAM, E. (1966). *Catch a little rhyme.* New York: Atheneum.
MILNE, A. A. (1958). *The world of Christopher Robin.* New York: Dutton.
MOORE, I. (1986). *Poems for young children.* New York: Doubleday.
NICHOLLS, J. (1985). *Magic mirror and other poems for children.* Winchester, Mass.: Faber & Faber.
O'NEIL, M. (1961). *Hailstones and halibut bones.* New York: Doubleday.
PRELUTSKY, J. (1983). *Random House book of poetry for children.* New York: Random House.
SENDAK, M. (1962). *Alligators all around us.* New York: Harper & Row, Publishers.

SILVERSTEIN, S. (1974). *Where the sidewalk ends.* New York: Harper & Row, Publishers.
SILVERSTEIN, S. (1981). *A light in the attic.* New York: Harper & Row, Publishers.
STARBIRD, K. (1960). *Speaking of cows.* New York: Lippincott.
STEVENSON, R. L. (1977). *A child's garden of verses.* New York: Platt & Munk.
UNTERMEYER, L. (comp.). (1959). *The golden treasurey of poetry.* New York: Western Publishing
    Co., Inc.

12. INFORMATIONAL BOOKS

BESSAR, M. (1967). *The cat book.* New York: Holiday house.
COLE, J. (1983). *Cars and how they go.* New York: Thomas Y. Crowell.
MAY, J. (1969). *Living things and their young.* New York: Follett.
MITZUMURA, K. (1971). *If I built a village.* New York: Thomas Y. Crowell.
ROCKWELL, A. (1971). *The toolbox.* New York: Macmillan.
ROCKWELL, A. (1972). *Machines.* New York: Macmillan.
SELSAM, M. (1973). *How kittens grow.* New York: Four Winds Press.
SKAAR, G. (1966). *All about dogs.* New York: Young Scott Books.
SWALLOW, S. (1973). *Cars, trucks, and trains.* New York: Grosset & Dunlap.
WHILE, R. (1972). *All kinds of trains.* New York: Grosset & Dunlap.
YEPSEN, R. (1983). *Train talk.* New York: Pantheon.

13. BIOGRAPHY

ALIKI. (1963). *The story of Johnny Appleseed.* Englewood Cliffs, N.J.: Prentice Hall
ALIKI. (1977). *The many lives of Benjamin Franklin.* Englewood Cliffs, N.J.: Prentice Hall.
AUSTIN, M. C. (ed.). (1960). Easy to Read Discovery Books (titles listed below). Champaign,
    Ill.: Garrard Publishing Co.
    *Daniel Boone: Lafayette; Theodore Roosevelt; Abraham Lincoln; George Washington Carver;
    Clara Barton; Paul Revere; The Wright Brothers.*
BURCHARD, M., and BURCHARD, S. H. (1976). *Sports star: Tom Seaver.* New York: Harcourt
    Brace Jovanovich, Inc.
BURCHARD, M., and BURCHARD, S. H. (1979). *Sports star: Tony Dorsett.* New York: Harcourt
    Brace Jovanovich, Inc.
GRAVES, C. P. (1966). *John F. Kennedy.* New York: Dell Pub. Co., Inc.
HALLIBURTON, W. J. (1984). *The picture life of Jesse Jackson.* New York: Franklin Watts, Inc.
MONTGOMERY, E. (1971). *Walt Disney: Master of make believe.* Champaign, Ill.: Garrard Pub-
    lishing Co.
QUACKENBUSH, R. (1985). (titles listed below). Englewood Cliffs, N.J.: Prentice Hall
    Ahoy! Ahoy! Are you there? A story of Alexander Graham Bell.
    Don't you dare shoot that bear! A story of Theodore Roosevelt.
    *Here a plant, there a plant, everywhere a plant, plant! A story of
    Luther Burbank.*
    *Mark Twain? What kind of name is that? A story of Samuel Langhorne
    Clemens.*
    Oh. what an awful mess! A story of Charles Goodyear.
    Once upon a time! A story of the Brothers Grimm.
    Quick, Annie, give me a catchy line! A story of Samuel F. B. Morse.
    The beagle and Mr. Flycatcher: A story of Charles Darwin.
    What got you started, Mr. Fulton? A story of James Watt and Robert Fulton.
    What has wild Tom done now!!!? A story of Thomas Alva Edison.
    Who said there's no man on the moon? A story of Jules Verne.
SUTTON, F. (1968). *Master of ballyhoo: The story of P. T. Barnum.* New York: Putnam's.
WEIL, L. (1983). *Christopher Columbus.* New York: Atheneum.

14. MAGAZINES FOR CHILDREN

Chickadee. Young Naturalist Foundation, 17th and M Streets NW, Washington, DC 20036. (ages 4–8)

Children's Playmate. 1100 Waterway Boulevard, Indianapolis, IN 46206. (ages 3–8)

Cricket. Open Court Publishing Co., Box 100, La Salle, IL 61301. (ages 6–12)

Ebony, Jr. Johnson Publishing Co., 820 South Michigan Avenue, Chicago, IL 60605. (ages 6–12)

Highlights for Children. 803 Church Street, Honesdale, PA 18431. (ages 2–12)

Humpty Dumpty's Magazine. Parent's Institute, 80 Newbridge Road, Bergenfield, NJ 07621. (ages 3–7)

Jack and Jill. Curtis Publishing Co., Independence Square, Philadelphia, PA 19106. (ages 5–12)

Ranger Rick. National Wildlife Federation, 1412 16th Street NW, Washington, DC 20036. (ages 5–12)

Sesame Street. Children's Television Workshop, One Lincoln Plaza, New York, NY 10023. (ages 3–6)

Stone Soup. Children's Art Foundation, P.O. Box 83, Santa Cruz, CA 95063 (ages 6–12)

WOW. Box 2007, Englewood, NJ 07631. (ages 4–8)

Your Big Backyard. National Wildlife Federation, 1412 16th Street NW, Washington, DC 20036. (ages 1–4)

15. PREDICTABLE BOOKS

a. Repetitive Phrases

ARNO, E. (1970). *The gingerbread man.* New York: Scholastic.

BROWN, M. (1957). *The three Billy Goats Gruff.* New York: Harcourt, Brace, Jovanovich, Inc.

DEPAOLA, T. (1975). *Strega nona: An old tale.* Englewood Cliffs, N.J.: Prentice-Hall.

EASTMAN, P. D. (1960). *Are you my mother?* New York: Random House.

GALDONE, P. (1970). *The three little pigs.* New York: Seabury Press.

GALDONE, P. (1975). *The little red hen.* New York: Scholastic.

LANGSTAFF, J. (1984). *Oh, a-hunting we will go.* New York: Atheneum.

LOBEL, A. (1979). *A treeful of pigs.* New York: Greenwillow.

MARTIN, B. (1967). *Brown bear, brown bear, what do you see?* New York: Holt, Rinehart & Winston.

PIPER, W. (1954). *The little engine that could.* New York: Platt & Munk.

POLUSHKIN, M. (1978). *Mother, mother I want another.* New York: Crown.

SENDAK, M. (1962). *Chicken soup with rice.* New York: Harper & Row, Publishers.

SEULING, B. (1976). *Teeny-tiny woman.* New York: Viking.

SHAW, C. G. (1947). *It looked like spilt milk.* New York: Harper & Row, Publishers.

VIORST, J. (1976). *Alexander and the terrible, horrible, no good, very bad day.* New York: Atheneum.

b. Rhyme

AHLBERG, J. A. (1978). *Each peach pear plum.* New York: Viking.

BONNIE, R. (1961). *I know an old lady.* New York: Scholastic.

BROOKE, L. (1967). *Johnny Crow's garden.* New York: Frederick Warne.

BROWN, M. W. (1957). *Goodnight moon.* New York: Harper & Row, Publishers.

CAMERON, P. (1961). *I can't said the ant.* New York: Coward, McCann & Geoghegan.

DEREGNIERS, B. S. (1968). *Willy O'Dwyer jumped in the fire.* New York: Atheneum.

DODD, L. (1976). *The nickle nackle tree.* New York: Macmillan.

EMBERLEY, B. (1967). *Drummer Hoff.* Englewood Cliffs, N.J.: Prentice-Hall.

HOBERMAN, M. A. (1978). *A house is a house for me.* New York: Viking.

KEATS, E. J. (1971). *Over in the meadow.* New York: Scholastic.

KRAUS, R. (1970). *Whose mouse are you?* New York: Macmillan.

LODGE, B. (1979). *Rhyming Nell.* New York: Morrow.
SEUSS, DR. (1965). *Fox in socks.* New York: Random House.
THOMAS, P. (1971). *"Stand back," said the elephant, "I'm going to sneeze!* New York: Lothrop, Lee & Shepard Co.
ZEMACH, H. (1969). *The judge: An untrue tale.* New York: Farrar, Straus & Giroux

c. Familiar Sequences (days of the week, numbers, letters, months of the year, etc.)

BAUM, A., and BAUM, J. (1962). *One bright Monday morning.* New York: Random House.
BROWN, M. (1957). *The three Billy Goats Gruff.* New York: Harcourt, Brace, Jovanovich, Inc.
CARLE, E. (1969). *The very hungry caterpillar.* New York: Philomel.
HUTCHINS, P. (1968). *Rosie's walk.* New York: Macmillan.
KEATS, E. J. (1971). *Over in the meadow.* New York: Scholastic.
MACK, S. (1974). *10 bears in my bed.* New York: Pantheon.
MARTIN, B. (1970). *Brown bear, brown bear, what do you see?* New York: Holt, Rinehart & Winston.
ROY, R. (1980). *The three ducks went wandering.* New York: Scholastic.
SCHULEVITZ, U. (1967). *One Monday morning.* New York: Scribner's.

d. Cumulative Patterns (as the story progresses, the previous line is repeated)

AARDEMA, V. (1975). *Why mosquitos buzz in people's ears.* New York: Dutton.
BERENSTAIN, S. and J. (1971). *The b book.* New York: Random House.
BRETT, J. (1985). *Annie and the wild animals.* Boston: Houghton Mifflin.
BROOKE, L. (1986). *Johnny Crow's garden.* New York: Frederick Warne.
EMBERLEY, B. (1967). *Dummer Hoff.* Englewood Cliffs, N.J.: Prentice-Hall.
GUILFOILE, E. (1962). *The house that Jack built.* New York: Holt, Rinehart & Winston.
KENT, J. (1971). *The fat cat.* New York: Scholastic.
LOBEL, A. (1984). *The rose in my garden.* New York: Greenwillow.
MAYER, M. (1975). *What do you do with a kangaroo?* New York: Scholastic.
McGOVERN, A. (1967). *Too much noise.* Boston: Houghton Mufflin.
PRELUTSKY, J. (1970). *The terrible tiger.* New York: Macmillan.
WABER, B. (1966). *"You look ridiculous," said the rhinoceros to the hippopotamus.* Boston: Houghton Mifflin.
WESTCOTT, N. B. (1980). *I know an old lady who swallowed a fly.* Boston: Little, Brown.
WOOD, A. (1984). *The napping house.* New York: Harcourt Brace Jovanovich, Inc.

e. Familiar/Popular Stories

ARNO, E. (1970). *The gingerbread man.* New York: Scholsatic.
BROWN, M. (1957). *The three Billy Goats Gruff.* New York: Harcourt, Brace.
GALDONE, P. (1972). *The three bears.* New York: Seabury Press.
GALDONE, P. (1975). *The little red hen.* New York: Scholastic.
GRABOFF, A. (1970). *Old MacDonald had a farm.* New York: Scholastic.
PIPER, W. (1954). *The little engine that could.* New York: Platt & Munk.
SENDAK, M. (1963). *Where the wild things are.* New York: Harper & Row, Publishers.
SEUSS, DR. (1957). *The cat in the hat.* Boston: Houghton Mifflin.
SLOBODKINA, E. (1947). *Caps for sale.* Reading, MA: Addison-Wesley.

f. Stories with Conversation.

ARNO, E. (1970). *The gingerbread man.* New York: Scholastic.
BROWN, M. W. (1972). *The runaway bunny.* New York: Harper & Row, Publishers.
EASTMAN, P. D. (1960). *Are you my mother?* New York: Random House.
FLACK, M. (1971). *Ask Mr. Bear.* New York: Macmillan.
GALDONE, P. (1972). *The three bears.* New York: Seabury Press.
GALDONE, P. (1975). *The little red hen.* New York: Scholastic.
HOBAN, R. (1964). *Bread and jam for Frances.* New York: Harper & Row, Publishers.

KELLOGG, S. (1971). *Can I keep him?* New York: Dial Press.
MCGOVERN, A. (1971). *Stone soup.* New York: Scholastic.
WABER, B. (1966). *"You look ridiculous," said the rhinoceros to the hippopotamus.* Boston: Houghton Mifflin.
ZOLOTOW, C. (1962). *Mr. rabbit and the lovely present.* New York: Harper & Row, Publishers.

16. BOOKS THAT CAN FOSTER CRITICAL DISCUSSIONS

FREEMAN, D. (1964). *Dandelion.* New York: Viking.
GALDONE, P. (1962). *The hare and the tortoise.* New York: McGraw-Hill.
GALDONE, P. (1972). *The three bears.* New York: Seabury Press.
GALDONE, P. (1975). *The gingerbread boy.* New York: Seabury Press.
GALDONE, P. (1984). *The three little pigs.* New York: Clarion.
HYMAN, T. (1983). *Little red riding hood.* New York: Holiday House.
LINDQUIST, W. (1970). *Stone soup.* New York: Western Publishing Co., Inc.
LOWREY, J. (1942). *The poky little puppy.* New York: Golden Press.
LIONNI, L. (1973). *Swimmy.* New York: Random House
PIPER, W. (1979). *The little engine that could.* New York: Scholastic.
SENDAK, M. (1963). *Where the wild things are.* New York: Harper & Row, Publishers.
SILVERSTEIN, S. (1964). *The giving tree.* New York: Harper & Row, Publishers.
VIORST, J. (1976). *Alexander and the terrible, horrible, no good, very bad day.* New York: Atheneum.
ZOLOTOW, C. (1972). *William's doll.* New York: Harper & Row, Publishers.

17. BOOKS FOR ENHANCING LISTENING AND DISCRIMINATION OF SOUNDS

BROWN, M. W. (1939). *The noisy book.* New York: Harper & Row, Publishers.
BROWN, M. W. (1947). *Goodnight moon.* New York: Harper & Row, Publishers.
GARELICK, M. (1963). *Sounds of a summer night.* Reading, MA.: Addison-Wesley.
HEIDE, F. (1970). *Sound of sunshine, sound of rain.* New York: Parents Magazine Press.
JOHNSTON, T. (1973). *Night noises and other mole and troll stories.* New York: Putnam's.
KAUFMAN, L. (1965). *What's that noise?* New York: Lothrop.
KUSKIN, K. (1962). *All sizes of noises.* New York: Harper & Row, Publishers.
MCGOVERN, A. (1967). *Too much noise.* Boston: Houghton Mifflin.
PERKINS, A. (1968). *The ear book.* New York: Random House.
QUACKENBUSH, R. (1972). *Old MacDonald had a farm.* New York: Lippincott.
SEUSS, DR. (1970). *Mister Brown can moo: Can you?* New York: Random House.
SEUSS, DR. (1978). *I can read with my eyes shut.* New York: Random House.
SHOWERS, P. (1961). *The listening walk.* New York: Thomas Y. Crowell.
STEINER, C. (1959). *Listen to my seashell.* New York: Knopf.
TEAL, V. (1967). *The little woman wanted noise.* Chicago: Rand McNally.
VICTOR, J. (1969). *Sh-h! Listen again.* Cleveland: World Publishing.

18. BOOKS FOR BUILDING SOUND–SYMBOL RELATIONSHIPS

a. Consonants
B

BERENSTAIN, S. and J. (1971). *The Berenstain B book.* New York: Random House.
BERENSTAIN, S. and J. (1986). *The Berenstain bears and too much birthday.* New York: Random House.

CALDER, L. (1985). *Blast off, barefoot bear!* New York: Tern Enterprises.
MONCURE, J. (1984). *My "B" sound.* Elgin, Ill.: Child's World Publishing.
PEET, B. (1977). *Big, bad Bruce.* Boston: Houghton Mifflin.

C (hard)

BERENSTAIN, S. and J. (1972). *C is for clown* New York: Random House.
KRAUSS, R. (1945). *The carrot seed.* New York: Scholastic.
SLOBODKINA, E. (1968). *Caps for sale.* New York: Addison-Wesley.

C (soft)

McPHAIL, D. (1974). *Cereal Box.* Boston: Little, Brown.
WILDSMITH, B. (1970). *Circus.* New York: Franklins Watts, Inc.
WOODMAN, J. (1986). *Bossy bear at the circus.* London: Brimax Books.

C (hard and soft)

MONCURE, J. (1984). *My "C" sound.* Elgin, Ill.: Child's World Publishing.

D

LEXAU, J. (1987). *The dog food caper.* New York: Dial Books.
MONCURE, J. (1984). *My "D" sound.* Elgin, Ill.: Child's World Publishing.
STEIG, W. (1982). *Doctor De Soto.* New York: Farrar, Straus & Giroux.
ZEMACK, H. and M. (1973). *Duffy and the devil.* New York: Farrar, Strauss & Giroux.

F

LITTLEDALE, F. (1987). *The farmer in the soup.* New York: Scholastic.
LOBEL, A. (1970). *Frog and toad are friends.* New York: Harper & Row, Publishers.
McPHAIL, D. (1984). *Fix-it.* New York: Dutton.
MONCURE, J. (1984). *My "F" sound.* Elgin, Ill.: Child's World Publishing.

G (hard)

BURINGHAM, J. (1976). *Mr. Gumpy's motor car.* New York: Thomas Y. Crowell.
GALDONE, P. (1981). *The three Billy Goats Gruff.* Boston: Houghton Mifflin.
SHARMAT, M. (1984). *Gregory the terrible eater.* New York: Scholastic.

G (soft)

GALDONE, P. (1975). *The Gingerbread Boy.* New York: Clarion Books.
REY, H. A. (1973). *Curious George.* Boston: Houghton Mifflin.
        (Other titles in this series include *Curious George Rides a Bike, Curious George Goes to the Circus,* and *Curious George Learns the Alphabet.*)

G (hard and soft)

MONCURE, J. (1984). *My "G" sound.* Elgin, Ill.: Child's World Publishing.

H

JOHNSON, C. (1960). *A picture for Harold's room.* New York: Harper & Row, Publishers.
KUSKIN, K. (1979). *Herbert hated being small.* Boston: Houghton Mifflin.
MONCURE, J. (1984). *My "H" sound.* Elgin, Ill.: Child's World Publishing.
ZION, G. (1976). *Harry the dirty dog.* New York: Harper & Row, Publishers.

J

ETS, M. (1965). *Just Me*. New York: Viking.
KUSKIN, K. (1959). *Just like everyone else*. New York: Harper & Row, Publishers.
MONCURE, J. (1984). *My "J" sound*. Elgin, Ill.: Child's World Publishing.
STOBBS, W. (1969). *Jack and the beanstalk*. New York: Delacorte.
WHITNEY, A. (1971). *Just awful*. Reading, Mass.: Addison-Wesley.

K

MAESTRO, B. and G. (1982). *The Key to the Kingdom*. New York: Harcourt Brace Jovanovich, Inc.
MONCURE, J. (1984). *My "K" sound*. Elgin, Ill.: Child's World Publishing.
PIERS, H. (1986). *Peek a boo*. New York: Harcourt Brace Jovanovich, Inc.
SCHONGUT, E. (1983). *Look Kitten*. New York: Little Simon.

L

COSGROVE, S. (1985). *Leo the lop*. Los Angeles: Price, Stern & Sloan Publishers.
DEREGNIERS, B. S. (1979). *Laura's story*. New York: Atheneum.
KRAUSS, R. (1971). *Leo the Late Bloomer*. New York: Windmill Books, Simon & Schuster.
MONCURE, J. (1984). *My "L" sound*. Elgin, Ill.: Child's World Publishing.

M

BEMELMANS, L. (1977). *Madeline*. New York: Puffin Books.
COSGROVE, S. (1985). *Little mouse on the prairie*. Los Angeles: Price, Stern & Sloan Publishers.
KELLOGG, S. (1976). *Much bigger than Martin*. New York: Dial Press.
MONCURE, J. (1984). *My "M" sound*. Elign, Ill.: Child's World Publishing.
WOLCOTT, P. (1974). *Marvelous mud washing machine*. Reading, Mass: Addison-Wesley.

N

BROWN, M. W. (1939). *The Noisy Book*. New York: Harper.
GUILFOILE, E. (1957). *Nobody listens to Andrew*. Chicago: Follett.
MCGOVERN, A. (1967). *Too Much Noise*. Boston: Houghton Mifflin.
RICE, E. (1975). *New blue shoes*. New York: Macmillan.
WEZEL, P. (1967). *The naughty bird*. Chicago: Follett.

P

BROWN, R. (1973). *Pig in the pond*. New York: D. McKay.
DEPAOLA, T. (1978). *The popcorn book*. New York: Holiday House.
DUVOISIN, R. (1950). *Petunia*. New York: Knopf.
KEATS, E. J. (1972). *The pet show*. New York: Macmillan.
ROTH, S. (1966). *Pick a peck of puzzles*. New York: Arnold Norton.

Q

BEATTY, J. (1967). *The queen wizard*. New York: Macmillan.
BLUE, R. (1969). *A quiet place*. New York: Franklin Watts, Inc.
HURD, T. (1978). *The quiet evening*. New York: Greenwillow.
JOHNSTON, T., and DEPAOLA, T. (1985). *The quilt story*. New York: Putnam's.
ZOLOTOW, C. (1963). *The quarreling book*. New York: Harper & Row, Publishers.

R

FISHER, A. (1983). *Rabbits rabbits*. New York: Harper & Row, Publishers.
KENT, J. (1982). *Round robin*. Englewood Cliffs, N.J.: Prentice-Hall.

SENDAK, M. (1975). *Really Rosie.* New York: Harper & Row, Publishers.
SHULEVITZ, U. (1969). *Rain, rain, rivers.* New York: Farrar, Straus & Giroux
WATTS, B. (1968). *Little Red Riding Hood.* New York: Scholastic.
ZOLOTOW, C. (1962). *Mr. Rabbit and the lovely present.* New York: Harper & Row, Publishers.

S

BROWN, M. (1947). *Stone soup.* New York: Scribner's.
KEATS, E. J. (1976). *The snowy day.* New York: Puffin Books.
KESSLER, E. and L. (1973). *Slush, slush!* New York: Parents Magazine Press.
LIONNI, L. (1973). *Swimmy.* New York: Random House.
RASKIN, E. (1973). *Who, said Sue, said whooo?* New York: Atheneum.
STADLER, J. (1985). *Snail saves the day.* New York: Thomas Y. Crowell.

T

COSGROVE, S. (1984). *Tee-tee.* Vero Beach, Fla.: Rourke Enterprises, Inc.
LEXAU, J. M. (1971). *T for Tommy.* New York: Garrard.
NESS, E. (1965). *Tom tit tot.* New York: Scribner's.
PRESTON, E. M. (1969). *The temper tantrum book.* New York: Viking.
SEULING, B. (1976). *Teeny-tiny woman.* New York: Viking.

V

CARLE, E. (1969). *The very hungry caterpillar.* New York: Philomel.
DEARMOND, F. U. (1963). *The very, very special day.* New York: Parents Magazine Press.
DUVOISIN, R. (1961). *Veronica.* New York: Knopf.

W

KEATS, E. J. (1964). *Whistle for Willie.* New York: Viking.
NYBLOM, H. (1968). *The witch of the woods.* New York: Knopf.
SENDAK, M. (1963). *Where the wild things are.* New York: Harper & Row, Publishers.

X

MONCURE, J. (1979). *My "X, Y, Z" sound box.* New York: Child's World Publishing.

Y

MARSHALL, J. (1973). *Yummers.* Boston: Houghton Mifflin.
SEUSS, DR. (1958). *Yertle the turtle and other stories.* New York: Random House.

Z

SEUSS, DR. (1950). *If I ran to the zoo.* New York: Random House.
SEUSS, DR. (1955). *On beyond Zebra.* New York: Random House.

b. Vowels (long and short)

A

BAYER, J. (1984). *A, my name is Alice.* New York: Dial Press.
BOYNTON, S. (1983). *A is for angry: An animal and adjective alphabet.* New York: Workman Publishers.
HIAWYN, O. (1982). *Angry Arthur.* New York: Harcourt Brace Jovanovich, Inc.
MONCURE, J. (1984). *Short a and long a: Play a game.* Elgin Ill: Child's World Publishing.

E

FRESCHET, B. (1977). *Elephant and friends.* New York: Scribner's.
KENT, J. (1975). *The egg book.* New York: Macmillan
MILHOUS, K. (1951). *The egg tree.* New York: Scribner's.
MONCURE, J. (1984). *Short e and long e: Play a game.* Elgin, Ill.: Child's World Publishing.
ROCKWELL, A. and H. (1985). *The emergency room.* New York: Macmillan.

I

BONSHALL, C. (1974). *And I mean it, Stanley.* New York: Harper & Row, Publishers.
FISCHER, A. (1965). *In the woods, in the meadow, in the sky.* New York: Scribner's.
MONCURE, J. (1984). *Short i and long i: Play a game.* Elgin, Ill.: Child's World Publishing.
ORAM, H. (1985). *In the attic.* New York: Holt, Rinehart & Winston.
ZOLOTOW, C. (1966). *If it weren't for you.* New York: Harper & Row, Publishers.

O

ALLEN, L. J. (1979). *Ottie and the star.* New York: Harper & Row, Publishers.
KESSLER, L. (1976). *Ghosts and crows and things with O's.* New York: Scholastic.
MONCURE, J. (1984). *Short o and long o: Play a game.* Elgin, Ill.: Child's World Publishing.
THALER, M. (1982). *Owly.* New York: Harper & Row, Publishers.

U

MONCURE, J. (1984). *Short u and long u: Play a game.* Elgin, Ill.: Child's World Publishing.
PINKWATER, D. (1982). *Umbrellas and parasols.* New York: Dutton.
YASHIMA, T. (1969). *Umbrella.* New York: Viking.

c. Digraphs

CH

BROWN, M. W. (1982). *Little chicken.* New York: Harper & Row, Publishers.
HOFF, S. (1961). *Little chief.* New York: Harper & Row, Publishers.
KWITZ, M. (1981). *Little chick's big day.* New York: Harper & Row, Publishers.
KWITZ, M. (1983). *Little chick's breakfast.* New York: Harer & Row, Publishers.
SENDAK, M. (1962). *Chicken soup with rice.* New York: Harper & Row, Publishers.

SH

ADAMS, A. (1981). *Shoemaker and the elves.* New York: Macmillan.
KLINE, S. W. (1984). *SHHH!* New York: Whitman Publishers.
ROGERS, P. (1986). *Sheepchase.* New York: Viking.
ZIEFERT, H. (1986). *Bear does shopping.* New York: Harper & Row, Publishers.

PH

GOVAN, C. (1968). *Phinny's fine summer.* New York: World Publishing.

TH

LOEDHAS, S. (1962). *Thistle and thyme.* Toronto: Alger.

d. Word Families

BROWN, M. W. (1984). *Goodnight moon.* New York: Harper & Row, Publishers.
EICHENBERG, F. (1952). *Ape in a cape.* New York: Scholastic.
LIVERMORE, E. (1979). *The three little kittens lost their mittens.* Boston: Houghton Mifflin.

PATRICK, G. (1974). *A bug in a jug.* New York: Scholastic.
SEUSS, DR. (1957). *The cat in the hat.* New York: Random House.

19. BOOKS FOR FOLLOWING DIRECTIONS

ASCHE, F. (1976). *Good lemonade.* New York: Franklin Watts, Inc.
BENJAMIN, C. (1982). *Cartooning for kids.* New York: Thomas Y. Crowell.
BOGLE, K., and CUTLER, K. (1974). *Crafts for Christmas.* New York: Lothrop.
DEPAOLA, T. (1978). *Pancakes for breakfast.* New York: Harcourt Brace Jovanovich, Inc.
DUNN, J. (1968). *Things.* New York: Doubleday.
HOBAN, T. (1971). *Look again.* New York: Macmillan
HUTCHINS, P. (1968). *Rosie's walk.* New York: Macmillan.
KUNHARDT, D. (1962). *Pat the bunny.* New York: Western Publishing Co., Inc.
LASKER, J. (1977). *Lentil soup.* Chicago: Albert Whitman.
MCGOVERN, A. (1971). *Stone soup.* New York: Scholastic.

20. SERIES BOOKS.

ALLARD, H. (1977). *The stupids step out.* Boston: Houghton Mifflin.
    The stupids die.
    The stupids have a ball.
BEMELMANS, L. (1977). *Madeline.* New York: Puffin Books.
    Madeline and the bad hat.
    Madeline and the gypies.
    Madeline in London.
    Madeline's Christmas.
    Madeline's rescue.
FREEMAN, D. (1968). *Corduroy.* New York: Viking.
    A pocket for Corduroy.
    Corduroy's day.
    Corduroy's party.
    Corduroy's toys.
GRAMATHY, H. (1978). *Little Toot.* New York: Putnam's.
    Little Toot on the Grand Canal.
    Little Toot on the Mississippi.
    Little Toot on the Thames.
    Little Toot through the Golden Gate.
HARGREAVES, R. (1980). *The Mr. Men books.* Los Angeles.: Price, Stern & Sloan Publishers
    Mr. Strong. Mr. Small. Mr. Fussy.
    Mr. Happy. Mr. Nosiy. Mr. Impossible.
HOBAN, R. (1976). *Bedtime for Frances.* New York: Harper & Row, Publishers.
    A baby sister for Frances.
    Best friends for Frances.
    A birthday for Frances.
    Bread and jam for Frances.
LINDGREN, B. (1982). *Sam's cookie.* New York: Morrow.
    Sam's bath.
    Sam's ball.
    Sam's car.
    Sam's teddy bear.
LOBEL, A. (1979). *Frog and toad are friends.* New York: Harper & Row, Publishers.
    Days with frog and toad.
    Frog and toad all year.
    Frog and toad together.

LOWREY, J. S. (1942). *The poky little puppy*. New York: Golden Press.
  The poky little puppy and the patchwork blanket.
  The poky little puppy follows his nose home.
  The poky little puppy's first Christmas.
MINARIK, E.H. (1978). *Little bear*. New York: Harper & Row, Publishers.
  A kiss for little bear.
  Father bear comes home.
  Little bear's friend.
  Little bear's visit.
PARISH, P. (1970). *Amelia Bedelia*. New York: Scholastic.
  Amelia Bedelia and the baby.
  Amelia Bedelia and the surprise shower.
  Amelia Bedelia goes camping.
  Amelia Bedelia goes shopping.
  Amelia Bedelia helps out.
  Good work, Amelia Bedelia.
REY, H. A. (1973). *Curious George*. Boston: Houghton Mifflin.
  Curious George and the dump truck.
  Curious George flies a kite.
  Curious George goes to the circus.
  Curious George learns the alphabet.
  Curious George rides a bike.
  Curious George goes sledding.
TAYLOR, M. (1976). *Henry the explorer*. New York: Atheneum.
  Henry explores the jungle.
  Henry explores the mountains.
  Henry explores the castaway.
WABER, B. (1975). *The house on East 88th Street*. Boston: Houghton Mifflin.
  Lyle and the birthday party.
  Lyle finds his mother.
  Lyle, Lyle crocodile.
WELLS, R. (1979). *Max's first words*. New York: Dial Press.
  Max's new suit.
  Max's ride.
  Max's toys.
ZION, G. (1976). *Harry the dirty dog*. New York: Harper & Row, Publishers.
  Harry and the lady next door.
  Harry by the sea.
  No roses for Harry.

Appendix B

Additional Literature Resources

1. BOOK CLUBS

The Book Plan, 921 Washington Avenue, Brooklyn, NY 11238.

Firefly Book Club, P.O. Box 485, Pleasantville, NY 10570.

Junior Deluxe Editions Club, Garden City, NY 11530.

My Weekly Reader Book Club, 1250 Fairwood Avenue, P.O. Box 2639, Columbus, Ohio 43216.

Parents' Magazine Read-Aloud Book Club for Little Listeners and Beginning Readers, Division of Parents' Magazine Enterprises, 52 Vanderbilt Avenue, New York, NY 10017.

Scholastic Book Services, See Saw Club (K–1), 904 Sylvan Avenue, Englewood Cliffs, NJ 07632.

Troll Book Club, 320 Route 17, Mahwah, NJ 07430

Trumpet Club, P.O. Box 604, Holmes, PA 19043

Young America Book Club, 1250 Fairwood Avenue, Columbus, Ohio.

2. COMPANIES THAT DISTRIBUTE STORYBOOKS, RECORDS, AND CASSETTES

Caedmon, 1995 Broadway, New York, NY 10023.

Doubleday, 277 Park Avenue, New York, NY 10017.

Kaplan School Supply Corporation, 1310 Lewisville–Clemmons Road, Lewisville, NC 27023.

Random House, Inc., 201 E. 50th Street, New York, NY 10022.

Scott Foresman Talking Story Book Box, 1900 E. Lake Avenue, Glenview, IL 60025.
Troll Book Associates, 320 Route 17, Mahwah, NJ 07430.
Weston Woods, Weston, CN 06883.

3. CHILDREN'S BOOK AWARDS

American Book Awards. Association of American Publishers, One Park Avenue, New York, NY 10016.
Annual awards for best books chosen by children. National Council of Teachers of English, 1111 Kenyon Road, Champaign-Urbana, IL 61801.
Caldecott Medal. American Library Association, 50 East Huron Street, Chicago, IL 60611.
Children's Book Showcase. Children's Book Council, 67 Irving Place, New York, NY 10003.
Newbery Award. American Library Association, 50 East Huron Street, Chicago, IL 60611.

Appendix C

Resources For Parents

1. BOOKS

BARTON, B. (1986). *Tell me another.* Exeter, N.H.: Heinemann Educational Books.
BUTLER, D. (1980). *Babies need books.* New York: Atheneum.
BUTLER, D., and CLAY, M. (1982). *Reading begins at home.* Exeter, N.H.: Heinemann Educational Books.
CHAMBERS, A. (1973). *Introducing books to children.* Boston: Horn Books.
GLAZER, S. M. (1980). *Getting ready to read.* Englewood Cliffs, N.J.: Prentice-Hall.
GLAZER, S. M., and BROWN, C. S. (1980). *Helping children read: Ideas for parents, teachers, and librarians.* Rider College, Lawrenceville. N.J. New Jersey Reading Association.
HEARNE, B. (1981). *Choosing books for children: A commonsense guide.* New York: Delacorte.
KAYE, P. (1984). *Games for reading: Playful ways to help your child read.* New York: Pantheon.
KIMMEL, M. M., and SEGEL, E. (1983). *For reading out loud.* New York: Delacorte.
LAMME, L. (1980). *Raising readers: A guide to sharing literature with young children.* New York: Walker & Co.
LAMME, L. (1985). *Highlights for children: Growing up reading.* Washington, D.C.: Acropolis Books, Ltd.
LARRICK, N. (1980). *Encourage your child to read: A parent's primer.* New York: Dell Pub. Co., Inc.
LARRICK, N. (1985). *A parent's guide to children's reading* (5th ed.). New York: Bantam.
PICKERING, C. T. (1977). *Helping children learn to read.* New York: Chesford, Inc.
ROSI, M. J. M. (1982). *Read to me: Teach me.* Wauwatosa, Wis.: American Baby Books.
TAYLOR, D., and STRICKLAND, D. S. (1986). *Family storybook reading.* Exeter, N.H.: Heinemann Educational Books.
TIEDT, I. M. (1979). *Exploring books with children.* Boston: Houghton Mifflin.
TRELEASE, J. (1982). *The read aloud handbook.* New York: Penguin.
WHITE, D. (1986). *Books before five.* Exeter, N.H.: Heinemann Educational Books.

2. PAMPHLETS AND BOOKLETS

Choosing a children's book. New York: Children's Book Council.
 A four-page folder giving advice on nine booklets along with sources and prices. Free

with stamped, self-addressed envelope sent to Children's Book Council, 67 Irving Place, New York, NY 10003.

JANES, D. *Reading in the home.* New York: Scholastic Magazines.
A six-page folder for parents. Free from Scholastic Magazines, 50 West 44th Street, New York, NY 10036.

SCHICKEDANZ, J. (1983). *Helping children learn about reading.* Washington, DC: NAEYC.
Free with stamped, self-addressed envelope sent to National Association for the Education of Young Children, 1834 Connecticut Avenue NW, Washington, DC 20009. (800-424-2460)

U. S. government publications. Available from U.S. Government Printing Office, North Capitol and H Streets NW, Washington, DC 20401.
Children and television (free).
Parents and beginning readers (free).

IRA Micromonographs. Published by the International Reading Association, 800 Barksdale Road, P.O. Box 8139, Newark, DE 19714.
This valuable series of twelve-to-twenty-four-page pamphlets focuses on answering questions parents often ask about the reading education of their children.
What books and records should I get for my preschooler? Norma Rogers. (No. 872)
How can I prepare my young child for reading? Paula Grinnell. (No. 881)
Why read aloud to children? Julie M. T. Chan. (No. 877)
How can I help my child build positive attitudes toward reading? Susan Mandel Glazer. (No. 879)
What is reading readiness? Norma Rogers. (No. 870)
How can I help my child get ready to read? Norma Rogers. (No. 876)

IRA Parent Brochures. Published by the International Reading Association, 800 Barksdale Road, P.O. Box 8139, Newark, DE 19714.
These brochures focus on practical reading concerns of parents and on ways for parents to help their children develop reading skills and a lifetime reading habit.
Your home is your child's first school.
You can encourage your child to read.
Good books make reading fun for your child. Glenna Davis Sloan.
You can use television to stimulate your child's reading habits. Nicholas P. Criscuolo.

Appendix D

Quality Television Programs with Associated Children's Books

EDUCATIONAL PROGRAMS

Sesame Street

GEISS, T. (1986). *Honk if you like honkers*. New York: Random House.
HAUTZEY, D. (1986). *It's not fair: A Sesame Street start to read book*. New York: Random House.
STILES, N., and WILCOX, D. (1974). *Grover and the everything in the whole wide world museum*. New York: Random House.
STONE, J. (1971). *The monster at the end of this book*. Racine, Wis.: Western Publishing Co., Inc.

Mr. Rogers' Neighborhood

ROGERS, F. (1983). *Mister Rogers' Planet Purple*. Dallas: Texas Instruments, Inc.
ROGERS, F. (1986). *Going to the doctor*. New York: Putnam's.
ROGERS, F. (1987). *Making friends*. New York: Putnam's.

Reading Rainbows

CAULEY, B. (1979). *The ugly duckling*. New York: Harcourt Brace Jovanovich, Inc.
KEATS, E. J. (1967). *Peter's chair*. New York: Harper & Row, Publishers.
LOBEL, A. (1972). *Frog and toad together*. New York: Harper & Row, Publishers.
SENDAK, M. (1963). *Where the wild things are*. New York: Harper & Row, Publishers.
STEVENS, J. (1985). *The tortoise and the hare*. New York: Holiday House.
VIORST, J. (1972). *Alexander and the terrible, horrible, no good, very bad day*. New York: Macmillan.
VOIGT, E. (illus.). (1980). *Peter and the wolf*. Boston: David R. Godine Publisher.

Muppets

BRUCE, S. B. (1982). *Gonzo and the giant chicken*. New York: Random House.
KATES, L. (1986). *Make believe with the Muppet babies: A storybook*. New York: Random House.

STEVENSON, J. (1986). *Bo saves the show.* New York: Random House.

Romper Room

ANASTASIO, D. (1985). *Romper Room book of ABC's.* New York: Doubleday.
FAVATA, R. (1984). *Romper Room song book of musical adventures: Alphabetcha!* New York: Caedmon.
KARNOVSKY, B. N. (1984). *Romper Room bedtime story book.* New York: Doubleday.

Nickelodeon (cable)

REY, H. A. (1973). *Curious George.* Boston: Houghton Mifflin.
REY, H. A. (1973). *Curious George learns the alphabet.* Boston: Houghton Mifflin.
REY, H. A. (1977). *Curious George flies a kite.* Boston: Houghton Mifflin.
REY, H. A. (1985). *Curious George visits the zoo.* Boston: Houghton Mifflin.

Disney (cable)

CHASE, A. (1964). *Mary Poppins.* Racine, Wis.: Western Publishing Co., Inc.
DISNEY, W. (1950). *Alice in Wonderland.* Racine, Wis.: Western Publishing Co., Inc.
GAG, W. (1938). *Snow White and the seven dwarfs.* New York: Putnam's.
KNIGHTS, H. (1978). *Cinderella.* New York: Random House.
MILNE, A. A. (1957). *The world of Pooh.* New York: Dutton.

POPULAR CARTOON SHOWS

Berenstain Bears

BERENSTAIN, S. and J. (1981). *The Berenstain bears moving day.* New York: Random House.
BERENSTAIN, S. and J. (1981). *The Berenstain bears go to the doctor.* New York: Random House.

Babar

DEBRUNHOFF, J. (1986). *Babar the king.* New York: Random House.

Charlie Brown

SCHULZ, C. M. (1976). *Life is a circus.* New York: Scholastic.
SCHULZ, C. M. (1976). *It's the Easter beagle Charlie Brown.* New York: Scholastic.
SCHULZ, C. M. (1976). *A Charlie Brown Thanksgiving.* New York: Scholastic.

Smurfs

PEYO. (1982). *A Smurf in the air.* New York: Random House.
PEYO. (1982). *Smurphony in C.* New York: Random House.
PEYO, (1982). *The wandering Smurf.* New York: Random House.

Popples/Wrinkles

GEORGE, G. (1986). *The popples and the puppy.* New York: Random House.
WEST, C. (1984). *The best place in the world: A Wrinkles storybook.* New York: Random House.

Dr. Seuss

DR. SEUSS. (1957). *How the Grinch stole Christmas.* New York: Random House.
DR. SEUSS. (1957). *The cat in the hat.* New York: Random House.
DR. SEUSS. (1960). *Green eggs and ham.* New York: Random House.
DR. SEUSS. (1961). *Sneetches and other stories.* New York: Random House.
DR. SEUSS. (1971). *Lorax.* New York: Random House.

OTHER BOOKS FEATURED AS TELEVISION SPECIALS

BAUM, E. (1984). *Wizard of Oz*. New York: Random House.
LOFTING, H. (1920). *The story of Doctor Doolittle*. New York: Lippincott.
TOLKIEN, J. R. (1984). *The hobbit*. Boston: Houghton Mifflin.
WILDER, L. I. (1935). *Little house on the prairie*. New York: Harper & Row, Publishers.

Appendix E

Computer Software for Early Literacy Development

1. *ADVENTURES OF KRISTEN AND FAMILY*   Grade: PreK–2
   DESCRIPTION: Prereader develops computer literacy through sequen-
   cing and storytelling activities that value family and
   community.
   HARDWARE: Apple II Family
   AVAILABILITY: Rhiannon Software

2. *BIG BIRD'S FUNHOUSE*   Grade: PreK–1
   DESCRIPTION: Children play hide-and-seek in a whimsical, interactive
   activity while practicing concentration, memorization,
   and sequencing.
   HARDWARE: Atari, Commodore 64
   AVAILABILITY: CBS Software

3. *CHARLIE BROWN'S ABC'S*   Grade: K–2
   DESCRIPTION: Uses animation to introduce children to letters and words.
   Includes off-screen activity cards.
   HARDWARE: Apple II Family, Commodore 64.
   AVAILABILITY: Random House School Division

4. *DELTA DRAWING*   Grade: PreK–7
   DESCRIPTION: User creates colorful drawings on the computer screen
   with single-key commands that control the Delta Cursor.
   HARDWARE: Apple II Family, Atari, Commodore 64, IBM
   AVAILABILITY: Spinnaker Software Corporation

5. *EZ LOGO, REVISED EDITION*   Grade: PreK–3
   DESCRIPTION: Children explore computer capabilities and experiment
   with turtle graphics using twenty-four open-ended
   activities.
   HARDWARE: Apple 64K
   AVAILABILITY: Minnesota Educational Computing Consortium

6. *FIRST–LETTER FUN*   Grade: PreK–3
   DESCRIPTION: Enjoyable animated stories that help chilren match letters
   with initial sounds of words.
   HARDWARE: Apple 48K, Commodore 64, IBM
   AVAILABILITY: Minnesota Educational Computing Consortium

7. *THE FRIENDLY COMPUTER*   Grade: PreK–3
   DESCRIPTION: Children learn the major parts of a computer system
   while playing games with Zebug, an animated charac-
   ter.
   HARDWARE: Apple 48K, Commodore 64, IBM
   AVAILABILTY: Minnesota Educational Computing Consortium

8. *KINDERCOMP*   Grade: PreK–3
   DESCRIPTION: A collection of six learning games that prepare children
   to read, spell, and count.
   HARDWARE: Apple II Family, Atari, Commodore, IBM, TRS-80
   AVAILABILITY: Spinnaker Software Corporation

9. *KIDWRITER*   Grade: PreK–3
   DESCRIPTION: Children create a graphically illustrated story.
   HARDWARE: Apple II Family, Atari, Commodore, IBM
   AVAILABILITY: Spinnaker Software Corporation

10. *LEARNING WITH LEEPER*   Grade: PreK–2
    DESCRIPTION: A bouncy character leads children through four animated
    games that teach shape matching, counting, eye–hand
    coordination, and creativity.
    HARDWARE: Apple II Family
    AVAILABILITY: Encyclopaedia Britannica

11. *LETTER MATCH*   Grade: PreK–2
    DESCRIPTION: A game for learning upper- and lowercase letters.
    HARDWARE: Atari, Commodore 64, TRS-80.
    AVAILABILITY: Computer Applications Tomorrow

12. *MAKE A MATCH*   Grade: PreK–1
    DESCRIPTION: Electronic book of favorite nursery rhymes with music
    and color graphics, used to enhance children's cognition
    and recall.
    HARDWARE: IBM, Tandy
    AVAILABILITY: Sunstar Systems

13. *MR. AND MRS. POTATO HEAD*   Grade: PreK–3
    DESCRIPTION: Children play animated games in which they create their
    own unique potato folk. Memory games help sharpen
    concentration and memory skills.
    HARDWARE: Apple II Family, Commodore 64
    AVAILABILITY: Random House School Division

14. *PAINT WITH WORDS*   Grade: PreK–2
    DESCRIPTION: Children exercise their creativity and develop their vo-
    cabulary as they choose words and turn them into color-
    ful images.
    HARDWARE: Apple 64K
    AVAILABILITY: Minnesota Educational Computing Consortium

15. *PICK–A–DILLY*   Grade: PreK–1
    DESCRIPTION: Color graphics and musical sounds used in a concentration game format to promote visual and sound memory.
    HARDWARE: Apple II Family
    AVAILABILITY: Actioncraft

16. *READ–A–LOGO*   Grade: PreK–1
    DESCRIPTION: A sequential program that helps preschoolers discover the world of meaningful print through symbols and signs that advertise products and services.
    HARDWARE: Apple II Family
    AVAILABILITY: Teacher Support Software

17. *RHYMES WITH*   Grade: PreK–1
    DESCRIPTION: Children use pictures with end-syllable rhymes.
    HARDWARE: Apple II Family.
    AVAILABILITY: Kidsware

18. *SENTENCE STARTERS*   Grade: PreK–2
    DESCRIPTION: Children use sentence beginnings and color graphics to create sentences and stories.
    HARDWARE: Apple II Family
    AVAILABILITY: Teacher Support Software

19. *SESAME STREET LETTER–GO–ROUND*   Grade: PreK–1
    DESCRIPTION: Provides practice in recognizing and matching letters and forming words.
    HARDWARE: Atari, Commodore 64
    AVAILABILITY: CBS software

20. *SNOOPY'S READING MACHINE*   Grade: K–3
    DESCRIPTION: Children create and learn different words from exposure to the following five word families (AT, ET, OP, UG, IG).
    HARDWARE: Apple II Family, Commodore 64
    AVAILABILITY: Random House School Division

21. *SPACESHIP LOST*   Grade: PreK–2
    DESCRIPTION: Uses the dynamics of interactive computer gaming to help children develop spatial concepts.
    HARDWARE: Apple II Family
    AVAILABILITY: Educational Activities, Inc.

22. *STICKYBEAR ABC / SHAPES / OPPOSITES*   Grade: PreK–1
    DESCRIPTION: Three software packages that help children learn about alphabet letters; shapes and their relationships; and opposites.
    HARDWARE: Apple II Family, Atari, Commodore 64
    AVAILABILITY: Xerox Education Publications

23. *STORY MIX-#3-NURSERY MIX*   Grade: K–1
    DESCRIPTION: Children compose a story by selecting story parts from a menu of four choices.
    HARDWARE: Apple II Family, Commodore 64, TRS-80
    AVAILABILITY: Bertamax Inc.

24. *TALKING TEXTWRITER*   Grade: PreK–3
    DESCRIPTION: Talking word processor can pronounce each letter, word, line, or page as children type it on the screen.
    HARDWARE: Apple II Family
    AVAILABILITY: Scholastic, Inc.

Appendix F

Resources for Teachers

1. SCHOOL SUPPLY COMPANIES

Chaselle, Inc., 9645 Gerwig Lane, Columbia, MD 21046.

Childcraft Education Corp., 20 Kilmer Road, Edison, NJ 08818-3018.

Didex Inc. Educational Resources, 5 Fourth Street, Peabody, MA 01960.

DLM Teaching Resources, P.O. Box 4000, One DLM Park, Allen, TX 75002.

Educational Teaching Aids, 159 West Kinzie Street, Chicago, IL 60610.

Harcourt Brace Jovanovich, Inc., One East First Street, Duluth, MN 55802.

H. L. Strickling, 55 West Quackenbush Avenue, Dumont, NJ 07628.

J. L. Hammett Co., Box 545, Braintree, MA 02184.

Kaplan School Supply Corp., 1310 Lewisville–Clemmons Road, Lewisville, NC 27023.

Scholastic Inc., P. O. Box 7501, 2931 East McCarty Street, Jefferson City, MO 65102.

Totline Press/Warren Publishing House, Inc., P. O. Box 2255, Everett, WA 98203.

Toys 'n' Things Press/Resources for Child Caring, Inc., 906 North Dale Street, Box 23, St. Paul, MN 55103.

2. REFERENCES FOR TEACHER-MADE MATERIALS

BARATTA, L. M. (1972). *Workjobs activity-centered learning for early childhood education.* Menlo Park, Calif: Addison-Wesley.

COUDRON, J. *Alphabet Puppets.* (1983). Belmont, Calif. Fearon Teacher Aids.

FLEMMING, B., and HAMILTON, D. (1977). *Resources for creative teaching in early childhood education.* New York: Harcourt Brace Jovanovich, Inc.

FORGAN, H. W. (1977). *The reading center: Ideas, games and activities for individualizing reading.* Santa Monica, Calif.: Goodyear.

FORTE, P. T. (1973). *Center stuff for nooks, crannies and corners.* Nashville: Incentive Press Inc.

GREFF, K., and ASKOV, E. (1977). *Learning centers: An idea book for reading and language arts.* Dubuque, Iowa: Kendall/Hunt.

NORTON, D. E. (1974). *Language arts activities for children.* Columbus, Ohio: Chas. E. Merrill.

RUSSELL, D., and KARP, E. (1975). *Reading aids through the grades.* New York: Teachers College Press.

SPACHE, E. B. (1976). *Reading activities for child involvement.* Newton, Mass.: Allyn & Bacon.

Spice Series Teacher Handbooks. (1960). *Spice primary language arts.* Stevensville, Mich.: Educational Service, Inc.

3. PROFESSIONAL ASSOCIATIONS AND RELATED JOURNALS DEALING WITH EARLY LITERACY

- American Library Association, 50 E. Huron Street, Chicago, IL 60611.
- American Montessori Society, Inc. (AMS), 150 Fifth Avenue, New York, NY 10010.
- Association for Childhood Education International (ACEI), 11141 Georgia Avenue, Suite 200, Wheaton, MD 20902.
  Journal: *Childhood Education*
- Behavioral Publications, 72 Fifth Avenue, New York, NY 10011.
  Journal: *Day Care & Early Eduation*
- Capital Publications, Inc., 2430 Pennsylvania Avenue NW, Washington, DC 20037.
  Journal: *Report on Preschool Education*
- Children's Bureau, Office of Child Development, U.S. Department of Health, Education and Welfare, Washington, DC 20201.
  Journal: *Children Today*
- Child Welfare League of America, Inc., 67 Irving Place, New York, NY 10010.
  Journal: *Child Welfare.*
- College Reading Association (CRA), Department of Curriculum and Instruction, College of Education, Applachian State University, Boone, NC 28608.
  Journal: *Reading Research & Instruction*
- Educational Resource Information Center/Early Childhood Education (ERIC/ECE), University of Illinois, 804 West Pennsylvania Avenue, Urbana, IL 61801.
- Education Today Company, 530 University Avenue, Palo Alto, CA 94301.
  Journal: *Learning*
- Gordon and Breach Science Publishers, Inc., One Park Avenue, New York, NY 10016.
  Journal: *Early Child Development and Care*
- Highlights for Children, Inc., P.O. Box 1266, Darien, CT 06820.
  Journal: *Early Years*
- The Instructor Publications, Inc., P. O. Box 6099, Duluth, MN 55806.
  Journal: *Instructor*

- International Reading Association (IRA), 800 Barksdale Road, P.O.Box 8139, Newark, DE 19711.
  Journals: *Reading Teacher; Reading Research Quarterly;*
  brochures, pamphlets, and monographs
- National Association for the Education of Young Children (NAEYC), 1834 Connecticut Avenue NW, Washington, DC 20009.
  Journal: *Young Children*
  pamphlets and monographs
- National Council of Teachers of English (NCTE), 1111 Kenyon Road, Urbana, IL 61801.
  Journal: *Language Arts*
  pamphlets and monographs
- National Education Association (NEA), 1201 16th Street NW, Washington, DC 20036.
  Journal: *Today's Education*
- National Reading Conference (NRC), 1070 Sibley Tower, Rochester, NY 14604.
  Journal: *Journal of Reading Behavior*
- Society for Research in Child Development, 5750 Ellis Avenue, Chicago, IL 60637.
  Journal: *Child Development*

Index